Tropical Whites

NATURE AND CULTURE IN AMERICA

Marguerite S. Shaffer, Series Editor

Volumes in the series explore the intersections between
the construction of cultural meaning and the history
of human interaction with the natural world. The series
is meant to highlight the complex relationship between
nature and culture and provide a distinct position
for interdisciplinary scholarship that brings together
environmental and cultural history.

Tropical Whites

The Rise of the Tourist South in the Americas

Catherine Cocks

PENN

UNIVERSITY OF PENNSYLVANIA PRESS

PHILADELPHIA

Published by
University of Pennsylvania Press
Philadelphia, Pennsylvania 19104-4112
upenn.edu/pennpress

Printed in the United States of America
on acid-free paper

10 9 8 7 6 5 4 3 2 1

Library of Congress Cataloging-in-Publication Data

Cocks, Catherine
Tropical whites : the rise of the tourist south in the Americas /
Catherine Cooks.—1st ed.
p. cm.—(Nature and culture in America)
Includes bibliographical references and index.
ISBN 978-0-8122-4499-1 (hardcover : alk. paper)
1. Tourism—Tropics—History—19th century. 2. Tourism—Tropics—History—20th
century. 3. Americans—Tropics—History—19th century. 4. Americans—Tropics—
History—20th century. 5. Race relations—Tropics—History—19th century. 6. Race
relations—Tropics—History—20th century. I. Title.
G155.T73C64 2013
338.4'7918093—dc 23   2012048416

For Hanley

CONTENTS

Plates follow page 126

A NOTE ON AMERICA AND AMERICANS

Throughout this book, I use "American" to describe people and things from the Western Hemisphere—all of it. When I mean people and things from the United States, I use the adjective "U.S." or some similar locution. In a book that is about the travels of people from the United States in other areas of the Americas, using "American" to mean "of the United States" would be confusing as well as arrogant. Not following the customary usage, in contrast, underscores one of the central points of my argument: that tourism helped to constitute and formalize national differences at the end of the centuries-long colonization of the Western Hemisphere.

All translations are mine unless otherwise noted.

Introduction

"Was there ever such a change?" asked Ida Starr, steaming south from New York City to the Caribbean and "feeling as serene and happy as a woman in a white linen frock can feel." She was not alone in her pleasure: "Every one must have gone down into every one's trunk this morning" to find white attire suitable for the warming temperatures. Travelers going south in winter at the turn of the twentieth century almost all changed into lightweight white clothing as the air warmed and the sun strengthened. "On the third day" of a Panama Mail cruise from San Francisco to New York, "all the officers appear in white duck trousers. Another day and their blue uniform coats give way to white." Among the passengers, "white flannel trousers vie with linen knickers among the men. The women . . . dazzle the ship with the sheerest of white summer things." Advertisements and illustrations for travel articles about the tropics regularly placed white-clad tourists in colorful market scenes. Even the ships carrying northern travelers into tropical waters were painted white, and the United Fruit Company dubbed its Caribbean passenger line "the Great White Fleet" upon its launch in 1899.[1]

The temptation to dismiss this change of clothing as a trivial performance of high society etiquette—only in summer did the fashionable wear white—may be powerful. Hard on the heels of that reflex judgment may come the belief that whites wore white in the tropics in a defensive doubling of their pale-skinned privilege.[2] Both of these analyses contain considerable truth, but they do not shed much light on what southward travel, ritually marked by the donning of white apparel, meant and why its popularity grew rapidly at the turn of the twentieth century. Because North Americans and Europeans believed that climate was one of the chief influences shaping their characters, travelers' change of dress was far more than mere convention, a shield against contamination by the dark fecundity of the tropics, or even a practical response to the rising temperatures.

Donning sheer, snowy garments, northerners opened themselves to summer, the season when—and in the case of travel southward, the place where—nature's powers reached their zenith and the virtuous necessity for human labor its nadir. A realm of steamy fertility, scantily clad dark-skinned primitives, leisure, and self-indulgence, the tropics were the opposite—and in the nineteenth century the enemy—of the winter-hardened civilization established in the earth's temperate zones by hard-working, self-disciplined, modestly attired whites. The region's sensuous pleasures aroused human appetites and could easily transform their relationships: "Why, the count and his brother are fairly blinding to the eyes, in their smart white flannels," purred Starr, a married mother of six who was traveling with her husband and two young daughters. "They actually look a bit interesting." This blossoming of the passions weakened the traveler's resistance to a far more perilous seduction. "The sudden call of Summer, the eternal loveliness of warmth, the expansion of the soul from out [sic] the chill of ice and snow, into the bliss of laughing seas and delicious sunlight; the sight of green, graceful palms," Starr confessed, "was all so intoxicating that . . . we would have bartered our very souls, with but little hesitancy, for a lifetime of such sensation!"[3]

The story of how such Faustian bargains became unnecessary—how whites learned to love the tropics without losing their souls—is the subject of this book. *Tropical Whites* sketches the American history of the development of the global tourist south, or what I call "the Southland," drawing on sources from Florida, Southern California, Mexico, and the Caribbean. In 1880, most European and North American whites regarded the tropics as the "white man's grave"; by the early 1940s, everyone knew that they constituted "the most ideal winter resorts" for vacationers from the temperate zones.[4] This about-face required a significant rearticulation of popular beliefs about the relationship between the environment and human bodies, a rearticulation that diminished nature's power to shape humanity and enhanced humanity's power to manage nature for its own benefit. Such a reweighting of the balance necessarily entailed changes in the way that North American whites conceived of human variation, especially the distinctions that constituted race and sexuality. In other words, the historical shift usually understood as the emergence of a modern society, one characterized by cultural pluralism and moral liberalization, owed much to the tourist industry's production of "tropical whites"—civilized, pale-skinned people with the youthful, sensuous joy of dark-skinned primitives.

Tropicality

Readers may protest that Southern California, Florida, and northern Mexico are not in the tropics. Indeed, these places do not lie between the Tropics of Cancer and Capricorn, or 23° 26′ 22″ north and south of the equator. Nor do Bermuda and most of the Bahamas, which also figure in this history. And although Mexico's central plateau and Jamaica's Blue Mountains do lie between those lines, they are cooled by their lofty altitude. But travel writers, boosters, and diarists readily labeled these places—or at least some of their features—as tropical. At the closing of the summer resorts in the northeastern and midwestern United States, *Travel* magazine reported in 1901, "Many eyes turn to the sunny South, to far away Hawaii or tropical California"; a column on travel books in the same magazine spoke of a brochure published by the Florida East Coast Railroad that featured "photographic reproductions of the tropical charms" of the state. Writing to his sister during his first visit to Florida in January 1880, John Gilpin reported that "we have been here now a day and a half and are beginning to feel established tho' every hour develops something new and strange in this tropical land."[5]

Geographically or botanically better-informed writers sometimes distinguished between "semi-" or "subtropical" and "tropical" zones, but these terms, too, were often used evocatively rather than scientifically. Adolph Sutro wrote in his 1889 diary that the town of Aguas Calientes, Mexico, just south of the line, "has an excellent climate with a semi-tropical vegetation and is said to be a place especially suited for consumptives," but he was not impressed with the country around the St. Johns River in northern Florida: "The shores are certainly picturesque especially to people who have never seen a tropical or semi-tropical country, but there is such a sameness about it that one soon tires." "Mediterranean" also appeared regularly to describe both Southern California and Florida, initially to deny their tropicality but later to align them with the blossoming resorts along the French Riviera and the origins of Western civilization; occasionally the term was extended to the Caribbean as well.[6]

Rather than simply evidence of scientific ignorance, the apparently indiscriminate use of the word "tropical" indicates that all of these places featured tropical traits. That is, certain kinds of landscapes and societies—those featuring "waving palms, slothful negroes, odd tropical fruits, and early venturings on the part of buccaneers from Spain"—signaled "tropicality" to U.S. visitors, whatever the geographic location. Southern California and Florida promoters made a point of importing royal and coconut palms, tropical icons not native to these areas, and the cultivation of oranges and architecture evocative of Spanish colonial and Mediterranean styles drove the point home. Parts of Mexico and many Caribbean islands were naturally and historically well endowed in these respects, but tourism promoters often had to work hard to design itineraries and landscapes that highlighted the tropical features that North American visitors expected to see in seasons or locations where they were not plentiful.[7]

These attitudes were nothing new by the late nineteenth century. More or less sophisticated versions of tropicality had long structured Europeans' encounter with the peoples and lands to their south, producing a temperate, civilized world in contrast to a tropical, primitive one. Janus-faced visions of the tropics as paradise or hell existed from the earliest European encounters with the Caribbean, and the preference for one or the other generally followed from the writer's optimism or pessimism about European (and later North American) society. By the nineteenth century tropicality became a critical element in the consolidation of racial difference. In those years, the idea of race derived to a considerable degree from a thoroughgoing environmental determinism, a belief that human beings were creatures of their places of origin and their places of residence. In this way of thinking, tropical places produced dark-skinned, lazy, passionate people and temperate zones pale-skinned, hard-working, cool-headed ones. The scientific and medical understanding of humanity held that the environment and human social relations were mutually and closely implicated. A people's natural setting could explain differences not simply of color but also of social organization, family form, gender roles, sexual morals and practices, religion, and capacity for self-rule. White North Americans and Europeans believed the tropics to be the "white man's grave" not merely because of their vulnerability to hot-weather diseases like yellow fever and malaria but because the tropical environment and tropical people might seduce them into abandoning their hard-won cold-weather virtues.[8]

To understand the successful development of the Southland as a tourist region, we must understand how the tropics ceased to represent nature at her most dangerous and came to represent her at her most loving, a change that necessarily had implications for racial and sexual mores. In other words, we must track the evolution of the idea of tropicality, a venerable instrument of colonization since the 1500s, through its adaptation to the interests of nationalists and tourism entrepreneurs (sometimes the same people) in the twentieth century. Remarkably, few scholars have studied the uses of this concept after 1900, and one result is that we know more about beach resorts in chilly England and the northeastern United States than we do about those in the Southland that now represent the ideal seaside experience. Tropicality has largely been abandoned on the verge of an era in which it arguably became one of the most lucrative geographic concepts in the world.[9]

The rearticulation of the relationship between human and nonhuman nature that updated tropicality in the early twentieth century occurred as part of intertwined transformations in medicine, horticulture, and transportation. Beginning in the 1880s, a network of fruit plantations, railroads, and steamships linked first Southern California and Florida to the rest of the United States and then Mexico and the Caribbean ever more closely to their northern neighbor. At the same time that medical researchers reduced the role of nature in human health to the management of infectious creatures via germ theory, commercial horticulture and steam transportation reduced the awesome seductive powers of the tropics to resources selectively available for the rejuvenation of weary northerners. Ideologically and economically linked with both medicine and agribusiness, the tourist industry formulated and advertised the social and personal significance of these changes—and made them tangible for the growing number of U.S. residents who could afford to travel for pleasure after 1880. Consequently, studying travel writing and industry marketing materials reveals the centrality of the tropics in the formulation among North American whites of self-consciously modern racial and sexual ideals, ideals premised on the belief that individuals' unfettered development of their own natures would naturally produce a good society. To put it another way, the rise of tropical tourism played a key role in popularizing culture, a new way of conceiving of human variation that diminished nature's social power while enhancing its symbolic role as the measure of human happiness. An examination of tourism in the Southland reveals the natural underpinnings of the idea of culture.

In its commonsense rendering, culture figures as the realm of human agency in opposition to race, which embodies the realm of biological determinism. The most streamlined telling of this story might begin with the rediscovery of Mendelian genetics in the late nineteenth century, which gradually led scientists to abandon the belief in the transmission of acquired characteristics and forced scholars interested in social problems to find grounds other than the body on which to build their theories. Contesting the biological reductionism of the eugenicists, a brave generation of social theorists broadened the idea of culture—a purely historical, human creation—to show that the prevailing notions of racial inequality had no basis in biology. Social differences, they proclaimed, were purely the product of human choices. In this narrative, it makes little sense to talk of culture being grounded in nature; it is a declaration of freedom from nature.[10]

But this origin story fails to capture the ambiguous, complex history through which race and culture came to be opposites. Among the many factors it obscures is that nature never ceased to play a role in the understanding of human variation. The reduction of race to biology is of recent vintage, dating only from the turn of the twentieth century. For centuries, *race* had long been a usefully vague term encompassing everything from skin color and skull shape to family organization and the likelihood of state formation. Whether referring to traits now glossed as continental origin, nationality, or ethnicity, it ranked people according to the universalizing scheme of Western civilization: everyone stood on some rung of the same, singular ladder leading upward from primitivism through barbarism to civilization. An integral element of this temporal universalism was the geographic universalism that underwrote the belief that environmental conditions determined human nature: similar natural zones produced similar kinds of people.[11] Geography, not biology in the form of the human body, was destiny during most of the long history of race. And if nature endowed people with specific qualities, a change in nature could transform them, too. In this way of thinking, long-distance moves of the kind millions made during the nineteenth century constituted a profound threat to the existing pattern of racial difference.

The popularization of culture in its anthropological sense vitiated the belief in a strong bond between people and their environments that was one of the pillars of this older understanding of race. The idea that people properly belong to social groups with coherent, closed systems of belief and practice that differ radically from each other and that cannot be ranked hierarchically on a universal scale shifted the source of human variation from the interaction of geography and biology to human history. This history often responded to environmental conditions, as in much romantic nationalism, but in such schemes nature worked locally, not globally. Culture required reimagining the spatial organization of the world so that social differences, rather than natural ones, constituted the most important boundaries. Increasingly in the twentieth century, the supposedly ancient bonds of nation came to stand in opposition to the large-scale geographic distinctions between human types more typical of race. In a world in which culture and nation legitimized each other—in aspiration if not in reality—nature lost its capacity to transform people who moved to a new environment.[12]

Despite these conceptual distinctions, *culture* inherited and perpetuated many of the same differences among humans previously labeled *race*, merely relegating those inextricable from bodies to the biologists and discounting the role of the environment. "Tradition" could be as heavy a burden as any supposedly inherent backwardness for those on the receiving end of anthropological classification, for the power to classify has never been equally distributed. Yet the shift in the content of and relationships between race and culture was not merely cosmetic. Nature, in the renovated understanding, ceased to be the inescapable source of human difference and thus social strife and became the privileged source of relief from it, the imagined past in which people knew their place and happily stayed in it. Whereas nature required a war among the races in the view of early twentieth-century white supremacists, culture in the eyes of the advocates of an emergent cultural pluralism required the mutual, respectful exchange of racial gifts (a term about which I will have more to say).[13]

The role of modern tropicality—and the tourist industry that promoted it—in popularizing the shifting role of nature in concepts of human variation and social organization becomes clearer if we look at two major tributaries to cultural pluralism: romantic racialism and heterosexual liberalism. Both entailed altered relationships between whites and nature that downplayed civilization's repressive role and emphasized the productive variety of human nature. Deeply invested in romantic individualism, both concepts also invoked a universal human nature that subtended every parochial manifestation of humanity. They celebrated the idea of the individual as the naturally distinctive expression of a universal truth, thus blurring the lines between primitive and civilized, nonwhite and white, male and female, and tropical and temperate. Perhaps most important, both romantic racialism and heterosexual liberalism celebrated human desires as the natural building blocks of healthy, happy societies. That is, they insisted that human nature produced civilization, rather than being an anarchic force needing to be harnessed by it.[14]

Conceptually similar, romantic racialism and heterosexual liberalism were historically intertwined as well. Growing out of the eighteenth-century romantic rejection of Enlightenment universalism, the former idea claimed difference as the condition for—not the enemy of—social progress. The notion that each people had a distinctive contribution—its "racial gift"—to make to the shared project of civilization was central to the ideologies of many nationalist, antiracist, and anticolonial movements at the turn of the twentieth century. This way of thinking reversed the civilized hierarchy of values to prize the characteristics long attributed to nonwhite peoples— their sensuality, their spirituality, their organic connection with land and community—and to condemn the repressive, materialist, and alienated conditions supposedly produced by civilized, industrial societies, thus preserving the differences constituted by white supremacy while challenging their ranking. To give one example, in 1924 the noted African American activist W. E. B. Du Bois celebrated "the peculiar spiritual quality which the Negro has injected into American life and civilization. It is hard to define or characterize it—a certain spiritual joyousness; a sensuous, tropical love of life, in vivid contrast to the cool and cautious New England reason." The epitome of a cool and cautious New England man of reason, Du Bois had famously written two decades earlier about the painful "twoness" of being a black person in the United States, so one may suspect that he, like many other minority and nationalist leaders, used such simplifications tactically in challenging racism. And yet this instance of romantic racialism was not merely a calculated descent into the vernacular. Particularly in his fiction, Du Bois frequently resorted to romantic language, themes, and plots to dramatize the emotional and intimate consequences of racism and the defiance of it.[15]

Indeed, because whites had long attributed to nonwhites excessive or undisciplined sexuality, abandoning the universal scale of civilization for culture's leveling play of difference necessarily threw sexual mores into question. Yet despite the long intimacy of race and sexuality in Western thinking, the rise of heterosexual liberalism, or the idea that consensual, monogamous, opposite-sex, adult sexual relations are the expression of natural impulses whose indulgence produces individual mental and physical health and social well-being, is usually portrayed as a transformation among white, middle-class, urban people, with some credit also given to working-class urbanites. In the usual story, for much of the nineteenth century, respectable women of all races who wished to claim a public role had to insist on their own superior morality, their lack of the base passions that drove men. By the early twentieth, a few of the middle-class white women empowered by two generations of political activism and growing opportunities for education and paid labor began to assert that women's sexual self-determination was the key to undoing civilization's repressive inequality. They then evangelized less privileged women, extending the "sexual revolution" to a wider range of women by the late twentieth century.[16]

As this hasty sketch should suggest, heterosexual liberalism was deeply racialized from the start. Ideals of female sexual modesty had long been critical measures of race, class, and ethnic status, and so alterations in the pattern of racial distinction necessarily stretched the fabric of sexual respectability. In the nineteenth century, northern European and North American whites faulted pretty much everyone living south of them or having darker skin for loose morals, and they associated their own "civilized" limits on women's sexual autonomy with raising women's status, scorning the greater or lesser restraints of other societies as oppressive. The twentieth-century challenge to respectable sexual conventions inevitably had racial implications. For instance, in the United States feminist demands for women's sexual autonomy made far less headway in the South, where the twin notions of white women's purity and African Americans' excessive sexuality justified rape and lynching in the maintenance of racial segregation and traditional gender roles. Many working-class women and women of color rejected the call for sexual self-determination precisely because it imperiled them to a far greater degree than it did well-to-do, white professional women.[17]

Both romantic racialism and heterosexual liberalism contributed to the emergence of the idea of culture by claiming nature as an ally, not an enemy, of civilization. Both concepts promoted the idea that people need not conquer nature or even human nature, but rather let both flower to produce harmonious social relations. From this perspective, cultural pluralism was more natural than racism and sexism and therefore would produce a happier society. Such ideas were critical for the success of tourism in the Southland, and in turn tropical tourism contributed to the popularization of the idea of culture. The tourist industry found culture, with its emphasis on the joys of variety, a congenial means of encouraging pleasure travel. Its marketing materials routinely advertised the idea that specific places were home to distinctive peoples regardless of similarities in geography, thus eroding the universalism implicit in environmental determinism. Tropical tourism contributed especially powerfully to this erosion because marketing hot climates as attractive vacation sites required precisely that reconceptualization of difference, belonging, and global geography summarized by culture. If human differences sprang from histories rather than geographies, then travel to new places could not remake those differences. Proving that a sojourn in the tropics would not turn civilized whites into primitive nonwhites

but merely rejuvenate them, faculties intact, meant profits for the Southland's promoters.

The idea of racial gifts implicit in the notion of culture was particularly
useful to tourism entrepreneurs because it reinforced the common portrayal
of pleasure travel as an institutionalized form of gift exchange—the gift of
hospitality for the gift of appreciation. In fact, tourism in the Southland
was frequently described as the trade of tropical joyousness and sensuality
in return for temperate business sense, engineering, and, of course, money.
The centrality of racial gifts to this commercial enterprise assisted with the
emergence of the idea of culture not least because it identified specific qualities (such as musicality among people of African descent, or visual artistry
among indigenous people) or discrete arts or objects (the rumba, serapes,
palm-frond hats) as the realization of cultural difference. Once defined in
this way, such differences could be easily circulated—usually sold, as with
performances and handicrafts in the Southland, but also absorbed as a way of
organizing and understanding human variation.[18]

In short, the idea of culture reduced the dangers and heightened the pleasures of the natural world, especially the tropics, nature's last redoubt against
the dominion of civilization. In the older view, nature was the source of the
problem solved by civilization; in the new one, it was the solution to the
problem posed by civilization. Advocates of romantic racialism, by portraying racial discrimination as the repression of a variety natural to humanity
and consequently beneficial to civilization, shifted nature's role in the formation of human individuals and societies. Advocates of heterosexual liberalism, in casting conventional sexual regulations as stifling perversions that
undermined both individual happiness and a society's viability, did the same.
Culture became the name of this rearticulation of the relationship between
humans and nature. In the language of race, nature was a realm of dangerously uncontrolled desires; in the language of culture, it was the realm of
freedom from oppressive social restrictions on healthy desires.[19] And as they
had for centuries, the tropics represented for North Americans and Europeans nature at her most powerful—so, under the regime of culture, the most
libratory. The perfect place to take a vacation.

The Development of the Southland

The tourist industry helped to forge the links of this altered bond between people and nature by offering U.S. whites a new relationship to the tropics— "the expansion of the soul from out the chill of ice and snow," as Ida Starr put it—without the risk of losing that soul to unregulated passions. It is true that the kind of leisure travel that I focus on here was the privilege of only a very small number of people—the "vacation gentry," in the words of a contemporary observer. The weeks free of labor and the large sums of money required for a stay at the luxurious resorts in Palm Beach, Florida, or Coronado Island, California, a first-class cruise around the Caribbean, or a Pullman-car tour of Mexico were more than most people could afford. Yet millions had the opportunity to see advertisements for such journeys, particularly after newspapers sprouted travel sections and printed more advertising and more graphics in the 1920s. Travel writing, public lectures, and stereographic and lantern slide images of far-off places beguiled many who would never eat strawberries in December in Mexico. The Florida golfing and fishing vacations of Presidents Warren Harding and Herbert Hoover and high society jaunts to Jamaica made the news, as did satires of them by Finley Peter Dunne and Ring Lardner. Hollywood kept Southern California in the public eye as a movie set and backdrop for the fabulous lives of the stars, as well as churning out hundreds of films set in real and imagined parts of the Southland. Professional athletes started migrating south for the winter some time around 1900, and the growing number of automobiles and paved roads after 1916 opened some places, especially Florida, to those with middling incomes.[20] Tropicality exercised its influence through its pervasive representation as much, or perhaps more, than through actual experience.

The Southland's tourism entrepreneurs convinced millions of the benignity of the tropics in several ways. First, the industry drew on medical geography and the rapid spread of commercial horticulture to show that the region, far from ensuring an early and miserable death, offered renewed health and vigor to both travelers and those stuck at home. Next, the industry rearticulated the bond between humans and nature through its rapidly expanding itineraries and also through new and improved modes of travel. Improvements in transportation, chiefly the extension of railroad and steamship routes and their growing speed and comfort in this era, with automobiles gaining in importance in the 1910s and passenger air travel beginning in the late 1920s, made it possible to go more places—and return home—faster and

more easily. These experiences and the fantasies that inspired them attenu-
ated the bond between people and their environment (that is, they weakened
the force of nature on body and soul) by making the experience of many
places more readily available, attractive, and free of undesirable consequences. Given enough money, one could subject nature's influence to the
evasive power of railroads and steamships and have summer year-round.

One of the chief signs of this new embrace of the tropics among North
American whites was a more positive view of warm weather. Increasingly,
residents of the temperate zone came to believe that whites might occupy
the tropics without being transformed by them, or only being transformed
in positive ways. New ideas about nature went hand in hand with new ideals
of selfhood and bodily propriety. The growing importance of beachgoing and
changing fashions in clothing, especially the radical shrinking of the bathing suit, amplified the signal given by travelers' donning of lightweight white
clothing on the trip south: a greater openness to the caresses of tropical nature. The unlikely new fashion for suntanning literally incorporated these
changes in attitudes and attire into white bodies. Innovative styles in dress
and bodily aesthetics in turn participated in the formulation of new norms
of sexuality. Redeploying venerable fantasies about people of Latin and African descent, North American whites simultaneously accepted the racial
gift of ready passion and bolstered white racial integrity to generate a self-
consciously modern heterosexual liberalism.

The popularization of the Southland through the concept of culture pre-
cipitated a transformation in the character of tourism throughout the hemisphere. In the Americas, pleasure travel and colonization had long been
phases of a single enterprise centered on rooting people in new places, but
after 1900 the two forms of travel became increasingly distinct. Even as white
North Americans came to believe that they could inhabit the tropics with im-
punity, Latin American and Caribbean leaders began to regulate foreigners'
access to the nation to ensure that they came to experience its culture, not to
put down roots. Regional elites devoted increasing resources to promoting
tourism in the 1920s and 1930s while enacting laws that defined wealthy visitors as transitory culture seekers, people who had no roots in tropical lands
and would never—could never—grow them. This codification of tourism
played a considerable part in rearticulating the relationship between people
and nature by locating belonging within culture and law and restricting the
capacity of visitors to naturalize.

The consequences of the development of the Southland are readily visible today in the archipelago of tropical beach resorts that girdles the globe. Then as now, the transaction at the heart of tropical tourism, the exchange of racial gifts, constituted a form of commercial multiculturalism in which the diversity of goods in the marketplace was presumed to resolve any antagonisms deriving from social inequalities. Throughout the Southland, the Latin, African-descended, and indigenous peoples who saw themselves celebrated as exemplars of youthful, healthy sensuality did not gain voting rights, access to jobs and land (much less political sovereignty), or even much money as a result of their roles as regional icons or commercial attractions. Indeed, in many cases governments and entrepreneurs bent on resort development seized the lands of poor and nonwhite people and suppressed their political participation and labor activism. Except as servants they were unwelcome on the new cruise ships and at the new beach resorts, whose pink-cheeked guests still didn't want their newly liberated daughters to marry one. And the tourist industry only reinforced the centuries-old assumption of those in temperate lands that the tropics are an inexhaustible source of natural wealth, sustaining economic and political systems that typically benefited outsiders more than locals and degraded the environment. Such criticisms remain valid today, despite nationalist revolutions and the widespread delegitimization of white supremacy.[21]

Nevertheless, the consequences of the rise of the Southland cannot be reduced simply to the perpetuation of unchanging North American and European racism and imperialism. The romantic racialism and heterosexual liberalism that accompanied and justified pleasure travel south of the border identified challenges to racism and sexism as modern pleasures. As white North Americans learned to love the tropics, they also learned to question one of the founding assumptions of white supremacy: that it represented the best and most moral way of life. They learned that in the tropics they might not be in danger of losing their souls but of recovering them. Although that new knowledge fell well short of a commitment to equality and justice for all, it increased the likelihood that some whites would make such commitments. The converse is also true: at the heart of modern challenges to nineteenth-century certitudes remain ideas about human differences ineradicably dyed with prejudice. Certainly the idea that nature is humanity's to manage has caused as many ills as benefits. But the fact that tropical tourism failed to keep the utopian promise of culture—that mutual understanding will produce social justice—should not blind us to the significant role that the industry and the experiences it sells played (and continue to play) in formulating and popularizing a renovated understanding of nature, including human nature. Dismissing pleasure travel as superficial or a perversion of genuine social relationships means refusing to take seriously one of the chief ways we interact with and imagine each other as creatures of this earth.

CHAPTER 1

A Regulated Arcadia

In a fable set in the 1850s and published in the U.S. magazine *Overland Monthly* in 1870, two young white men from the United States sail from New York for the California goldfields. As they wait for canoes to take them across the Isthmus of Panama, one falls ill with "isthmus fever" and is tended by a young local woman. She is beautiful, the narrator tells us, in spite of her mixed Indian, African, and Spanish heritage, for "in that climate, it was not to be expected that a dark skin should excite the same aversion with which at home we generally regard it." Her loving care preserves the man's life, but it leads to a fate worse than death: he decides to stay in Panama with her. "It was a regular Arcadia that he had contrived in his imagination," sighs the older and wiser narrator: "we other poor devils were to go up to the mines, and there delve and wear out our strength, and become toil-bent and haggard in our profitless pursuit of the glittering metal." If they succeeded against long odds in striking it rich, their "labor [would] lead to no pleasant result, since our very riches would involve us in the entanglements of a vicious and artificial civilization." Spurning the fate of those who toiled in civilization's mines, the convalescent man "would marry his native flame. . . . The fruits of the ground would be their food, and the birds should sing around them. . . . In such an oasis of pleasant days their lives would gently glide along." After the fashion of fables, his friends—and the timely reappearance of the young woman's husband—save him from this folly and return him to the bosom of civilization in the shape of a far more suitable wife, "a tall, elderly woman, with a hook-nose and bony frame, who . . . perhaps made him pretty comfortable, after a cold, morbid manner."[1]

This long-forgotten tale succinctly captures the seductive perils of the tropics for adventurers from the temperate zones, as well as the chilly comforts of civilization. Having overcome the physical peril, the "isthmus fever" that indexes the deadly diseases and high mortality rates that accompanied European expansion and slave trading in the world's warm places, this deluded young man succumbs to the moral peril of the tropics—the fantasy of a life free of work, privation, and the color line, and full of leisure and sensual pleasure afforded by generous nature. For the sake of white civilization, he cannot be permitted to give his life to the tropics, yet the loss of this youthful passion reduces him to a mean, prim man; "all the romance of his disposition seemed driven out of him."[2] The price of civilization's victory over the tropics is steep.

This portrayal of the contest between temperate civilization and tropical backwardness sums up the complex ideas about the relationships among nature, race, and sexuality out of which the tourist industry constructed the Southland and invited whites to inhabit it. Before they could build, entrepreneurs and local governments had to assure potential visitors that the life-threatening diseases with which tropical regions were associated had been overcome; they had to assure whites that the tropics, though beguiling enough to visit, would not seduce them into abandoning their ambitions and crossing the color line. Rather than imperil civilization by eroding the virtue of the civilized, the tourist industry promised that the warm places of the world would be a well-deserved reward for those who "delve and wear out [their] strength"—a reward integral to civilization's continuance. Aided by changing medical theories and the spread of large-scale fruit plantations throughout the Southland, tourist entrepreneurs popularized the romantic critique of civilization as a source of personal well-being and economic opportunity for whites. In short, the industry helped to make the tropics safe for whites by altering their relationship with nature, their own as well as the lush landscapes of the Southland.

The process of rearticulation had to begin with the venerable environmental determinism that undergirded medicine, imperial policy, and popular conceptions of human variation during the nineteenth century. The central principle—that the natural environment shapes its human inhabitants—combined with high mortality among Europeans and North Americans in southern lands to convince most whites that the tropics were a serious threat to white bodies and white civilization. Tourists faced these risks because of the form leisure journeys often took in those days—long, slow voyages leading to long stays—but also because tourism and colonization were close kin in the Americas throughout the nineteenth century. Throughout the nineteenth century and into the twentieth, distinguishing between visitors and emigrants, tourists and investors, was often impossible, because the final battles between settler states and native peoples were still being fought, national borders and imperial dominions were shifting, millions of people were traveling from Europe and Asia and among the American states and colonies, and economies were developing rapidly in response to the world's uneven industrialization. Even the most self-effacing pleasure traveler cast a colonizing gaze under these circumstances, and even the most calculating imperialist visited the same nascent sights as did sojourners without pecuniary motives.[3]

Southland promoters had one especially useful ally in their efforts to reassure potential visitors: physicians. They commonly sent well-to-do patients south for the winter, offering as therapy the same warm climate that imperiled whiteness in debates about race and empire. These invalid hegiras laid the foundations for what would soon become a booming tourist industry in Florida and Southern California, and to a lesser extent in the Caribbean and Mexico. Then, at the turn of the twentieth century, two developments—germ theory and the expansion of commercial agriculture throughout the region—undermined environmental determinism and the concepts of human difference that it supported. By containing the dangers of tropical nature and turning its fecundity to civilized ends, these developments aided the tourist industry in making the Southland a source of pleasure, rather than danger, for visiting whites—a regulated, rather than a regular, Arcadia.

White Man's Grave

Building on ancient Greek ideas, Europeans and then Euro-Americans for centuries believed that the environment played a large role in shaping human beings and their societies: individually and collectively, people were creatures of the place they lived in. Among many environmental factors, climate loomed large. At the largest scale, warm climates produced dark-skinned people who were hot-blooded, emotional, and indolent, while temperate climates generated light-skinned people who were cool, rational, and hardworking. Writing to a European naturalist in the late eighteenth century, Thomas Jefferson categorized residents of Virginia, including himself, as southerners who partook of the "fiery, voluptuary, indolent" characteristics of that breed. The classic elaboration of this line of thought came from the eighteenth-century French philosopher Charles de Montesquieu, who asserted that heat relaxed the fibers of men's bodies, making them weak, timid, and overly sensitive to stimulation. Conversely, cold shortened the fibers, making men strong, courageous, and indifferent to pain. Climate likewise governed sexual passions: "With the delicacy of organs found in hot countries, the soul is sovereignly moved by all that is related to the union of the two sexes; everything leads to this object. In northern climates, the physical aspect of love has scarcely enough strength to make itself felt."[4]

Although few twentieth-century U.S. residents were likely to have read much Montesquieu, the ideas he had formulated continued to structure racial attitudes well into the twentieth century. When the American Social Surveys firm conducted a study of U.S. citizens' perceptions of Latin Americans for the U.S. Office of Inter-American Affairs on December 10–20, 1940, it found that, given a choice of nineteen adjectives with which to describe residents of Central and South America, 49.3 percent chose "quick-tempered" and 43.7 percent "emotional," with "lazy" not far behind at 38.5 percent. The questionnaire did not ask the respondents to explain the origins of these characteristics or their policy implications, but the report on the findings noted that the better educated were more likely than the less educated to attribute these characteristics to Latin Americans.[5]

Although obviously heir to this venerable environmental determinism, the Euro-American concept of race in its simplest iteration—that is, that white and nonwhite humans differ radically and the former are superior—did not spring fully formed from the forehead of ancient Greek climatology or even Montesquieu's influential work. Through the first two to three hundred years of European expansion, both intellectuals and colonists believed that whites could—and should—acclimatize to hot climates, including the tropics. If they lived past the initial "seasoning," adopted sensible clothing and customs from the local people, and learned to use local medicines and therapies, Europeans could thrive in their newly conquered lands. This confidence persisted despite very high mortality rates among new arrivals, endemic malaria, and chronic, devastating epidemics of diseases like cholera, dysentery, typhoid, and yellow fever. After all, such diseases also occurred in temperate areas.[6]

Even as mortality rates fell in the early nineteenth century, this confidence began to wane in tandem with the hardening of racial distinctions. The nineteenth-century argument between monogenists and polygenists over whether humans had a single origin or many was in part about whether climate produced race or race was divinely ordained and unchanging. The advent of evolutionary thought in both its Lamarckian and Darwinian forms intensified the argument about human origins and how the species might change over time and in different environments, topics intensely racialized by the late nineteenth century. The abolition of slavery in the Americas between the 1820s and the 1880s, the accelerating migration of people from Asia and Europe to the Western Hemisphere, and the renewed imperialism at the turn of the twentieth century helped to promote an extreme form of white supremacy that asserted an essential difference between white and non-white, temperate and tropical. Whereas Europeans and North Americans had long believed that different climates produced certain kinds of human beings, by 1900 most believed that distinct races of humans were suited to distinct climates, a change in emphasis that underscored the threat of the tropics to natives of the temperate zone—that is, whites.[7]

The U.S. geographers Ellsworth Huntington and Ellen Churchill Semple were among the best-known advocates of climatic determinism and racial hierarchy in the early twentieth century. Like most scholars, they agreed that civilization simply could not arise in the tropics, because there humans had no incentive to transcend their animal natures. Huntington claimed as one of the fundamental principles of his field that "the world contains a few great centers of evolution"—by which he meant the progressive development of complex civilization—and "these are located in the interiors of the continents in medium or high latitudes" because there "the physical environment is most variable. In a warm, moist plain in low latitudes an animal never experiences any great extremes of either heat or cold. . . . [As a result] even if [these animals] are not sluggish, they are usually primitive." Man was born in the tropics, Semple argued, and "in his primitive, pre-civilized state, he lived in a moist, warm, uniform climate which supplied abundantly his simple wants, [and] put no strain upon his feeble intellect and will." Temperate areas, by contrast, "are characterized by the intermediate degrees of annual temperature and marked seasonal diversity which are so favorable to human development" and therefore these zones "are richer in cultural possibilities and hence in historical importance."[8] Only when humans moved out of the tropics did they encounter the challenges that produced evolution and, eventually, civilization.

Although Semple and Huntington wrote in a scientific, secular mode, the idea that the tropics exercised their fatal influence by offering a fantastic, seasonless luxuriance that enabled people to live without working had deep roots in Christian theology. To Christians, the idea of a life without effort necessarily brought to mind Eden, that garden home before original sin condemned humans to labor for their sustenance. For some among the early European explorers and colonizers, the American tropics in particular constituted the earthly realization of a prelapsarian state of grace. In the sixteenth and seventeenth centuries, the "New World"—especially the West Indies—seemed to be free of both the economic hardships and the political corruption of Europe. Some of those engaged in debates over colonization and religious and political change in Europe dwelt lovingly on the natural Christianity of the native peoples of the Americas. Their physical beauty and paucity of clothing underscored their purity of body and soul—they had no need of that fig leaf.[9]

In the pessimistic version of climatic determinism typical of the late nineteenth century, though, the very absence of want and bareness of bodies among tropical peoples signaled their failure to achieve civilized morality. Without the spur of adversity and the fear of future scarcity, they never learned to work hard; without the modest clothing required by cold weather or the scourge of hungry children, they never learned to control their passions. James Froude, on a tour of inspection in the British West Indies in the late 1880s, reported that the black residents "live surrounded by most of the fruits which grew in Adam's paradise. . . . The curse is taken off from nature, and like Adam again they are under the covenant of innocence." Too ignorant to know that nonmarital sexuality was a sin, they lived amoral lives and allowed those of their many children who did not die young to "scramble up anyhow, and shift for themselves like chickens." These contented peasants "have no aspirations to make them restless," and "if happiness is the be all and end all of life," then they are "the supremest specimen of present humanity." Not confined to dark-skinned peoples of the tropics, such traits emerged gradually as one traveled south, according to the climatologists. Semple pronounced, "The southerners of the sub-tropical Mediterranean basin are easy-going, improvident except under pressing necessity, gay, emotional, imaginative, all qualities which among the negroes of the equatorial belt degenerate into grave racial faults."[10]

The absence of seasons was more than an incentive for laziness and immorality. For many Europeans and North Americans, the natural cycle was a worldly enactment of the Christian promise of resurrection and eternal life. In this scheme, spring was a time of rebirth and courtship, summer of fruitfulness, autumn of mature preparation for the scarcity to come, and winter of old age and inevitable death. Without the latter two, there was no hope of a proper Christian atonement for sin and renewal of life. Writing from the Florida plantation where she spent her winters from the late 1860s, Harriet Beecher Stowe reminded her readers that "we are seeing all things in winter, and not as they will be when God shall wipe away all tears, and bring about the new heaven and new earth, of which every spring is a symbol and a prophecy." Until the happy day of the millennium, however, those who lived in perpetual spring or summer remained careless children, unable to achieve spiritual redemption or material civilization. As Semple argued, "Everywhere a cold climate puts a steadying hand on the human heart and brain. . . . Among the folk of warmer lands eternal spring holds sway. National life and temperament have the buoyancy and thoughtlessness of childhood."[11]

In short, the pessimistic climatic determinism of the nineteenth century cast the tropics and their residents as necessarily primitive and lacking the capacity to become civilized. From this perspective, they had neither the morals nor the ambitions of the pale-skinned peoples of the world's temperate zones. But despite this dire diagnosis, white people had long lived in the tropics and were colonizing ever more of them in the imperial scramble of the turn of the twentieth century. The possible racial consequences of such migrations—and the long visits, often presaging a more permanent move, that were typical of leisure travel in this era—preoccupied many thinkers and imperial officials. Some believed that climate no longer exercised the same power over humans as it had in the past and that the races were now stable and unchanging. If that were true, however, then whites could never adapt to the tropics and would face significant handicaps in exploiting their riches. Others, believing that humans continued to be malleable (and now often casting this belief in evolutionary terms), feared that the tropics would remake white colonists in their own image.[12]

The possibility itself was not new; seventeenth-century English colonists in the Chesapeake Bay region (today's Maryland, Virginia, and the District of Columbia) feared their transmutation into Spaniards from living in a place on the same latitude as Spain. But it took on a new intensity in the late nineteenth century, when the fear that whites who lived in the tropics might become dark-skinned was labeled "racial degeneration." "The real problem is this," Harvard professor Robert De C. Ward pronounced in summing up a century's thinking in 1930: "Can men and women of the white race immigrate in large numbers to the moist hot Tropics and live there on the same high plane of civilization as that characteristic of their former homes, retaining their physical health and vitality, their mental and moral standards, and reproducing their own kind?" And the danger was not confined to the first generation: "Further, can future generations of white people, born in the Tropics, maintain, in the years to come, these same standards of civilization and of physical, mental, and moral vigor?" Ward's answer was no, a pessimism echoed by many experts and travelers in the tropics. Semple concluded, "The intense heat and humidity of most tropical lands prevent any permanent occupation by a native-born population of pure whites."[13]

As Ward and the *Overland Monthly* story published sixty years earlier made clear, the dangers to whites in the tropics were both physical and moral. Although death rates had declined significantly by the late nineteenth century, epidemics and efforts to control them with quarantines and large-scale fumigation had a significant economic and political impact. Medical officers inspected every passenger on every ship entering Caribbean ports, and many American countries required certificates attesting to travelers' health and vaccination against smallpox well into the twentieth century. The commercial effects of epidemics of yellow fever believed to originate in Cuba helped justify U.S. military interventions in that country in 1898 and 1906. Steaming around the Caribbean in 1897, Joseph Kirkbride scribbled in his journal, "The next stop will be St. Vincent—an island not on list but to take the place of Guadeloupe, where Yellow fever prevents us from stopping." He and his fellow passengers missed seeing Curaçao for the same reason. Even if visitors to the tropics did not come down with a specific disease, the enervating wet heat still threatened their racial vigor and bodily health, because in nineteenth-century medical understanding, miasmas, or the damp, putrid air rising from low-lying land, were a major source of illness. Ward wrote, "The muggy, oppressive 'hothouse' air is not only uncomfortable and difficult to endure, but it has a distinctly enervating effect, which is more or less widespread among all white residents of the Tropics."[14]

Compounding the peril of high humidity was the blazing tropical sunshine: "'Beware of the sun' is a good rule for the Tropics. There is, in general, too much sunshine in the Tropics." Eighteenth- and nineteenth-century physicians especially worried about the effects of the sun's rays on whites' heads and kidneys, advising them to wear hats and special underwear and avoid the noonday sun. Even in the cool tropical highlands the sun could be harmful. Guidebook writer T. Philip Terry advised against "sun baths" in Mexico's high country: "In elevated districts the golden rays of the sun possess a subtle banefulness which sometimes produce curious disorders. . . . After hours of exercise in the sun at high altitude strong men have been known to faint. . . . The nerves of the most phlegmatic will sometimes twitter and become jangled."[15]

By the turn of the twentieth century, developments in the study of the electromagnetic spectrum imparted a modern sheen to this long-standing fear. In an influential study based on research in the U.S.-occupied Philippines, army doctor Charles Woodruff argued that the greater proportion of "actinic" (ultraviolet) rays in tropical sunshine penetrated the vulnerable pale skins of whites and overstimulated them, leading to nervous exhaustion or "tropical neurasthenia." They could survive—but probably never thrive—in the tropics only with the proper prophylaxis: "*Day clothing should be opaque*"—certainly not the sheer whites most tropical visitors donned—and the "hat must be of wide brim and thick enough to exclude all the rays [of the sun]." Finally, houses, schools, and hospitals must be kept dark.[16] In short, whites had to shield themselves assiduously from tropical nature if they were to retain command of both their faculties and their colonies. Donning sheer whites and rejoicing in the sun's warmth, as so many southbound travelers did, could only lead to mental and bodily decay.

The physical degeneration caused by the heat and sunshine inexorably led to moral depravity because, as the relentlessly grim Semple wrote, the tropics "produce certain derangements to the physiological functions" that lead to "intense enervation; this starts a craving for stimulants and induces habits of alcoholism," while also tending "to relax the mental and moral fiber" and inducing "indolence, self-indulgences and various excesses which lower the physical tone." Huntington concurred: "In tropical countries weakness of will is unfortunately a quality displayed not only by the natives, but by a large proportion of the northerner sojourners," citing gambling, lying, drunkenness, laziness, and sexual promiscuity.[17] (Exciting pastimes, freedom from home constraints, lavish food and drink, complete relaxation, and sexy, sexually available companions: what self-respecting tropical resort does not advertise these as its prime attractions today?)

Such ideas were not limited to scholarly studies or imperial policymaking; travel writers often rehearsed them as well. Reminding his readers that "it is thought that unless people are spurred on incessantly by the exigencies of the changing seasons they will lose energy, and fall into an idle floating along with gracious nature," journalist Charles Dudley Warner asked, "will Southern California be an exception to those lands of equable climate and extraordinary fertility where every effort is postponed till 'to-morrow?'" One Florida visitor, regretting the end of her tenth winter there, confided in a letter that "I have had a most complete vacation—such a resting time! I fear it has made me lazy & slow." Stephen Graham shook his head sadly over the U.S. colony in Panama in the 1920s: "Apathy, listlessness, no doubt, is the chief danger [to whites] in Panama, and that being a spiritual danger it is more to be regarded than the material danger of disease." C. W. Johnston, who approved of few people and places outside his home state of Iowa, believed that whites living in Panama would inevitably degenerate to the level of the natives: "The [local] people have no life nor energy to do anything, the same as all humanity similarly situated in hot climates. . . . That which is accomplished worth while is done by constantly infusing new blood from colder climates."[18] In these cases, the tropical climate was eroding the physical and moral superiority of white colonists, reducing them to the indolence and immorality of the dark-skinned locals.

And what about the new generation, born in the tropics? Influenced by the sultry climate, they would emulate their dark-skinned peers in being physically and sexually precocious but failing to mature into disciplined, capable adults. As A. Grenfell Price wrote in a 1939 study summing up a wide array of earlier research, "Under the [Jamaican] climate the [white] children's mental powers developed early," but "subsequent mental acquirement did not keep pace with early progress." As if that was not bad enough, "the climate undoubtedly encouraged early and habitual licentiousness." White Australian children living in tropical Queensland similarly "develop rapidly and are of good physique, tall, highly strung, excitable, and sexually advanced," although they also "show a marked falling off in intellect after sixteen." Writing to a friend in Illinois from Jamaica, Ruth Bryan Owen reported of a child she was caring for that "Kitty is improving very much. Her adoption of local color would amuse you. (Perhaps local *color* is an unfortunate phrase on this island.) I refer to English manner."[19]

Long before Price's survey of the field, there were anecdotal reports of troubling changes in whites living in warm climates. Addison Awes, accompanying his ailing wife to Southern California in the 1890s, deplored the presence of what he called the "Sunday Picnic Girls": "If anything they exceed their pious sisters in physical strength and beauty; they are skilled in swimming, boating, fishing and shooting," but these prototypical California girls also "are immodest, rude and boisterous, and have a peculiar dare-devil way about them which makes them repulsive to the true gentleman." The climate, Awes believed, was so pleasant that people had no incentive to stay home and learn the behavior proper to their gender and age. The decline in manners and morals had a racial element as well: "having many of the characteristics of the Spanish race, and fast accumulating what they have not already acquired," Awes wrote of his hosts, they were "passionately fond of dancing, sports, gambling, holidays, [and] speculating," and he quickly fled back to his home in New England to publish this diatribe. Whether his wife recovered from her illness he did not mention.[20]

As Awes's complaint suggests, proximity to people already degraded by tropical influences (that is, the locals) heightened the purely climatic dangers. In the tropics, whites might lose the most important aspect of their racial identity—social dominance—along with their morals. Julius Muller warned readers of the *Century*, a popular magazine, that "the tourist who occasionally sees a white man in rags slink through the streets of a Caribbean port does not realize that what he sees is not so much a personal tragedy as a tragedy of his race." Wondering if whites really had to suffer freezing winters to maintain their superiority, Warner noted that "in the Barbadoes the white man is always thawed to the point of perspiration. And I am told by a man resident there that the whites in Barbadoes have no rights which the black man is bound to respect. There is an attempt to make him feel that he belongs to an inferior race." Worst of all, "often he has not energy enough to resist this prevailing impression."[21]

Indeed, the popular wisdom had long had it that a key element of white virtue—hard work—converted into a fatal flaw in the tropics, for as soon as whites attempted to do manual labor there, even on their own land, they descended socially, and eventually physically, to the level of the natives: "Only as a master can the white man survive in the tropics." The belief that only dark-skinned people could safely undertake hard labor in hot climates, thus making their enslavement by whites necessary, had a long pedigree. Montesquieu endorsed it, and the idea had shaped arguments for and against slavery in the 1830s and again when U.S. citizens debated their nation's expansion into Latin America, the Caribbean, and the Pacific in the 1890s and 1900s. Whereas many saw white rule as the key to making the tropics safe for white exploitation, others—repeating the abolitionist accusation that slavery made slave owners into tyrants—believed that this adoption of aristocratic ways endangered U.S. republican virtue. Either way, the white person in the tropics risked body and soul.[22]

In the absence of a steep and strictly policed racial hierarchy, many whites feared, proximity might lead them to abandon their racial-sexual scruples, as the *Overland Monthly* story dramatized. Muller repeated the point more euphemistically: "At first the poor Northern white man may loathe [the brown-skinned peasants of the Caribbean] with all the fierce prejudice of the North; but sooner or later tolerance is bound to come, if not to the original colonists, to their children." Following quickly on the heels of tolerance, re-production across the color line would fatally hasten the climate's slow work in transforming whites into people of color. For many white supremacists, Latin America (as well as Spanish and Portuguese colonies in Africa and India) constituted the chief examples of the intimate congress between de-generation and miscegenation. Prominent white supremacist Lothrop Stod-dard declared that "there can be no doubt that the [Latin American] Creole whites, as a class, showed increasing signs of degeneracy. Climate was a prime cause in the hotter regions" but "even more than by climate the Creole was injured by contact with the colored races. . . . Colored strains percolated in-sidiously into the Creole stock." With faint praise for highland Costa Rica, Stoddard dismissed its entire region as "the tropical jungle of degeneration, mongrel Central America."[23]

Although Stoddard's views are infamous today, they were not unusual in the early twentieth century. The belief that all people below the Rio Grande—as well as the descendants of Spanish colonists in the United States—were lazy, sexually immoral mixed-bloods prone to revolt shaped U.S. foreign pol-icy toward Latin American and Caribbean countries and structured popular attitudes toward U.S. imperialism in the region. The problem of the trop-ics became an urgent concern as the United States began to develop its far southeastern and southwestern peripheries—areas previously under the rule of Spain and its rebellious heirs—in the late nineteenth century. As Price put it in 1939, "The white penetration of Florida represents a penetration of the tropical margins," with all the racial dangers that entailed. "There is more sunshine, the atmosphere is more genial. It is a better place in which to loaf," Warner said of California. "Will these mild qualities of climate and condition in any injurious degree undermine and deteriorate the Anglo-Saxon energy and thrift?"[24] If Florida and California were dangerous, how much more so the nation's increasing economic, military, and political engagement with na-tions and colonies in Latin America and the Caribbean?

Of course, there are critical differences between Florida and California—fully privileged members of the United States for decades by the 1880s and dominated politically and demographically by white U.S. citizens—and the nations and colonies of the region that were not and did not become part of the colossus of the north or those that became subordinate parts of it, such as Puerto Rico, the Virgin Islands, and, to lesser extents and for shorter peri-ods, Cuba, Haiti, the Dominican Republic, and Nicaragua. But whether these places or others that the United States controlled for long periods would eventually be fully absorbed was still in play in the early years of the twentieth century, and tourism remained a forerunner of colonization. Both Southern California and Florida owed their rapid settlement to this relationship, and for a while it looked as if people from the United States would also flood Mexico and Cuba's Isle of Pines.[25] Any rise in pleasure travel to the Southland, inside or outside U.S. borders, might lead large numbers of white U.S. citizens to settle in tropical areas permanently, with troubling racial and political consequences. Travel businesses and regional promoters would have to address these fears if they expected to prosper.

Travel Therapy

The same ideas that motivated fears of white degeneration in the tropics generated the body of thought known as medical geography, which parsed the effects of climate and other environmental phenomena into prescriptions for individual well-being. Throughout the nineteenth century, both physicians and ordinary people in the United States understood health to be a matter of carefully calibrating the relationship between individual bodies and their environments, and so people took careful note of their natural and built surroundings in an effort to achieve and maintain physical well-being. Devoting themselves to this nexus of body with nature, medical geographers or climatologists produced reams of papers and books examining the precise effects of a place's "temperature, atmospheric vicissitudes, prevailing winds, humidity, its elevation above the sea level, its proximity to the ocean or oceanic currents, its contiguity to mountains, lakes, rivers, arid areas, soil, drainage, vegetable productions, malaria, general sanitation and other factors" on a variety of human types. This particular passage, significantly, comes from a pamphlet promoting the healthfulness of Florida's climate. Local boosters here and in Southern California drew heavily on the medical literature in the 1880s to promote their states—otherwise suspect for being so far south—as healthy places to live.[26]

While race theorists, geographers, and imperial officials worried about the effect of migration on racial difference, physicians regarded travel as a potentially valuable therapy for ailing individuals. If a person sickened because of a lack of harmony between her or his environment and that person's physical constitution, then going to another place better suited to that constitution was an obvious strategy. Today the travels of consumptive patients seeking high, dry, or at least warm locations far from the harsh northern winters are best remembered, but sufferers from digestive, renal, nervous, and other conditions also went from doctor's office to train station and wharf. Physician and San Diego booster Peter C. Remondino insisted that his region had "a variety of climates suited to all and every diathesis; the gouty and the rheumatic, the bronchitic and the asthmatic, the victim of demoralized liver or malarious spleen as well as the slave to periodical sore throats, enlarged tonsils, or the not overhappy possessor of a pair of rebellious lungs, backsliding kidneys or of a disgusted and enfeebled heart."[27]

But deciding which of these climates was appropriate required a well-informed physician: "Careful and thorough consideration should precede [the] decision where to send invalids for climate treatment," wrote William F. Hutchinson in an 1891 guide to the West Indies and Central America for physicians. Although "certain places are favorable for certain diseases . . . judicious selection is not an easy matter." Florida booster Charles J. Kenworthy agreed and quoted a colleague to support the point: " 'Of the large and annual increasing number of invalids, more especially consumptive patients, who are now sent abroad to winter in vapious [*sic*] health resorts, probably as many are injured by a wrong or by too tardy a change of climate, as are saved by the timely and judicious use of this most valuable remedy.' "[28]

Physician-prescribed travels underwrote the development of health resorts in Florida, Southern California, and the desert and mountain Southwest in the United States, and did the same to a lesser extent in Cuba and Jamaica, laying the foundations for the tourist trade soon to come. In Europe, the same process helped to create the resorts of the French Riviera. The close link between therapeutic and pleasure travel was neither accidental nor new; the mineral springs around which spas grew up in Europe and the United States had long offered both cures and recreation, and the belief that seawater and later sea air were healthful encouraged the growth of seaside resorts from the late eighteenth century. Wealthy enough to travel for extended periods, most ailing travelers and their healthy companions expected ample accommodations and pleasant diversions when they got to their destination. As the Atlantic Coast Railroad put it, "It is generally accepted as a truism, that recreation is just as necessary as occupation, if healthy life is to be attained." Consequently, Hutchinson pointed out, physicians had to take into account more than simply the climate: "How shall the sick man amuse himself? Are there rides or drives to take? Are there out-of-door games going on? What sort of society is down there? These are important points to all who are not prostrate."[29]

The British physician F. C. S. Sanders preferred California to other locations because "other climates may be better, but belong to countries objectionable either on account of their isolated situation, or the semi-civilized condition of their inhabitants." Although no fan of California, Kenworthy endorsed the sentiment: "The locality selected should present various attractive features, so as to keep the patient from brooding over his infirmities. The invalid requires cheerful society, sources of amusement and occupation, an opportunity to walk, ride, drive, boat, fish, botanize and enjoy sunshine." In contrast, Remondino was exasperated at how often medically necessary travel became pleasure travel and advised his readers not to "make a tourist's picnic out of your trip. I have seen many who have done so wear themselves out sight-seeing." "I have been sick ever since I left home" in Rhode Island for Southern California, Anna Dexter confided to her children, "although not so but what I could go about. Of course I couldn't stay in and [lose] anything."[30]

One of the great attractions of tropical places for physicians and the sick was their equable climates, precisely the characteristic that geographers and white supremacists believed would undermine racial vigor and civilizing dynamism. The variability of weather and sharp seasonal changes that Stoddard, Semple, Huntington, and many other like-minded thinkers regarded as essential racial stimulants, physicians regarded as threats to their patients' frail constitutions. "Sudden changes in temperature, however slight, must be carefully guarded against," Hutchinson warned, advising his readers always to wear a hat indoors and never to sit in a draft. Kenworthy blamed much illness in the North on the "cold and changeable climates" there and the necessity of artificial heat. Remondino claimed that San Diego County enjoyed the "coolest summers and warmest winters in the United States"—that is, the least change in temperature year round—"a climate that is the best, either for production, comfort, health, or long life."[31] Equable temperatures neither too warm nor too cold made it possible for people to live out of doors as much as possible and to ventilate their homes thoroughly, two key therapies of the period.

Medical climatologists also began to rework the old fear of the brilliant sunshine of the tropics. Many physicians regarded sunshine as a good general tonic mostly because when it shone, people could get outside and exercise in the fresh air: "It is the exercise and the open air which does [sic] the good, and the strong sunlight is of secondary importance." A logical extension of the view that environmental factors shaped health, "phototherapy" emerged as a field of research and application in the mid-nineteenth century, and by the late nineteenth century it had achieved a measure of respectability and was incorporated into medical education. The sun, of course, does not only shine in the Southland (though the travel literature would soon imply as much), and phototherapists did not limit their practice to that part of the world; alpine peaks were a favorite locale. Nor did they prescribe the casual use of this powerful tool. Remondino cautioned that "sunshine is healthy, but basking in the sun whilst sitting against some strongly reflecting surface in a still air and being immersed in a cool but not chilly sunshiny air in a tolerable degree of motion are wholly different and have entirely different results."[32] Nevertheless, to the extent that this carefully circumscribed medical redemption of sunshine countered Woodruff's view that strong sunlight would inexorably reduce healthy whites to nervous wrecks, it reduced fears about the impact of the tropics on visitors from the temperate zone. In the 1920s, Southland promoters and physicians would make much more of the health benefits of sunshine (see Chapter 4).

At the same time, such environmental explanations for poor health faced challenges from the new germ theory of disease. In the mid-nineteenth century, some scientists began to argue that microscopic creatures, not environmental phenomena such as foul smells, newly turned earth, damp air, or a mismatch between a person's constitution and the environment, caused disease. As scientists isolated bacteria and proved their role in generating specific illnesses, the approach enjoyed growing success, while medical geography lost influence. Although climatologists quickly pointed out that environmental conditions, including climate, often affected the ability of bacteria and parasites and their insect vectors to cause illness in humans, germ theory undermined the structure of ideas underlying this approach and the related concerns about white settlement in the tropics. If health required not a careful calibration of constitutional and environmental conditions but simply the eradication of particular microscopic creatures, then white settlers in the tropics—and their children—only needed to identify and eliminate germs in order to thrive there. Germ theory promised to reduce nature's power over human health, and that promise generated a new confidence among travelers, especially those with a weak grasp of the details. In 1935, Michael and Virginia Scully blithely assured their readers that "it is possible to travel over Mexico without encountering a single germ," but the rural areas were still primitive, "and all primitive countries have germs." But this unfortunate truth need not derail one's vacation plan; one needed only to "be sure your vaccination is recent enough to be effective."[33]

The process by which germ theory replaced medical geography was, as such paradigm shifts typically are, slow and partial, not least because germ theory did not immediately produce successful vaccines or cures and because patterns of illness clearly do vary according to geography and season. Yet in the tropics germ theory enjoyed a few spectacular successes at the turn of the twentieth century, as researchers discovered that two of its worst scourges, yellow fever and malaria, were caused by parasites carried from person to person by mosquitoes—not the wet, fetid climate or a lack of acclimatization to it. The 1898 war between the United States, Spain, and Cuba provided the institutional matrix in which ongoing research in Cuba and the United States led to the proof that mosquitoes spread yellow fever. The ability to prevent mosquito-borne disease then enabled the United States to keep enough laborers alive long enough to construct a canal across the Isthmus of Panama, a long-sought achievement that the French had most recently failed to attain.[34]

But this triumph of etiological detection led not to vaccines or targeted therapies but to more of what had already been prescribed in the name of environmental causation: improving drainage and installing sewer systems. Medical officials simply added to these older approaches a new emphasis on eliminating or sealing fresh water sources to prevent mosquitoes from breeding in them. Whatever the medical theory, it was clear to many U.S. whites that the near elimination of yellow fever from Havana and the Panama Canal Zone confirmed their own imperial benevolence, technological skill, and racial superiority. With scientific expertise, enterprise, and cleanliness, the United States had opened the dreadful tropics to white colonization, travel, and commerce. Briton Stephen Graham noted admiringly, "America . . . made the Canal, but she overcame the forces of death first. She overcame the idea of the white man's grave. She rolled away the stone from the sepulchre. What was one of the most pestilential swamps in the world is now something like a health resort."[35]

The triumph of germ theory over tropical disease was just one aspect of the conquest of the tropics. It became increasingly obvious to U.S. residents after 1914 that their know-how could control even the frighteningly fecund nature of the tropics: "Jungles on all sides teeming with life, but rendered harmless through engineering."[36] Nowhere was the power of rational enterprise more evident than in the planting of thousands of groves and fields growing tropical fruit, especially oranges (in Florida and Southern California) and bananas (in the Caribbean and Central America). These, as much as window screens and mosquito eradication campaigns, transformed the tropics into a source

of healthy pleasure for whites from temperate climes. The increasing availability of tropical fruit in U.S. markets, accompanied by the widespread circulation of images of the landscapes from which these fruits came, revived the
old vision of the tropics as Eden—and this time associated that paradise with
U.S. entrepreneurial vigor and industrial power.

Flowers and Fruits

The abundant fertility of the tropics had long sparked envy and fear in temperate hearts. There nature was so generous one did not need to work; there
nature's generosity snuffed out the possibility of human transcendence. European and North American naturalists and painters communicated this
double sense of luxury and danger in portrayals of overgrown, gigantic, lush
landscapes that circulated publicly via engravings and exhibits. Doing their
part, travel writers described the profusion of flowers as "rioting" with numb-
ing frequency: "tropical fruit and flowers riot in the sheer joy of living" in
Southern California, which "isn't beautiful in a sedate, reserved way—there
is a prodigal, riotous, abandoned spendthriftiness to its beauty." When travelers approached the island of Dominica, "the tropical luxuriance in all its
riotousness rushed to the sea's edge to greet us." In Florida, "blooms of a hundred varieties run riot," especially in Key West, where "yards and gardens are
ablaze with gorgeous blooms that riot because they can't help rioting. They
don't have to be incited to riot, as in the North." This figure of speech at once
expressed and belittled the fear of tropical fecundity.[37]

European and North American whites had long shipped representatives
of the abundant, unruly tropics northward. Symbols of the region's exotic,
primal power, tropical plants—especially the iconic royal and coconut palm
trees—by the mid-nineteenth century graced royal courts, botanical gardens,
and, especially in the United States, hotel lobbies. Gradually, and in small,
expensive quantities, some of the sweet fruits grown in the tropics also survived the journey northward. Oranges had long been known and prized in
Europe; bananas, grapefruits, mangos, and others were strange new wonders
in the mid-nineteenth century. Taking advantage of groves started by earlier Spanish colonists, U.S. farmers began growing oranges in Florida in the
1860s, and the fruit was a major element of Southern California's economy
from the 1880s. Bananas, long cultivated in glorious variety in the Caribbean and Central America, first made their way to the United States in small

quantities in the 1870s, selling for an expensive 10¢ (equivalent to $2.02 in 2010) each at the 1876 Centennial Exposition in Philadelphia. Thanks to U.S. dollar diplomacy, corporate gamesmanship, weak governments eager for infrastructural development and revenue, and ruthlessness, the U.S.-based United Fruit, Standard Fruit, and Cuyamel Companies created gigantic plantation archipelagos across the region to grow and ship the fruit north in vast quantities by the 1920s. Jamaica grew only 21,000 metric tons of bananas in 1887, but 356,000 in 1930; the United States produced 250,000 metric tons of citrus fruit in 1899, but 2.9 million in 1930. By the early decades of the twentieth century, the fruits of these labors appeared in quantity on the shelves of grocery stores across the country. One 1917 estimate had every U.S. resident eating seventy-two bananas every year, for a grand annual total of seven billion nationwide.[38]

The vast acreage devoted to a single type of a single cash crop, and the vast network of railroads and steamships linking those acres to grocery stores throughout the United States, embodied the taming of tropical nature in a way that was apparent on a daily basis to ordinary people. The plantations, like pioneers' farms on the prairies not long before, turned nature to human purposes, making civilization out of wilderness, fulfilling the divine mission that Christians believed God had given to humanity and that many white U.S. citizens considered their mission in the Western Hemisphere. Fruit growers did their part to spread the word that this transformation in the use of the land also transformed the meaning of warm climates: now they were sources of well-being, pleasure, and beauty. Advertising their products as marvelously healthful, they plastered their shipping crates with brightly colored labels portraying, among other things, lavishly fruitful landscapes and beautiful maidens, embodiments of tropical fertility and hospitality.[39] The proliferation of tropical fruit in U.S. markets went hand in hand with the increased circulation of images of tropical landscapes and tropical people, underscoring the new safety of the world's warm places (Plate 1).

The fruit crate label landscape—and similar images in travel writing— addressed in a highly compressed way the widespread concerns about the effect of the tropics on white people. Many such images, particularly those of California, showed a landscape of tidy green orchards, tilled fields, and whitewalled, red-roofed houses. By portraying a centuries-old idealization of rural life, such images countered two contemporary phenomena—the emergence of agribusiness and the widespread publicity about the poverty, backbreaking work, and loneliness of rural life for small farmers. The white-walled,

red-roofed houses evoked a mythic Spanish colonial past when genial aristocrats lived leisured lives amid fields of plenty. Guidebooks and postcards
generally portrayed orange picking as the happy pastime of pretty white girls
or white families, obscuring the labor of growing legions of mostly nonwhite
migrant workers who made tropical luxuries readily available to better-off
residents of the United States. Here in California, the images promised, the
ideal rural life was still available; one might be both a gentleman and a farmer.
Such imagery seems to have been less common in Florida, but the early developers credited themselves with bringing a northern work ethic to a land
neglected by earlier Spanish and southern white colonists.[40]

Fruit advertisements might be inducements to travel as much as railroad and tour company flyers, for flowering orange groves and oranges were
among Florida and Southern California's chief attractions for several decades.
Above images of an orange grove and a packing house in a souvenir booklet,
frequent traveler Lottie S. Tillotson scrawled "familiar scene." The "ultimate
object" of many visitors, a travel writer claimed, was "to eat oranges that they
have themselves picked." "Every grove Mama sees she wants to go in and pick
the oranges or shake a tree or two," Samuel Dexter told his children. When
the couple asked for some oranges before departing from their hotel in San
Diego, they "were told to go out in the yard at the rear of the hotel and pick
and eat what [they] liked." Riding through the streets of Pasadena, California,
in 1893, Augustus Tripp and his wife visited several groves and at one got
permission to eat all they liked: "We 'pitched in' and made a laughable exhibit
of ourselves with our faces buried in the delicious fruit"—exemplifying, in
a small, self-deprecating way, the erosion of civilization in the form of table
manners by tropical abundance.[41]

There was money to be made in this mania; outside St. Augustine, Florida,
one man improved upon nature when he "wired golden fruit and leafy twigs
on his trees by the bushel and then, because nature has made it difficult to
photograph oranges in their native color, he whitewashed the fruit." His stage
properly set, he offered to take tourists' pictures: "As a result you may send
home from the ancient Spanish city a picture of yourself, supremely happy,
standing beneath trees loaded with real fruit, picking them as nonchalantly
as if it was your constant occupation." Indeed, picking oranges became such a
cliché that humorist Irvin Cobb portrayed the Spanish explorer Balboa, after
dipping his toes in the Pacific, having had "his photograph taken showing
him standing in the midst of the tropical verdure, with a freshly picked orange in his hand"[42]—just as many latter-day tourists did (Fig. 1).

Figure 1. Picking oranges was one of the tropical fantasies many visitors to Southern California and Florida indulged. The tiny figure on the mountaintop in the distance says, "That, Elsie, is Old Baldy! Notice the snow"—reassuring fearful easterners that California had the full range of seasons. Adolph Christian Fera, *Post Cards of a Tourist (Mr. "Skinny" East): Cartoons of Southern California* (Los Angeles: Henry J. Pauly, 1910): 3, call no. 351476. Reproduced by permission of The Huntington Library, San Marino, California.

Picking and eating oranges was, for such a simple act, full of meaning. One of the chief cultural definitions of the tropics was a place where a person could sustain her- or himself simply by plucking fruit from the trees, as in the *Overland Monthly* story with which this chapter opens. "It seems as we pass this orange grove that I feel an almost irresistible urge to go in and pick up some of the golden fruit," Mrs. Neal Wyatt Chapline wrote, and then "pillow my head on the softness of Mother Earth freshly turned and be lulled to restfulness," the picture of an indolent tropical native. The apparent tendency of tourists to indulge themselves well past the point of comfort—Kenworthy blamed any ailments among visitors to Florida on their "eating excessive quantities of fruit"—suggests the tropics' dangerous allure. Oranges themselves, a fruit that cannot be grown in temperate climates, were a potent symbol of wealth, and European kings and aristocrats had nurtured them in greenhouses for centuries. The ability of U.S. farmers to grow the fruit within the boundaries of their own country, and to grow them on a scale that made them widely available, represented the capitalist taming of the tropics to republican ends.[43]

And oranges were not all; the abundance of all kinds of fresh fruit in the tropics delighted northern travelers in this era when refrigerated transport was new and fruit still mostly a local, seasonal pleasure. The sheer variety and availability of tropical fruit caused frequent comment, usually in the form of lists: "Mangoes, tamarinds, pine-apples, guava, lemons, grapes, oranges, bananas, melons, cocoa-nuts, jamboos, pomegranates, custard-apples, grandadillas, jambolans, nam-nams, limes, mangostan, pomeloes" beguiled the artist B. Kroupa in the markets of Panama. "And think of us eating watermelon for dessert which we got in a neighboring garden yesterday," Emma Gilpin marveled to her sister-in-law Sue, "and the pineapples fresh from the fields and bananas grown right here of a very delicious sort—ripe tomatoes of course, all the time." If Sue was not yet astonished and envious, Emma pressed the point: the Gilpins also enjoyed "cocoanut which we select for their delicious milk and in the custard condition eaten with a spoon. We always have [limes] to [improve] our drinks and lemons & sour oranges—Sapadillos [*sic*] and guavas we have learned to like very well & we see many other curious things growing which ripen later in the season as mangoes, avocado pears, [tamarinds] etc. etc." U.S. Navy sailor Robert Bloomfield jotted in his diary that vendors rowed out to the USS *Vermont* while it was anchored near Port of Spain, Trinidad, selling "oranges 10¢ a doz. bananas 5¢ doz Coconuts 3 for 5¢ limes 10 for 5¢. Can not realize it is the day before

Xmas, just like midsummer. Having a watch feast tonight in dynamo room."
Traveling south from Empalme, Sonora, to Mexico City in 1909, Selena Ingram recorded in her diary, "All the natives flock to the station bringing great
baskets of cantaloupes watermelons, mangoes pineapples cocoanuts & other
tropical fruits."[44]

As much as it invited pleasure, the fantastic natural abundance of the
tropics had long provoked fears that nature had run out of human control and
might devour the built environment on its way to reducing people to wretched
backwardness. Not long after listing all the fruits for sale in Panama's markets,
Kroupa remarked that "the same circumstances which render it unwhole-
some [for people], make it the gardener's paradise." But in places like Florida
and Southern California, where growing oranges was supposed to cure consumptive patients, provide healthful food to millions in colder climes, and
foster successful small businesses, human and vegetable health had become
boon companions. In chronicling the exploits of "Mr. 'Skinny' East," who had
come west aiming to improve his physical and financial health, Los Angeles
cartoonist Adolph Fera portrayed the region as a place where both men and
strawberries grow fat (Fig. 2).[45]

The connection between horticulture and tourism was stronger than simply the one being an attraction or an advertisement for the other. As well
as being important local boosters in California and Florida, fruit growers
were also sometimes tourist entrepreneurs. When John Gilpin spoke of eating berries off the vine and oranges off the tree, he was referring to fruits
cultivated for market by the owners of the boardinghouse where he and his
family stayed that winter; the same was true of the orange grove behind the
Dexters' hotel in San Diego. The connection also operated on a grander scale.
Florida developer Henry Flagler subsidized agriculture at the same time that
he constructed beach resorts and railroads. Legend has it that Miami land-
owner Julia Tuttle convinced Flagler to extend his line south of Palm Beach by
sending him fresh orange blossoms after a terrible freeze destroyed the crop
in the northern part of the state in 1895. Two of the big U.S. banana firms,
Standard Fruit and United Fruit, operated Caribbean cruises and passenger
services as a complement to their freight operations and included plantation
tours in the itineraries. Tour companies not owned by fruit companies also
included plantations and packing houses in their offerings: Gates Tours told
travelers to Mexico that on one day, "lunch will be served on a large coffee
plantation, shaded by orange and banana trees in full bloom—a charming
spot and a never-to-be-forgotten occasion."[46] The promotion of tourism and

Figure 2. Men weigh themselves on produce scales, flanked by giant fruits and vegetables. On the right, a portly gentleman says, "I've been here five years. How long you been here?" His bony companion admits, "Just came." Adolph Christian Fera, *Post Cards of a Tourist (Mr. "Skinny" East): Cartoons of Southern California* (Los Angeles: Henry J. Pauly, 1910): 6, call no. 351476. Reproduced by permission of The Huntington Library, San Marino, California.

of plantation agriculture often went hand in hand, and both promulgated the vision of an orderly and welcoming land of plenty.

Images and descriptions of landscapes in the Southland—particularly those of mountainous California and Mexico—also countered assumptions about the region's dangerous tropicality by portraying the availability of multiple climates, from verdant coasts to tree-clad hills to snowy mountains. These were images of the proper cycle of seasons transposed onto a single landscape, visual confirmation that, in fact, the climate was perfect because it encompassed every climate (Plate 2). One much-repeated California version of this refrain went like this: "There is no lack of variety in southern California. On almost any day in the winter you may take a comfortable morning plunge in the ocean at one of the nearby beaches, within two hours pick oranges and roses at Pasadena and in two hours more play snowball at the Alpine Tavern on Mount Lowe." John Sebastian invoked both the horizontal motion—from frozen east to summery west—and the vertical in a single paragraph. He was exalted "to be transported in perfect, luxurious comfort from the chilling blasts of an eastern winter to Smiley Heights [in Redlands, California], with its masses of bud and blossom on every hand . . . [and] from this vernal paradise to lift the eyes and behold, only a little way beyond, lofty summits shining serenely white with snow." Samuel Dexter wrote to his children, "There is no part of this city or the outskirts but what you can see oranges & palms growing and from where you may be standing look at the mountains in most any direction and see snow in large quantities."[47]

The same claim was made for Mexico and similar landscapes appeared, although cactuses, burros, and church towers were more common than orange groves. The spectacular railroad trip between tropical Veracruz on the gulf coast to Mexico City, in a 7,000-foot high valley amid towering volcanic peaks, vividly illustrated that the country, despite its tropical location, possessed all the proper seasons. "One may drink chocolate and cinnamon on the warm Gulf [of Mexico] shore in the morning," Chautauqua author E. H. Blichfeldt marveled, and then "pass upward through the altitudes of cocoanut, orange, coffee and banana, sugar and cotton, during the next two or three hours." By eleven o'clock the passenger would need to "draw on a heavy coat for warmth, while looking upward across the dry table-land to slumbering volcanoes capped with snows that never melt." On the cover of one guidebook, a pale road snakes up mountainsides flanked in the foreground by organ cactus, in the background by royal palms, and in the center by spiky pines. Tropical foliage wells up from hidden valleys below and snowcapped peaks hold up the sky: this was Mexico in and for all seasons.[48]

In combination, germ theory, phototherapy, and commercial horticulture proved to most U.S. residents that the tropics could be made healthy for whites; the "regular Arcadia" of the *Overland Monthly* story could be tamed and put to civilized uses, a regulated paradise. But these phenomena did not necessarily lessen the moral dangers that environmental determinists attributed to life in hot climates. Preventing yellow fever and malaria did not automatically diminish tropical lassitude or immorality, and tropical abundance still might erode the white newcomer's ambition and racial fastidiousness. Ward, permanently unconvinced that the tropics could be safe for whites, wrote, "Entirely apart from the presence or absence of disease, hot, damp tropical climates have a deleterious influence upon white men, especially upon white women and children, which operates and will operate as an apparently insuperable obstacle to the complete acclimatization of our race in the Tropics." One response came out of Australia, where physicians and scientists had a great deal at stake in advocating the idea that whites could settle the tropics without degenerating. By the 1920s, they attributed the dangers of tropical life not to the climate but to the lack of hygiene among nonwhites. The solution was strict racial segregation, a kind of social sanitation, in tandem with sewers and window screens.[49]

This was a solution highly congenial to whites in the United States; racial segregation was, after all, being firmly established in their country at the same time that germ theory became common currency, and they brought it with them as their nation extended its reach throughout the region. As the *Science News-Letter* reported, apparently without shame, "Because of the expense, the anti-malaria efforts [in the U.S.-controlled Panama Canal Zone] have been confined to the large towns where the white population is concentrated, and native farmers are required to live at least one mile beyond the borders of the sanitated [*sic*] towns."[50] Bolstered by new medical theories, new landscapes, new healthy foods, and racial segregation, the tourist industry took up the other part of regulating Arcadia—recasting lassitude, childishness, self-indulgence, and sexual expressiveness as traits beneficial, not detrimental, to white people.

CHAPTER 2

More and More Attractive Each Year

"Day cold rainy and generally disagreeable," adventure writer Kirk Munroe jotted in his diary on November 28, 1881, the day he paddled a canoe south from Jacksonville, Florida, launching a 1,600-mile, water-borne tour of the state. After foundering in some rapids on November 30, he hauled his gear onto land to dry it out and wrote, "Very wild country and have not seen a human being either on river or shore. Turned in at 8 o'clock." He stopped to buy supplies and mail letters at several farms and villages on his travels but encountered few people except when visiting Cedar Key, Fort Myers, and Key West. In contrast, the mosquitoes and sometimes fleas were many, as were more welcome creatures, including alligators, turkeys, ducks, snappers, groupers, and yellow tails, all of which he shot or hooked with gusto. In February, he ventured inland and lost his way in a cypress swamp and tall stands of sawgrass: "Ran out at dark and am camped on narrow sand beach. Southerly gale is flowing and sea threatens to innundate my camp. Am in despair. . . . It seems as though I should never escape. I wonder how long it will be before my friends send in search of me and whether I shall be found alive."[1]

Munroe survived this trip and even indulged in a similar, though less adventurous, journey with his new bride, Mary Barr, in 1884. His experiences cast into relief the undeveloped condition of Florida—and much of the Southland—in the early 1880s. In light of these difficulties and the well-known dangers of disease and degeneration in the tropics, the cautious investor probably regarded the prospect of tourism in the southeastern and southwestern peripheries of the United States and its closest southern neighbors, Mexico and the islands of the Caribbean, with some skepticism in 1880. Getting there was slow and arduous; once a traveler was there, accommodations were few and rough, and few refined amusements or companions were available. Compared to the luxuries available at eastern resorts or the attractions of high culture in Europe, the Southland did not have much to offer to wealthy pleasure travelers. Yet an increasing number of people found reasons to go there, and not all of them were avid outdoorsmen like Munroe. During a brief stay in Cedar Key in December 1881, he reported that he "met a party of excursionists from Illinois who go to Tampa and Manatee for winter." Within twenty years, Southern California and Florida were important tourist destinations, growing "more and more attractive each year"; within thirty, some islands in the Caribbean were as well, and Mexico's rise in the firmament of pleasure travel occurred rapidly after the end of its revolution in the late 1920s.[2]

The key to understanding this transformation is the close relationship between tourism and colonization at the turn of the twentieth century. The initial investments, mainly by railroads and steamship companies, aimed to create or serve new industries that produced freight to be hauled. Pleasure travel was integral to this plan, not an afterthought or a by-product, even though moving people would never be as profitable as moving things. In the United States, the transportation companies that advertised the beauties of their routes and bankrolled hotels and resorts calculated that some passengers would elect to buy land granted to the railroads by the government to found new communities and establish new businesses. At a time when travel was slow and expensive and travelers' stays comparatively long, large resort hotels like San Diego's Hotel del Coronado and Palm Beach's Royal Poinciana were literally centers of development. "A veritable 'American Riviera' could be established" in the Virgin Islands, one hopeful entrepreneur wrote to the U.S. secretary of the interior, humbly offering to spearhead the project because "colonization and similar developing projects have been my life work." Exemplifying the overlap between pleasure travel and settlement on a smaller scale, Kirk Munroe built a winter home on southern Florida's Biscayne Bay in 1886, and he and his wife settled there permanently in 1903, the same year in which his cousin, Ralph, established the well-known Biscayne Camp for boaters in the town of Coconut Grove (now part of Miami).[3]

Like real estate prospectuses, tourism flyers fostered and advertised the taming of tropical landscapes for refined pleasures. Just as large-scale commercial horticulture produced landscapes embodying the tropics in service to human ends, travel writing (broadly understood to include everything from travelogues and adventure tales to advertisements and transportation schedules) rendered places bodily and visually accessible and pleasurable for visitors. At the same time that developers and tourists altered tropical land-scapes, however, they also began to offer and seek services that would allow travelers to be transformed by the tropics—to a degree. In the Caribbean an innovative service, the cruise, played an important role in creating tropical whites in part because it pulled tourism and colonization apart. This mode of travel encouraged tourists to regard the places they visited solely as play-grounds, not sites of potential settlement or investment. Further, traveling on a floating exemplar of European or U.S. technological and sanitary superior-ity underscored the ability of tourists to indulge in the pleasures of the trop-ics without risking their perils. (When the United States' neighbors began promoting tourism more consistently in the 1920s, many leaders found it in their best interests to reinforce this emerging distinction, a topic I address in Chapter 6.)

Getting There

Although both Southern California and Florida already had a trickle of visi-tors in 1880, neither was yet fully connected to the U.S. rail system nor had many good-sized towns. Northern Florida had begun to attract visitors, par-ticularly those suffering from respiratory ailments, after the end of the Civil War in 1865, with the old Spanish colonial town of St. Augustine becoming so popular that by 1885 "everyone knows that St. Augustine is the oldest city in the U.S. and nearly everyone knows it is one of our most noted health resorts," according to the Florida Excursion Company. Others came to cultivate the oranges first sowed here by Spanish colonists, settling along the many rivers and lakes. Perhaps the most famous was abolitionist novelist Harriet Beecher Stowe, whose house at Mandarin was one of the earliest tourist sights in the area. The new northern immigrants to Florida often opened boardinghouses and hotels to supplement their income from horticulture, thus helping to ac-commodate the increasing number of winter visitors. John and Emma Gilpin and their toddler son Vincent stayed with a Mr. and Mrs. Jones in a boarding-house along the Homosassa River during their first visit to Florida in 1880: "They are Northern people—came here 10 or 11 years ago on acct. of Mrs. Jones' health which has here most wonderfully improved."[4]

In many ways, the state's initial growth partook of the general develop-ment of the South after the war. The work of one early investor, Henry Plant, exemplifies the process. He had invested in freight services and railroads throughout the South before the war and continued his work after it. His "Plant System" eventually absorbed the relatively short lines of its many competitors, encouraging commercial horticulturalists and hotelkeepers to set up shop now that passage between Florida and northern markets was faster, cheaper, and more regular. Atlantic coast steamship lines also carried passengers from northern cities to southern ones, like Charleston, South Carolina, and Savannah, Georgia, that had rail links to Florida. On the state's western coast, Plant launched a steamer service between Tampa and New Orleans and eventually ran ships to Key West, Cuba, and the Bahamas. He also built hotels in a number of towns along his railroad routes. Following the usual business model for railroads, Plant's companies and their rivals put out promotional materials that promised transient pleasures, good returns on investment, and ideal home sites.[5]

Nevertheless, in the 1880s travel to and within Florida was still difficult and time consuming even for those who eschewed canoes. On his first trip to Florida in 1880, John Gilpin wrote to his sister with pleasure that the steamship journey from Philadelphia to Savannah took just under three days and the family did not suffer much from seasickness. Having arrived in the early morning, he, Emma, and Vincent stayed in a hotel until late afternoon, when they boarded a train for Florida, expecting to arrive in Cedar Key, on the state's western coast, by the following evening. From there, they got a boat to Mr. and Mrs. Jones's boardinghouse, where they spent nearly three months. On March 24, the family reluctantly decided to head home but discovered that no boat was available to take them to Cedar Key until the following week. Finally on board, they had an overnight sail to town, where they waited another night for a train that departed at 4:15 A.M., at last arriving in Jacksonville in the northeastern part of the state at 3:00 P.M. to find that there were no boats plying the St. Johns River to their intended destination, Sanford. They managed to get to Palatka instead, and after a brief stay there, they took the train to St. Augustine, arriving April 1.[6] The Gilpins did not seem to find these travels unduly difficult, but they might well have tested the endurance or the finances of less sturdy and well-heeled travelers.

These difficulties diminished rapidly after 1890, as Plant consolidated many short railroads into his system and a new investor appeared on the scene—Standard Oil mogul Henry Flagler. Ceding the west coast to Plant, Flagler focused his formidable energies on the east, which he had initially visited in the late 1870s with his ailing first wife. In 1883, he stayed in St. Augustine with his second wife, and by 1884 he had decided to build a hotel there—the soon-to-be-famous Ponce de Leon. To a greater degree than Plant, he recognized the possibilities of elite tourism as an element of economic development, perhaps because he was a member of the New York–based high society that summered in Newport or Saratoga and wintered in St. Augustine or at the Hotel del Monte in northern California. After building lavish new hotels in St. Augustine, Flagler bought a railroad and extended it down the coast, erecting a series of new resorts at Ormond, Palm Beach, and eventually Miami to attract passengers to his line. He also launched a steamship line to serve hotels he acquired and renovated in Key West, the southernmost point in the United States, and Nassau in the Bahamas. His most ambitious project—extending the railroad across the ocean to Key West—was surely marvelous publicity, even if it was financially risky and dangerous for the workers, more than one hundred of whom died in three hurricanes that occurred during construction. Other, less well-known developers busily lined Plant's and Flagler's railroads with towns, farms, and hotels.[7]

Twenty-five years after their first journey southward, the Gilpins were still vacationing in Florida, but now, on February 22, 1905, they boarded a Pullman train in Philadelphia with through tickets to Miami. Despite the crowds that had gathered to see President Theodore Roosevelt off on a different train, the Gilpins departed on time and the very next afternoon detrained in Jacksonville and went to see the local ostrich farm. They then took the night train to Miami—a city that had not even existed in 1880—and registered at the Hotel Biscayne on the afternoon of February 24. By the 1920s, one could travel from the major East Coast cities to northern Florida in as few as twenty-four hours on a luxurious Pullman train, and in ten more hours one could reach Miami, with easy connections to Key West, Havana, and Nassau. During the winter tourist season, ten trains departed from Jacksonville, the northeastern portal to Florida, every day.[8]

Much farther away from the nation's population centers than Florida, Southern California began its rise more than a decade later in the 1870s and benefited from a brutal competition between two major western railroads, instead of the relatively amicable division of labor that Florida enjoyed. Although the northern part of the state had a rail link to the eastern United States in 1869, upon the completion of the nation's first transcontinental railroad, the counties south of the Tehachapi Pass did not get one until 1876, when the Southern Pacific Railroad ran tracks from San Francisco to Los Angeles. Nine years later, the rival Atchison, Topeka, and Santa Fe Railroad arrived, breaking the Southern Pacific's monopoly and setting off a fierce rate war that—predictably—fueled a real estate boom and an equally predictable bust. Many of the towns platted on paper were never realized, but light and heavy rail lines laced the region, colonies of midwesterners founded several towns (most famously Pasadena), citrus orchards and vegetable farms rapidly replaced ranches and wheat fields, and the population of Los Angeles grew by some 500 percent in the 1880s.[9] (Miami experienced much the same in the mid-1920s, just as Los Angeles followed the path blazed by scores of earlier boomtowns, reckless land speculation being a typical U.S. approach to colonization.)

In the early years, not a few of the visitors were ailing. By the turn of the twentieth century, tens of thousands of mostly healthy people visited each winter—this despite the fact that even on a luxury limited train, the journey from the East Coast took about five days and passed through sparsely settled deserts and high mountains. Samuel and Anna Dexter seem to have left their home in Rhode Island on January 18 or 19, 1901; they arrived in Southern California on January 24. In 1903, John and Emma Gilpin received word of an acquaintance, Mrs. Darlington, whose heart had failed during the journey. Emma wrote home, "Some guests here, sitting at our table, spent last winter in Southern California. . . . [They] told of the difficulty of the journey over the 'divide' in Arizona, just before you reach Southern California. The altitude is too great for those who have weak hearts." Until the completion of the Panama Canal in 1914, few would choose to take the long, slow, expensive steamship journey between the East and West Coasts of the United States; most of the steamers serving California were either coastal or transpacific.[10]

In contrast to the focus on leading individuals in Florida's tourism development, Southern California's story emphasizes organizations—first the railroads, then the Los Angeles Chamber of Commerce, founded in 1888 in the wake of the collapse of the real estate bubble, and later the All Year Club, established in 1921 to do what its name proclaimed—broaden California's seasonal appeal. Along with development companies and many municipal governments, these organizations published reams of flyers, guidebooks, and advertisements, sponsored traveling lecturers, and exhibited at expositions. The chamber also underwrote and was the largest subscriber for the journal *Land of Sunshine* (later *Out West*). Tourism for all of these entities remained intimately tied to colonization, and nearly all the publicity materials extant from the turn of the twentieth century reflect the same assumption that visitors were essentially prospective citizens. In a booklet entitled *Redondo Beach and the Pleasures You May Have There*, the Los Angeles and Redondo Beach

Railway summarized the town's desirable features as "magnificent views, a perfect bathing beach, sanitary sewers, artisan [sic] water, gas, electricity, shade trees, telephones and direct car service to Los Angeles," and highlighted the smoke-belching power plant. In 1886, the Coronado Company issued a prospectus for a magnificent hotel and town across the bay from the city of San Diego that described "the property . . . which we confidently believe will become the most popular seaside resort in the United States"—in no small part because the soil was "nature's storehouse of inexhaustible fertility." This is not, perhaps, a piece of information that people planning a beach vacation today consider critical in making their decision, but it was certainly important for would-be horticulturalists.[11]

Indeed, many visitors, like Samuel and Anna Dexter, undertook their vacations with the idea of settling down and investing in new businesses. On his first visit, the Rhode Island businessman told his children that "Mama & I went down to the Chamber of Commerce building to see the exhibit of the products of this section. . . . The exhibit consisted of the various kinds of fruits & vegetables, fishes in spirits, and products of the seas in way of sea[weeds], shells & the like and also a mining exhibit which include [sic] the different minerals & the rocks stones &c which showed indications of oil." Though he had nothing more to say about the region's resources aside from marveling at the lavish fruit and flowers, Anna Dexter wrote home on February 21 to report that "on our way to the park this afternoon we walked round to see the oil section [of Los Angeles] which is close to the park and right in among the pretty houses it seems to me that most of the wells were pumping oil, but . . . there are so many swindlers here"; she then hastened to reassure her children that "the men that papa is with for oil in San Diego are a nice set of men."[12]

The link between tourism and colonization would weaken as the Southland expanded beyond the borders of the United States, but not as much as one might assume from the perspective of the early twenty-first century. Borders now solidified by time were considerably more fluid around 1900, as the United States rode a centuries-long wave of expansion and U.S. businesses found they could rely on Washington to secure their increasing investments in Latin America against local demands. Selena Ingram, having followed her railroad executive husband from Kentucky to Vermont and on to Northern, then Southern, California, uprooted again in 1908 to establish a new home in Empalme, the Southern Pacific company town in Sonora, Mexico. In fact, this was only the second home the couple owned (the first was a ranch in

California's Imperial Valley)—they had rented in San Francisco and Los Angeles. A ready traveler who visited Mexico City and regularly journeyed around Sonora on her husband's private railroad car, Ingram, like the several thousand other U.S. expatriates in Mexico by 1910, entertained both family and business visitors during her stay.[13]

Still, in 1880 Mexico must have seemed a much less attractive prospect for an investment in tourism than Florida and Southern California. No one could have known then that Porfirio Díaz, who had seized power in 1876, would rule directly or indirectly until 1911 and give Mexico its longest sustained period of stability since independence. Largely because of the chronic warfare of the nineteenth century, Mexico at the beginning of the 1880s still had only a few hundred miles of railroad tracks, and they ran from Veracruz on the Gulf of Mexico to the capital, Mexico City. A rudimentary road system threaded through the nation's challenging mountains, deserts, and jungles, traveled mainly by foot, horse, and mule. Building a modern transportation network was one of the top priorities of the Díaz regime, which offered subsidies to U.S. and British investors as part of a general economic development plan that at times relied heavily on foreign capital.[14]

As soon as the Mexican Central Railroad linked El Paso, Texas, to Mexico City and the Mexican National Railway did the same for Laredo, Texas, in the mid-1880s, U.S. residents began traveling southward in greater numbers, as the publication of a spate of travel books in the late 1880s attests. In an account published in 1888, O. F. Fassett noted that in addition to his party from Vermont, an excursion from Kansas was visiting Mexico City. The Mexican National Railroad offered "Tropical Tours to Toltec Towns" as early as 1892, although alliteration more than the actual itinerary determined the title, and Gates Tours ran annual Mexico trips on chartered railroad cars beginning in 1894. In September 1899, the editors of *Modern Mexico*, a journal published in Mexico City for U.S. expatriates and would-be investors, declared that "Mexico is destined to see more tourist travel this winter than ever before. Already the excursion managers are perfecting their railroad and hotel arrangements for many special trains that will come after the holidays. The individual travelers scattered through all the year have been much more numerous during the past summer and fall than in former years." It is impossible to quantify "more" in this era, but it seems likely that these early tours were fairly small, elite events. In the same issue of *Modern Mexico*, the Wabash Railroad advertised two spring 1900 tours of no more than fifty people each. Such figures, combined with the frequency of advertisements for Mexico tours, suggest that from several hundred to several thousand U.S. tourists visited Mexico each year between the mid-1880s and 1911, in addition to the thousands running U.S.-owned or managed mines, railroads, ranches, and plantations there.[15]

Lying at the center of the rail network and by far the largest urban area in the country, Mexico City remained the chief destination for U.S. tourists at the turn of the twentieth century, but the possibility of broadening the field of pleasure travel and establishing North American– and European-style resorts seemed promising. Mineral springs in Monterrey, Nuevo León, and Tijuana, Baja California, seemed sure to become attractions, just as such medicinal waters supported health and pleasure travel elsewhere in the Americas and in Europe. The country's spectacular waterfalls and mountain gorges rivaled those of the Alps and came decorated with lush tropical valleys and splendid Spanish colonial cathedrals and monasteries to boot. Early travelers did not fail to notice the beauty of the local handicrafts, from baskets and pottery to leather and lace, hinting at the future boom in artisanal production specifically for visitors.[16] But plans for luring tourists to see the sights were derailed by the onset of the Mexican Revolution in 1911. Not until the late 1920s would U.S. travelers begin to venture south again in large numbers, and by then the Mexican government would play a much larger role in fostering the industry.

The islands of the Caribbean and their northeastern neighbors were, like Mexico, difficult for North Americans to reach in the 1880s. Although the imperial powers—Spain, Britain, France, the Netherlands, and Denmark— maintained mail and freight services to their colonies, passenger accommodations were decidedly limited and secondary to the mission of these ships. In the 1860s and 1870s, a few U.S. steamship lines launched regular freight services to the Caribbean, Mexico, and Central America, and from the 1880s to South America, but they, too, regarded passengers as secondary. Such companies typically offered bimonthly or monthly sailings on relatively small ships traveling fixed routes determined by freight and mail contracts; the best-served cities were Nassau and Havana.[17]

The development of Florida improved the situation somewhat. In the 1890s, the Plant System offered steamer service from Tampa to Key West and Havana three times a week in winter and twice in summer, and its publicity noted that the Ward Line (based in New York and also known as the New York & Cuba Mail) offered weekly service from Havana to the Mexican cities of Progreso, Tampico, and Veracruz. An 1895 compilation of U.S. hotel and transportation services reported that the Ward Line had fourteen ships in operation with weekly service to Havana and Mexico and bimonthly service to Nassau and Santiago de Cuba. As this information suggests, in the early years of the twentieth century service remained limited. In 1904, Frederick Ober noted that although steamships ran regularly from New York City to Havana and Nassau, and both cities were readily accessible from the infant city of Miami during the winter vacation season, few steamships headed south from there and inter-island traffic still often traveled on sailing ships. He advised would-be tourists to charter a steam yacht, and some did just that. Two years later, when the Hamburg American Line, a German company with a global presence, launched its Intercolonial Service, it could claim that "this new service will be particularly appreciated by tourists who visit the West Indies and stop at one of the leading resorts. They frequently express a desire to see more of these beautiful islands, but after realizing the difficulty of making proper connections at the various islands, the plan is abandoned."[18]

As these complaints about a lack of transport and claims to have redressed it suggest, interest in Caribbean tourism was burgeoning in the early twentieth century, and in this interest local elites saw a ray of hope for their struggling economies. The gradual abolition of slavery in the region over the course of the nineteenth century and the preference of emancipated people for independent subsistence farming had weakened once lucrative plantation economies. At the same time, growers of sugar, tobacco, coffee, and tropical fruits elsewhere challenged the Caribbean islands' dominance of these crops, and protective tariffs in the United States limited access to the closest major market for Caribbean produce. By the 1880s, the islands' leaders and imperial officials had good reason to be looking for alternative businesses, and the signs that the success of the French Riviera in drawing leisure travelers might be replicated in Florida and Southern California made tourism a promising new option.[19]

The increasing political, economic, and military involvement of the United States in the islands also played a key role in facilitating tourism, even though European steamship lines continued to dominate the region through the 1920s. In 1898, the United States intervened in the Cuban revolt against Spain and assumed control over Spain's last remaining colonies, including Cuba and Puerto Rico in the Caribbean. In addition to military interventions in Haiti, the Dominican Republic, Honduras, and Nicaragua in support of its economic interests, the colossus of the north underwrote the secession of Panama from Colombia in 1903 and then constructed the Panama Canal through the tiny new nation. When the canal opened for business under U.S. management in 1914, the number of ships passing through the Caribbean rose rapidly and U.S.-owned steamship companies based on the Pacific coast, such as the Grace Line, the Panama Mail, and the Panama Pacific, began to compete in the region.[20]

The other major players in Caribbean tourism were the U.S.- and British-owned banana companies. Their political, economic, and environmental impact on the region is well known, but their simultaneous investment in tourism has not earned as much attention. Freighters had long carried a few paying passengers, and the early banana boats were no exception. Because there was no mass market for U.S. manufactured goods in the Caribbean in the late nineteenth century, carrying tourists south brought in revenue when the banana companies might otherwise have had only expenses. And yet as in Southern California and Florida, the connection was deeper: pleasure travelers might also become investors, if not in the fruit business then in related enterprises, and at the very least their adventures advertised the transformation of the tropics into a font of health and joy. The mythmaking central to tourist industry publicity—from strifeless histories to the riches always promised to result from modest investments—also sometimes obscured or even dampened local discontent. United Fruit, which invested the most in Caribbean leisure travel, built what was for a time Jamaica's most successful resort hotel, the Titchfield, in Port Antonio in the mid-1890s. Appealing to elite travelers, the company wrote, "Built and owned by the United Fruit Company, [the Titchfield Hotel] is under American management whose policy is to keep thoroughly abreast of the times and to maintain a strictly up-to-date house." At the same time, the government-subsidized Myrtle Bank and Constant Spring Hotels in Kingston, the capital, languished. Their struggles may have had less to do with poor management and service (as local critics believed) than with the fact that United Fruit controlled transportation to its resort—it launched its "Great White Fleet" passenger service in 1899—and had deep pockets to fund improvements there and publicity throughout the United States. Jamaican tourist promoters had neither of these advantages.[21]

As the examples of Jamaica's hotels, Flagler's chain of resorts, and San Diego's Hotel del Coronado suggest, lodgings were as important as trains and ships to the development of tourism. Building a hotel to catalyze development was business as usual in the settlement of the United States—city boosters from the early nineteenth century had often launched their efforts by opening one, as well as platting land and sending out publicity. Hotels anchored resort towns like Saratoga and Atlantic City and made big cities comfortable for business and pleasure travelers alike. The inadequacy of the hotels in St. Augustine supposedly inspired in Henry Flagler his decades-long commitment to the development of Florida. Although early visitors to the state like the Munroes and the Gilpins, who notably were more interested in fishing than dancing, lived happily in boardinghouses, attracting the luxury trade required luxury hotels. "Enormous sums of money combined with the natural resources & possibilities have certainly made an attractive spot" of Palm Beach, Emma Gilpin conceded, and "there seems to be nothing that guests (who get in) cannot get here—good hotels—fine climate—sports of all sorts—bathing in surf or pool—swimming—bicycling—golfing—music—dancing—sailing—rowing walking—riding of several sorts etc. etc." The tour company Raymond-Whitcomb built its own hotel, the Raymond, in Pasadena when it began bringing large tours to a then relatively undeveloped Southern California in the 1880s. Amy Bridges, arriving there in December 1886, approved of its "beautiful parlors reading, writing and billiard rooms. . . . Our rooms are very pleasant and nicely furnished." The quality of the hotels affected the success or failure of a destination with tourists: "We had been told the hotels [in San Diego] were miserable," Bridges noted; "—if we went to one, we should wish we had gone to the other—Everything would disgust us with the dirt about it etc. In fact San Diego was not worth visiting except to say—you had been there."[22]

The discourse on lodgings in Mexico and the Caribbean, as United Fruit's comment about its Jamaican hotel being "under American management" suggests, quickly came to revolve around the inferiority of local hostelries. Such criticism reflected both tourists' general affluence and the widening gap in wealth and technology between the United States and its hemispheric neighbors. In the 1880s and 1890s, the Mexican railroads, with some self-interest, claimed that the cities along their routes had decent hotels. The Mexican National Railroad, for example, mentioned good hotels in Monterrey, Saltillo, San Luis Potosí, San Miguel de Allende, Toluca, Morelia, and Guadalajara in 1892. Four years later, however, Gates Tours housed its travelers in Pullman sleeping cars for the duration, assuring them that there were no good hotels anywhere in the country, although they were free to pay an additional fee to lodge in the Hotel Iturbide, a former royal palace in Mexico City. By 1904, the tour company had conceded the merits of the Iturbide but continued to insist that "as the hotel accommodations outside of Mexico City are very poor, we have arranged to retain our own train at all other places." As the tour expanded along with Mexico's rail network, the company broadened its offerings; by 1911, travelers could opt to spend a night in "unique tule cottages" near Lake Chapala instead of on the train.[23]

Similarly, steamships often served as hotels when in port, presaging the emergence of the cruise. Finding lodgings in Caribbean island towns could be more difficult than in Mexico, especially on the smaller islands where little domestic demand for hotels existed. Ella Wheeler Wilcox wrote of her first visit to Havana, "The hotels were dirty and ill-kept; the beds, instruments of torture"; after the U.S. takeover in 1898, she found conditions much improved. She was very fond of United Fruit Company's Hotel Titchfield and wrote of Puerto Rico, "There is a crying need now of an American hotel where travelers may find real comfort"—in contrast to a hotel in St. Thomas, Virgin Islands, where her room "lacked every possible convenience . . . no bureau, no dresser, no hooks, no wardrobe, no clothes press"; and to top it off, the beds were uncomfortable and the windows opened onto noisy streets. Wilcox was not alone among U.S. travelers in finding the minimal furnishings and unglazed windows common in many tropical hostelries disconcerting and uncomfortable. Vernon Briggs, traveling through Mexico in 1891, said stoically, "We have learned by this time not to expect home comforts." Selena Ingram noted of a hotel in Guadalajara, Mexico, "This is a handsome *looking* hotel—but has not many real comforts—no private baths &c."[24]

Ingram's complaint, which did not feature in the accounts of Wilcox and Charles Dudley Warner ten and twenty years earlier, by the 1910s constituted the minimum requirement of many U.S. tourists: a private bathroom with a toilet, hot and cold running water, and a bathtub or shower. "The tale is told," Briggs reported, "of an American who came to a fashionable hotel here [in Mexico City] and told the proprietor that he wanted two connecting rooms with a bath"—which, of course, in 1891 did not exist to be provided to him. "Few, if any, of the hotels have baths," Briggs conceded, "but there are clean and well-ordered public bath houses" that, while evidence of one way in which the Mexicans "excel us in civilization and refinement" for Warner in the mid-1880s, would soon become a sign of their backward lack of privacy and proper sanitation. Standards in hotel accommodations and sanitation were rapidly rising in the United States in just the years when the Caribbean islands and Mexico launched their efforts to attract U.S. visitors. Before 1900, travelers expected to share bathing facilities and toilets in hotels and on steamships (few trains offered more than toilets and sinks), and advice books urged steamship passengers to schedule their baths with the steward a

day before embarking or as soon as possible thereafter in order to get a desirable time of day.[25]

Later travelers increasingly insisted on having these services provided inside their hotel rooms or steamship cabins, as cleanliness and bodily privacy
became tightly intertwined markers of civilization. Under the regime of germ
theory, personal cleanliness became a guarantee of good health; it seemed to
give the individual perfect personal control over his or her health, regardless of what others might do or fail to do. The technologies of sanitation,
from piped water to sewage systems, lessened the daily labor such fastidiousness required—no more pumping, carrying, and heating water or emptying
chamber pots and night closets. Regular bathing thus subsumed earlier, more
varied efforts to regulate the individual's bodily interaction with the natural
environment. In the tropics in particular, the insistence on managing bodily
processes to keep them private and remove contagion established the difference between superior whites and inferior nonwhites.[26]

The constantly rising standards increased the cost of attracting the richest
travelers—those most likely to make the trip in the first place. A 1937 report
on hotel construction in Mexico remarked, "The conditions that modern
hotels must meet to fulfill the contemporary demands of travelers require
considerable investments of money, since it is indispensable that they include
well-built rooms of a good size, well ventilated, with comfortable furniture,
and in a majority of cases a bathroom in each room." The Mexican government struggled to provide loans to enable national entrepreneurs to bring
hotels up to the emerging standard, while in Cuba hotels followed sugar plantations in falling into U.S. hands, and Puerto Rican promoters called on U.S.
companies and the federal government to invest in or provide loans for hotel
projects in San Juan. British colonial governments directly and indirectly
supported hotel development projects in the Caribbean, and the Canadian
National Steamship Line also seems to have done so.[27]

The onset of World War I in Europe temporarily reduced tourism in the
Caribbean. Despite hopes that the war would force wealthy U.S. travelers to
go south instead of east on vacation, the combination of the drafting of commercial ships for war service and German submarine warfare in the Atlantic
drastically undermined steamship travel. When it resumed in the 1920s, an
innovation in ocean travel that began in the 1880s would become the tourist
industry's chief form in the region. That innovation was the cruise.

The Caribbean Cruise

The usual story of the cruise industry has it rising, phoenix from the ashes to which the affordable jet travel of the 1950s reduced the passenger steamer, in the 1970s.[28] But the foundations of the cruise industry had already been laid well before World War II—indeed, before World War I. From their small beginnings in the 1890s, cruises played a critical role in establishing the Caribbean as a tourist destination with a global profile. The tropical cruise exemplified its historical moment—and modeled the future of much tourism—in several ways. As a floating resort hotel, it created more distance between travelers and the places they visited, helping to separate tourism from colonization in the Americas. It offered the height of metropolitan luxury and cleanliness amid the backward tropics, modeling the diminishing power of nature to reshape humanity. In its sheltered embrace, white travelers in the Caribbean could indulge themselves in the region's famed sensual pleasures without selling their souls, as Ida Starr had declared she would. They could become tropical whites.

The history of the pleasure cruise begins with improvements in steamship technology and therefore passenger comfort at the end of the nineteenth century. As they acquired steel hulls and more efficient engines, steamships grew larger and were less at the mercy of wind and waves, therefore less likely to reduce their passengers to retching misery. The increasing size also meant that more cabins and broader areas of the deck became available to passengers. By the 1880s, first- and second-class passengers slept in cabins with two to four berths, cabinets, and wash basins equipped with tanks of fresh water for drinking and washing. The invention of refrigeration in the late 1870s meant that ships no longer needed to carry livestock to provide fresh meat and could provide a wider range of fresh fruit, vegetables, dairy products, and eggs. Dining room menus—and decor—improved accordingly. The number of toilets and baths on board rose, and fresh water gradually replaced salt in the bathing facilities. After 1900, more and more first-class cabins had running water; by the 1920s, ships were converting the despised "inside" or windowless rooms into private bathrooms for the wealthiest travelers.[29]

Luxury passenger liners also offered a growing range of public rooms over the course of the first few decades of the twentieth century: "Drawing Room, Lounge, Smoking Rooms, Ladies' Room and Dining Saloons" were available to passengers on a 1911 American Lines cruise. At the turn of the century, though, the very best ships served the busy transatlantic route, and they offered far more: bars, cafes, gymnasiums, pools, beauty salons, libraries, and many scheduled activities, from bridge tournaments to costume balls. In 1913 longtime steward R. A. Fletcher boasted, "The floating palaces which now cross the Atlantic are supplied not only with every luxury, but with suggestions also for inventing fancied necessities and the opportunities of gratifying supposed desires which are really efforts to pass the time away as quickly and agreeably as possible."[30]

All this luxury was fueled by coal, although oil would begin to replace it the 1910s. The construction of ever-larger, more expensive ships that consumed ever-greater quantities of coal meant that companies had to keep their ships in service and earning revenue as much as possible to earn a profit. However, transatlantic travel was decidedly seasonal, with few venturing to cross in winter. Consequently, the steamship companies actively encouraged more wealthy people to travel in the off season and on other routes. The first advertisements for pleasure cruises appeared as early as the 1840s, but for the most part these were promotional efforts to attract travelers to liners, that is, ships running specified routes on a regular schedule. The common practice was to place tour groups on existing liners, just as they were placed on regular service trains, and by the late nineteenth century tour companies sometimes chartered entire ships for cruises, as they did trains. The first cruise properly understood—a voyage purely for the purpose of amusing passengers—seems to have been sponsored by the North Company of Scotland, which began offering regular summer cruises from Scotland to Norway in the 1880s and by 1887 had built a ship designed entirely for this trade.[31]

At the same time, other steamship companies began advertising wintertime tours in the Mediterranean and the Caribbean. The earliest evidence I have found of the latter is an 1879 flyer for winter tours on the Quebec & Gulf Ports Steamship Company. Like early ocean tours in other regions, this one simply advertised passenger cabins available on existing freight liners. In the 1880s, the Quebec Steamship Line published more substantial guides to its pleasure trips from New York City to Bermuda, but these remained liner services carrying passengers in addition to freight and mail.[32] That both of these companies were based in Canada signals the importance of the British Empire in efforts to diversify the Caribbean economy in these years; that both identified New York City as their main port of departure signals the predominance of U.S. residents among potential and actual travelers to the Caribbean.

The ships serving the Caribbean at the turn of the twentieth century were considerably smaller than the palaces steaming across the Atlantic, and as a result they were often less comfortable. Nevertheless, some hardy pleasure travelers made the journey. Poet Ella Wheeler Wilcox reported with surprise that the 1,800-ton freighter with only fourteen first-class staterooms on which she and her husband spent several days in the late nineteenth century was "spic and span," and she was charmed to find a small circus company traveling in steerage, along with a cargo of coffee, cocoa, sugar, tobacco, and cotton. Embarking on the S.S. *Ohio* for a West Indies cruise in February 1897, Joseph Kirkbride reported that the weather was "very rough almost from the start & was soon sent below, where I remained with all clothes shoes &c on, until Sunday eve when I took off shoes—Room mate also sick, so we had a beautiful time." Ida Starr's only consolation during days of stomach-turning heavy weather was a kind steward who supplied her with a popular remedy for seasickness, champagne and ship's biscuit. When the bill came, her husband was quite startled at the amount she had drunk.[33]

Even if the weather was fine and no stomachs were uneasy, traveling on a freighter had drawbacks. Harry Franck complained that the passenger's "comfort is everywhere second to that of the steamer personnel" and that "the inexplicable uproar with which the crew seem to pass its time during the journey" made sleep unlikely. Sailors swabbing the deck at four in the morning sent water cascading through the porthole of William Corlett's cabin. That forgiving soul allowed as how he was "fond of sea-water" and glad to find that a night's travel south from New York had already warmed it up a bit. With an eye on his sailing schedule, the ship's captain might forbid the passengers to disembark at ports. Colombian businessman Carlos Patiño Jaramillo, once stuck on board staring at the shore for six hours while the cargo was loaded, excoriated the captain as "a savage and ignorant Yankee who probably worked his way up from cabin boy."[34]

Even when the accommodations were good and the passengers allowed to go ashore, the ports of call might have little to offer. Indeed, Kirkbride found that Roseau, Dominica, was "a poor sort of place," Kingstown, St. Vincent, was "not a very interesting place," and neither was Castries, St. Lucia, whereas La Guayra, Venezuela, was a "small uninteresting place." The determinedly sweet-tempered Wilcox reported that "the only memorable thing we saw in St. Croix was an old cement stairway" and "there is little in St. Kitts to interest strangers," though when stranded there, she spent several pleasant days reading and writing letters at the public library. Corlett, an otherwise cheery and inquisitive traveler, claimed that "few are the attractions offered to detain the traveler in the capital city of Martinique" aside from the marble statue of the Empress Josephine, a local girl. The Pacific coast of Central America was no more exciting, Patiño discovered on one of the occasions when he was allowed to disembark: "Some of the passengers, the most curious ones, went ashore to acquaint ourselves with the town [La Libertad, El Salvador]. This has nothing of note; some of its streets are narrow and its buildings unimportant."[35]

Despite the limits of transportation, accommodations, and sightseeing in the Caribbean, the region's future as a tourist destination must have seemed promising to the steamship companies at the turn of the twentieth century. The first genuine Caribbean cruise service seems to have been launched some time around 1891, for the following year the Plant System announced that "owing to the success of last season's excursions, it is the expectation of the Plant System to again run a series of winter trips from Port Tampa, Florida, down the Gulf of Mexico, past the Keys, east through the outlying Bahamas, thence south into the placid Caribbean Sea, to Jamaica, and home northward around the capes of Cuba." By 1895 Hamburg American also began offering Caribbean cruises properly understood. A 1912 brochure claimed that "for twenty-five years the Line has devoted special attention to pleasure-cruising. Winter cruises to the West Indies, in particular, have been conducted during the past seventeen years, and have met with steady and growing popularity. No less than 12,000 delighted travelers have thus been conveyed to the West Indies." Its success, the company claimed, stemmed in part from its careful discrimination in selecting ports to visit—a critical sign that these journeys were full-fledged cruises. They had no purpose other than pleasure, and their itineraries were determined by what the company thought that the travelers wanted to see, not freight or mail contracts. The British Royal Mail was running Caribbean cruises by 1905, the same year that the U.S. tour company Raymond-Whitcomb first chartered a ship for this purpose.[36] It seems very likely that other companies were also testing these waters between the 1890s and the first decade of the twentieth century.

Temporarily curtailed by World War I, the Caribbean cruise industry got an unexpected boost in the 1920s when the United States sharply limited European immigration with emergency legislation in 1921, subsequently made more draconian in 1924 and 1929. Companies serving the transatlantic routes could no longer rely on millions of steerage passengers to keep their ships full and profitable. Although cruises had already become a regular part of many companies' business before World War I, they became increasingly so afterward as a means of replacing the revenue lost through immigration restriction.[37] Moreover, the war catapulted U.S. citizens into the role of the world's wealthiest and most willing travelers, replacing the British. Taking advantage of the growing market, by the mid-1920s Holland America, Cunard, Swedish America, Hamburg American, North German Lloyd, and other European companies were advertising Caribbean cruises regularly alongside pleasure travel in the Mediterranean and other seas and round-the-world trips.

Initially, the ships serving the new routes in the Caribbean (like those in the Mediterranean) were the same ones that in other seasons or earlier in their lives had served the transatlantic crossing. But as the promotional material for Caribbean cruises emphasized, tropical cruising demanded quite different amenities than did the blustery North Atlantic. The interior corridors and tiny windows that ensured a meager measure of warmth and comfort on the journey between New York and Southampton or Bremen turned a steel-hulled, coal-burning steamship into a gigantic convection oven under the blazing sun and in the warm temperatures of the Caribbean. A decade before other European lines, Hamburg American in 1911 refitted one of its transatlantic liners for Caribbean cruises. By taking out the boilers and smokestacks no longer needed to fuel a quick ocean crossing, the company was able to expand the deck and interior space available to passengers. The company boasted that its ships had "special constructive features [that] render them somewhat unique and delightfully appropriate for cruises of this nature" among them "the swimming pool, gymnasium, grill room, etc." and "superior ventilation. . . . Every cabin has an electric fan." A 1937 Cunard cruise ship had a swimming pool, gymnasium, squash courts, a card room, main and garden lounges, and a sports deck, in addition to the dining saloon.[38]

Operating only in the Caribbean, United Fruit boasted that its ships were "built specially for tropical service and for the most exacting of passengers"; the music room was surrounded by "windows, some of them bay windows, on three sides, and in the tropics, when they are opened there is never a want of a breeze." In an architectural trick that other ships would later emulate, in 1913 United Fruit's three newest ships featured a palm court that "in the north . . . is closed and snug; but as the ship swings into the warmth of the tropics the whole rear wall is taken out and the room is made one with the deck . . . a veritable open-air café." By the mid-1930s, the Grace Line went one better by offering a dining room whose roof could be rolled back on clear nights. Perfection in ventilation and the "refreshingly cool trade winds" were such constant themes in the publicity as to awaken suspicion, like the ubiquitous claim that the staterooms were all large and airy.[39] Whatever the truth, the Caribbean cruise ship modeled the greater intimacy with nature that the southbound traveler expected and, by the 1920s, welcomed.

Cruises also entailed changes in the type of customers and thus the architecture suitable for lodging and boarding them. On regular liners, the passengers were carefully segregated into first, second, and third class (better known as steerage). The classes embarked and disembarked at different times, occupied distinct vertical slices of the ship, ate in different dining rooms from different menus, socialized in different lounges, bathed (if at all) in different facilities, and disposed of their bodily wastes in different toilets. Spaces reserved for first-class travelers comprised as much as two-thirds of the passenger accommodations aboard, even though these travelers were usually a distinct minority relative to those traveling second and third class combined. One Southern Pacific steamer accommodated 152 first-class, 72 second-class, and 500 third-class passengers. Chief Steward Fletcher noted in 1913 that, of the 350 stewards staffing a typical high-end transatlantic ship, 250 served first class, 70 second, and the rest third.[40]

But cruises were by their design luxuries; the ships providing them would not serve passengers whose aim was to get from here to there as cheaply as possible. Although some ships, especially those dressing up liner service as cruises, continued to serve multiple classes, many followed the pioneering example of the North Company in the 1880s: they sold only first-class tickets. Having only first-class passengers on board made shipboard segregation unnecessary and eliminated the need for separate public spaces. Dining rooms and lounges once reserved for second-class passengers could be refurbished as card rooms, gymnasiums, and so on. But what to do with all the unused second- and third-class staterooms—too small, too overstocked with berths, and too understocked with windows for first-class passengers? At first, many ships simply closed off these staterooms and sailed mostly empty.[41]

As the demand for steerage passage remained low, some steamship companies took another approach to unused space aboard. Although still cramped, uncomfortable, and smelly, third class by 1900 had already become less dangerous and unpleasant than it had been fifty years earlier. A combination of legal mandates and competition for the millions moving westward from Europe had impelled the larger companies to offer cabins instead of dormitories, more toilets, simple meals served in a dining room, and even some deck space to steerage passengers. As a result, it was not as difficult as it might otherwise have been to recast steerage as "tourist third class" in the

1930s. The spartan four- and six-person cabins, simple meals, and functional public spaces extended the possibility of pleasure travel to a growing number of North Americans who had education and vacation time but not money, especially professors, teachers, and students.[42] This class of travel helped the Caribbean cruise industry prosper during the Great Depression; it also widened the growing rift between tourism and colonization, as few third-class passengers would be investing in orange groves or winter homes.

Deck Sports

As ships offered a growing amount of interior and deck space to passengers, the things passengers did on board expanded to fill them. At the turn of the twentieth century, regular liners provided pianos, shuffleboard, libraries, and writing paper in an attempt to keep passengers amused; men enjoyed liquor and cigars in the smoking room, while women took tea in the ladies' salon or on deck. Patiño greatly appreciated the presence of a skilled pianist and a good singer among the passengers during his long journey from Ecuador to San Francisco. As this example suggests, in the late nineteenth century on most ships, passengers themselves organized the onboard entertainments. F. Frankfort Moore's fictional travelers "got up bean-bag tournaments, cricket, bull, and hockey, and there was quite a run upon lemon-squashes." Passengers on transatlantic liners usually bet on how many miles the ship would travel each day, and on the larger ships the pool might go as high as $300 (the equivalent of about $3,700 in 2010). On many ships passengers staged a concert to benefit a sailors' charity, and travel advisor Josephine Tozier suggested that "the audience should be as lenient and admiring as possible."[43]

Since most of what they were selling was time on board ship, companies offering cruises had to keep the travelers amused. The elaboration of onboard entertainment naturally required greater coordination and staffing on the part of the steamship company. Already in 1908 William Corlett had mentioned a "manager of shore excursions" on board his ship; the American Line had an "Office of the Pleasure Cruise Department" located on the "Promenade Deck Aft" and staffed by Mr. Harvey L. Mead and two assistants during one 1911 cruise, and Hamburg American had a similar tourist department by 1912.[44] The chief duty of these services seems to have been organizing and selling tickets for shore excursions (about which more shortly), not staging onboard entertainment, but that would change rapidly.

Two decades later, a Cunard cruise from Quebec to Bermuda had a cruise staff of seven, including a director, a "directress," and five male assistants. These seven ran a relentless round of what were called "deck sports"—shuffleboard, deck tennis, and ping pong tournaments—as well as offering bridge lessons, setting up bridge and backgammon games, overseeing horse and turtle races, and hosting tea parties. In their spare time, they also sold tickets for shore excursions. The ship also hosted an orchestra to play at tea and evening dances, professional cabaret performers who put on a nightly show, and a lecturer who regularly spoke about upcoming ports and current events (the island of St. Pierre and "Will Adolph Hitler Wreck Germany?" on Friday, September 1). The pool, gym, and squash court were always open, and on some trips the onboard golf pro would cable ahead to arrange for passengers to play on island courses upon request. Rival Hamburg American's Caribbean cruises offered "Fun . . . a Rollicking Lot of It at Sea! Horse races, illustrated travel lectures, talking pictures, concerts and Tea Dances, sports tournaments, turtle races, bridge and other card games; keno; amateur theatricals, treasure hunt, 'Pirates' Ball'; Country Fair; Swedish Smörgasbord, a masquerade, a 'traditional German bierfest'; a 'Winky Dinner, a delightful forest elf affair' and a farewell dinner and dance." At some point in the 1930s, the United Fruit Company issued a manual for its cruise directors that described in great detail the games and events to occur during each journey.[45] Although dwarfed by twenty-first-century cruises, these Depression-era voyages were clearly their progenitors.

The provision of such entertainments, especially dances and dinners, was much easier when passengers were all of one class. Not only did having a single class open up more and larger public spaces, but the passengers themselves could assume that they were among decent people—whatever that meant. United Fruit claimed that its passengers were all "diplomats and debutantes, captains of industry and congenial vacationists," or less euphemistically, "the kind of traveler who wants the best and is willing to pay for it." Guidebook writer and cruise lecturer George Seaton advised would-be travelers to ask their travel agent about the class of the people who patronized various ships, "since on a vacation you will naturally prefer to be with people of the same general position and outlook on life that you yourself have." Although he denied that finding one's class level was a matter of price—"Some of the most delightful people are generally found on the smaller and slower ships"[46]—the cost of tickets necessarily limited the kind of people who would inhabit passenger cabins on board ship.

Cruises were generally an expensive way to spend a vacation, although the shipping lines emphasized that they were a better bargain than rail travel, since a steamship fare included a berth and meals and a railroad ticket did not. In 1912, Hamburg American's twenty-eight-day Caribbean cruises offered a luxury suite for $1,700 (about $37,900 in 2010). The highest fare for a regular stateroom (per berth, assuming double occupancy) was $450 ($10,000); the lowest was $125 ($2,800), and one such room was labeled "for servants." By comparison, a set of 1913 Thomas Cook & Son eighteen- to twenty-day railroad tours from New York down the east coast of Florida cost a minimum of $167 ($3,600); that price rose to $237.50 ($5,200) for those going on to Havana—and these rates included transportation, lodging, and meals.[47]

Prices also fluctuated over time, as more lines diverted ships to cruise service or dressed up regular liner services, especially when steamship companies confronted the economic crisis of the 1930s. In the flush 1920s, the Panama Pacific charged $400 (roughly $4,900 in 2010) for a first-class cabin on the journey from San Francisco to New York City (second class was $250, or about $3,100); during the Depression, prices dropped to $170 ($2,700) and up for first class and $120 ($1,900) and up for tourist class. The Canadian National Steamship's thirteen-day tour to Mexico in 1937 offered eight types of first-class rooms, ranging from an outside room with a bed and a Pullman berth for $100 (about $1,500) per person, double occupancy, to a suite including a bedroom with two twin beds, a living room, a private bath and toilet, and a baggage room for $225 ($3,400) per person. Seaton calculated in 1938 that for the "ideal trip" of fourteen to eighteen days, the lowest price came out to about $10 ($150) per day for a "stateroom on one of the lower decks, probably inside" (meaning windowless), and assignment to the first sitting for dinner or the less desirable dining salon. The maximum rate, excluding luxury suites, he estimated as $20 ($300) per day for a room with a window and other amenities.[48] Such prices were prohibitive for most U.S. residents, and even more so for the people in Mexico, Central America, and the Caribbean who hosted these ships.

But prices were not the only barrier to steamship tourism. Not surprisingly, United Fruit's "congenial vacationists" most likely meant "white." In brochures printed in the 1920s, the United Fruit Company instructed passengers making reservations to identify their gender, marital status, and familial relationships—all necessary for making appropriate cabin assignments—and ended with "(If colored, so state.)"—italics in the original. The Grace Line issued the same instruction and put it in bold for good measure, while the Standard Fruit and Steamship Company left the words discreetly unemphasized.[49]

Given U.S. racial norms, it seems likely that any would-be passenger foolish enough to "so state" would promptly be informed that the ship was already full. It is notable that all three of these companies were based in the United States; the European steamship lines apparently did not see the need to have passengers identify themselves by race, although in the Caribbean most of their passengers were U.S. residents and citizens.

By comparison, when Pan American Airlines launched its Caribbean passenger service in 1928 with a flight from Key West to Havana, it refused to enforce U.S.-style racial segregation: "Pan American draws no color line. Perish the man who does in West Indian and Central and South America." This policy may have stemmed from the fact that many of its early passengers were Latin Americans and Caribbean inhabitants whose social status was not as closely tied to their ancestry as would have been the case in the north, or the fact that providing "separate but equal" accommodations would have been difficult and expensive on the tiny planes of this era.[50] Or perhaps Pan American's managers were more enlightened than their peers in the steam-ship industry.

Elite—and most likely socially and phenotypically white—Latin Americans were welcome aboard cruises and liners as first-class passengers and participated fully in social events. At a costume ball on the S.S. *Ecuador* in 1930, one Señora Alvarez won the prize for best costume for her "richly embroidered, typically Spanish costume"; her typically clad husband had to cede the men's prize to Señor A. Escolan, "who represented a Spanish Caballero." Traveling on the Panama Pacific's S.S. *Virginia* in 1937, Mexican official Manuel Toussaint's only complaint about onboard hospitality was the bland U.S.-style food. Passenger lists indicate that Latin Americans remained a minority among people from the United States and Canada with English, German, Irish, and other western European surnames. Of the eighty-six passengers who signed the back of the passenger newspaper *Tropical Chatter*, published on the Panama Mail's S.S. *Ecuador* in 1930, fourteen gave both Hispanic surnames and hometowns in Central America and the Caribbean; the rest were non-Hispanic.[51]

Souvenir passenger lists compiled by the steamship companies enable a sketch of the demographics of cruise ships and first-class passenger liners. A Grace Line ship running from New York City to San Francisco in 1936 carried 178 first-class passengers, of whom only six had Hispanic surnames; one surname was French, a few might be Scandinavian, and two or three were probably German-Jewish. The rest were English, German, Scottish, and Irish—at this class level, virtually certain to enjoy the status of white North Americans or western Europeans. Unfortunately, this list did not include hometowns, so one can only speculate about the citizenship or ethnicity of Pauline de Alvarez and Mary Nieves, among others with suggestively hybrid names. Ethnically, liners seem to have had a more heterogeneous mix than cruise ships. Only one Hispanic and one Italian surname appear among the passengers on a 1928 Holland America cruise, while perhaps twenty-eight might be German (including some who were probably Jewish). By comparison, a New York & Cuba Mail ship, plying a regular route between New York City and the Caribbean, carried sixty-five first-class passengers of whom about ten had Hispanic surnames and the same number Italian. German surnames were also common, and the list was annotated in German: its owner jotted down "am Tisch [at table]" to indicate who was seated at his table for meals, as well as some mostly illegible notes about the august social connections of a few of his fellow passengers. Japanese and Chinese names also sometimes appeared, although these were rare.[52]

Whatever their origins, first-class passengers had paid for and expected luxurious accommodations aboard ship. A tremendous amount of work had to be done to ensure they got it. In addition to the crew needed to keep the ship operating and moving in the right direction, a small legion of stewards and stewardesses, cooks, and cooks' helpers staffed every passenger liner. Most visible to the passengers were the stewards, all-purpose servants who cleaned staterooms and public rooms, served meals, washed dishes, provided room service, served tea, bouillon, and ice cream on deck and cigars and alcohol in the smoking room, suggested amusements to bored passengers, and scheduled and cleaned the shared bathrooms. In addition to providing these services to female passengers, stewardesses might be called on to hand launder clothing, keep the sheets and towels mended and inventoried, and tend passengers' children. A 1918 handbook for prospective stewards describes regular fifteen- to eighteen-hour days beginning well before dawn, ending after 11:00 P.M., and allowing for only an hour or two's rest between rounds of cleaning rooms and serving meals.[53]

Although photographs in the publicity materials suggest that the crew members directly serving patrons on Caribbean cruise ships and liners were white, other sources suggest that the crews probably included nonwhites, likely Caribbean residents. In a fictional tale of a cruise on the British Royal Mail steamship line published in 1903, F. Frankfort Moore offered as an example of the ridiculous demands of passengers this comment addressed to the chief steward: "If I had known that there were nigger waiters aboard this steamer I shouldn't have come. Could you manage to keep them in another part of the ship while the meals are going on?" Most passengers favored condescension to open hostility. U.S. writer Isabel Anderson described the stewards on the United Fruit Company's S.S. *Cartago*, headed for Panama, as "West India negroes, well-mannered and soft-spoken." On a ship headed from New York to Puerto Rico, the stewards were "mostly South American or Porto Ricans—which is to say not negroes, but *café au lait* mixtures of Spanish and Indian. They are a friendly lot, rather childlike, fairly efficient, for Southerners." For the most part the ship's officers appear to have been white, male, and citizens of the country where the steamship company had its headquarters; they were often former naval officers.[54]

Like hotels, steamships had to promise perfect sanitation as a prophylactic against the perils of the hot climate. On its ships, the United Fruit Company promised, "everything about the ship is spick, span and spotless," with decor in white enamel and mahogany—a nice mix of sleek modernity and tropical luxury. The conversion of ships from coal to oil in the 1910s and 1920s made it much easier for steamships to maintain the appearance of perfect cleanliness, since oil neither produced dust nor had to be carried on board in baskets. Its new oil-burning ships, United Fruit promised, were "spotlessly white and clean and with a total absence of vibration, jar or noise of machinery . . . [and] a total absence of 'ship smell.' Everything is clean and immaculate"—the napkins even came sealed in parchment envelopes. The room most critical for assuring civilization's safety in the tropics was, of course, the bathroom; the Great White Fleet's were "spotless white enamel with tiled flooring, porcelain tub and lavatory." In 1910, before the room with bath had become the sine qua non of first-class travel, Hamburg American emphasized that "another point which has received particular attention is the equipment of the bathrooms, of which there are no less than thirty on this steamer, an invaluable advantage for a cruise in the tropics."[55] The fact that most Caribbean passenger ships were painted white emphasized their symbolic cleanliness and gave them an air of technological modernity that their growing size and luxury reinforced.

Shore Excursions

In addition to onboard entertainment, companies offering cruises had to ensure that their passengers had pleasant visits at the various ports of call. On regular liners, the crew took no responsibility for this, as Patiño's experience demonstrated; their duties focused mainly on ship maintenance and freight contracts. The *Ocean Records* handbook informed readers that the purser "and his assistants have a vast amount of clerical work to do between ports and have little time for sociability, mapping out tours, or reciting the history or anecdotes of foreign countries." Joseph Kirkbride, traveling on a freighter in 1897, hired a carriage at each port and drove around to whatever points of interest he could find, and this approach seems to have been common among his fellow travelers. Nearly all visitors gravitated to the best local hotel—if there was one—for a meal.[56] But such autonomous amusements created problems for cruise ships; having promised their passengers a wonderful trip, they were more likely to be blamed by disappointed or defrauded passengers. Worst of all, excursionists might be delayed in getting back to the ship, which had a tight schedule to maintain.

Keeping passengers safe, on schedule, and entertained was no small challenge in the early twentieth-century Caribbean. Many ports were too small to allow large ships to dock. Passengers had to get into small craft—initially sailboats or rowboats, later motor boats—to get to shore. If the winds and waves were high, the process of going over the ship's side could be quite nerve-wracking, as could the trip across the harbor. After the small boat in which he sat almost overturned on the way to the dock, Kirkbride noted of his return that he "had a nasty trip out to [the S.S.] Ohio being rowed by natives. The getting on board was rather exciting—Several sharks seen close up—Evidently interested." On the boat from her ship to the dock in Kingston, Jamaica, Susan De Forest Day reported, "the spray works havoc with our perishable gowns. Soon the solid water breaks over the bow, reducing our poor dresses to strings and our hats to pulp." At some Central American ports, passengers were loaded into contraptions that looked like two wooden benches strapped back to back; this was then attached to a crane that lifted the travelers off or onto the ship.[57]

There also remained ports, despite the steamship line's claim to have chosen them with all deliberate care, where there was not much for tourists to do. The *Cruise News* of the White Star Line's S.S. *Laurentic* advised in 1912, "Also please do not expect too much on the shore excursions as conditions in the West Indies are still primitive." That same year—the seventeenth year in which Hamburg American had run Caribbean cruises—the company's only comment about Fort de France on Martinique was that there were not enough carriages on the island to arrange for the travelers to tour it. "In the

West Indies," the tour company Raymond-Whitcomb explained fourteen years later, "travelers are rarer than in Europe and sightseeing less systemized." Some thirty years after Patiño's glum report on La Libertad, El Salvador, Madeline Allen wrote that the town "is only a wharf full of coffee in sacks and a few streets" whose only notable features were a tame vulture and "very brown and very naked" children. La Guayra, Venezuela, apparently had so little to interest travelers that ships putting in here arranged for special trains (and later automobiles) to whisk passengers to Caracas, in the mountains a short distance away, as soon as they landed. Or the port's residents might be all too well prepared, to the discomfiture of the arrivals. "The landing of three hundred and fifty tourists" on the dock in Bridgetown, Barbados, Corlett noted, "had a demoralizing effect on the dozen or more cab drivers in waiting. Prices soared to the limit and stayed there until our departure."[58]

Cruise ships therefore began to organize their own shore excursions. This service ensured that passengers would have something to do and would do it under the best of circumstances. Raymond-Whitcomb, a high-end tour company that promised seamless service in all its excursions, asserted that "the traveler . . . naturally . . . prefers to be spared the trouble of hunting out his own conveyance, driving a doubtful bargain with a voluble but unintelligible driver and trusting helplessly that all will go well." This was precisely Clare Sheridan's experience on her arrival in Havana: "we stumbled into the arms of a guide, who stood in wait. Unable to speak a word of Spanish, we allowed him to attach himself to us." Fortunately, the worst result of her helplessness in this case was boredom; the cathedral was closed for repairs, the locals were all sleeping through the noontime heat, and "the town seemed to have innumerable, modern marble monuments, each one more in ill taste than the other and each Cuban patriot thus commemorated had to be described at length by our unshaven guide."[59] The cruise ships tried to minimize the occasions when tourists had to suffer such authentic interactions with the locals.

The cruise ships or the tour companies that chartered them could investigate and hire only the best, and their demands for quality and security materially affected the services that local entrepreneurs and governments offered. In Cuba, the tourist police—a specialized force—regulated automobile rentals (which included chauffeurs in this era) and generally assisted tourists; both police and chauffeurs typically had to speak English. In the late 1920s and 1930s, a time of considerable political turbulence in Cuba, the National Commission on Tourism aimed to regulate guides so that they did not take tourists to improper places or make negative statements about Cuba, to prevent hotel touts and vendors from besieging passengers on the dock, and to banish beggars from the streets. Puerto Rico's Institute of Tourism established an information bureau on the dock where passengers disembarked, providing there "courteous English speaking guides and hostesses . . . to give information and to take care of visitors desiring the services of a guide for sightseeing tours; and cultured Puertorican [*sic*] girls are prepared to conduct ladies on shopping trips."[60]

Steamship companies or tour agencies could negotiate the price in advance, preventing vendors from suddenly inflating prices, but also probably ensuring that tourists would pay a premium. "They are a bunch of robbers and charge $2.50 [about $35 in 2010] for going ashore in the launch," Allen complained, and that trip did not even include a tour once she landed. Industry insider Seaton noted in 1938, "By agreement among the lines, all the travel companies charge the same rate for the excursions," and that rate included cars on standby to pick up travelers delayed by flat tires or mechanical problems and a low limit on the number of people placed in each car. No doubt local entrepreneurs had to meet these demands or lose business, and such demands tended to squeeze out the smaller enterprises. Company-planned excursions also claimed to ensure that visitors would see "everything": "They are carefully planned to give you the best," as Seaton put it. What they usually did, for a charge of $2 to $5 (roughly $30 to $75 in 2010), was emulate what independent travelers had long done: take a carriage (later an automobile) ride around the port city and its vicinity, with visits to major public buildings, monuments, gardens, and the neighborhoods of poor or minority residents who might qualify as picturesque (usually those of African descent, although Chinese and East Indian locals might also serve this purpose, while in Central America indigenous people had the role), ending with lunch at the best hotel to be found. At larger, more popular ports like Havana, where ships tended to stay more than a few hours and often overnight, there might be several shore excursions extending farther into the countryside and possibly including ocean bathing, golf, tennis, and other activities at local clubs and hotels. Evening tours to Havana's famous nightclubs, bars, jai alai games, and casino were popular offerings by the 1920s.[61]

But by the 1930s, one of the main attractions seems to have been shopping—that is certainly the impression given by George Seaton, who included a section titled "What to Buy in [place name]" in each chapter of his 1938 book on the West Indies, from mahogany furniture in Haiti to Wedgwood china in Jamaica, lace and drawn work in Puerto Rico, and rum everywhere.

Even as U.S. factory products flooded the region, local, handmade crafts became major attractions for visitors. The growing importance of shopping for
local handicrafts meant that travelers mainly encountered the people of the
Caribbean as the makers and vendors of goods that increasingly symbolized
their culture—preindustrial and therefore replete with meaning. Embroidered clothing made by orphans under the benevolent care of Catholic nuns
evoked a backward and, for that reason, caring patriarchal society in which
even misfortune produced beauty.[62] By buying such exotic goods, white U.S.
travelers gained not simply a souvenir but a role as patron, sustaining orphans in one place, simple natives in others.

Baskets and hats woven by hand from palm fronds or even locally produced rum—that quintessential beverage of the slave economy—embodied
an intimacy between people, place, and things lost in the industrialized
United States.[63] The sale of such handmade souvenirs in a market far larger
and more lucrative than the local one circulated a fragment of this lost intimacy as a means of sustaining practices deeply rooted in the native soil in a
new economy driven by the winds of travel. After the United States purchased
the Virgin Islands from Denmark in 1917, the U.S. Department of the Interior struggled to find alternatives to sugar cultivation and coaling, which
were no longer viable. Selling souvenirs to the growing number of tourists
seemed like the only real possibility, but it required a material reorientation:
"Although citizens were skilled in the art of palm-weaving, their styling of
products was not such as would attract modern tourists. Enlargement of activities and scope was made possible through an allotment of Federal funds
and classes of instruction were organized." The result was happy, at least for
federal officials in 1939: "Today the island is selling baskets, hand-woven hats
and embroidered linens by hundreds of thousands to vacationing northerners—and making a neat profit. Approximately one third of the population is
wholly or partially dependent for a livelihood upon the work."[64]

The sale of handicrafts constituted the most literal realization of the idea
of racial gifts—the idea that each division of humanity brought a special tal-
ent to the joint project of civilization—and helped to popularize cultural
pluralism. The conversion of local, handmade goods into tourist souvenirs
facilitated the spread of the idea of culture because it cast the intriguing difference between home and away in terms of tangible, purchasable goods that
symbolized the mutually beneficial interdependence of industrial and artisanal, temperate and tropical, white and nonwhite peoples. Civilization in the
form of advanced technology and business organization (steamships and tour

companies) bought the tourists in, while tourists' patronage ensured that less advanced peoples and technologies could survive even as local economies were transformed. Tropical tourism relied on difference and celebrated it, within narrow bounds; in doing so, it popularized the notion of culture and weakened the link between tourism and colonization—between visiting and rooting oneself in local soils.

As the examples I drew from Seaton indicate, however, duty-free luxury goods from Europe also attracted tourists. This kind of shopping corresponded to the double status of the Caribbean as the natural home of tropical natives and the site where European sophistication had been grafted onto the Americas. Many guides commented that Curaçao was just like a bit of Holland, or Martinique of France, or Jamaica of "Colonial Britain at its best. Though purely tropical and though steeped in the piratical history of Morgan and his buccaneers, Jamaica is actually as British as Piccadilly."[65] Such comments assured travelers that European civilization could triumph even in the tropics and among populations dominated by those of African descent.

How reassured white U.S. visitors were varied, with fears generally diminishing over time in tandem with declining fears of racial degeneration. At the turn of the twentieth century, Ida Starr was horrified to find herself seated among nonwhite worshipers at an Anglican church in Kingston, asking, "Where is the white man in Jamaica? What is his position, and what has brought him into his present deplorable situation? Has the white blood after all so little potency?" In contrast, when World War I–era traveler Philip Marden went to Sunday services in the same city, he was only surprised to find that the local people of color worshipped at the Church of England rather than the African Methodist Episcopal Church (a major black denomination in the United States)—that is, surprised to find that not all people with African ancestors shared the same culture. "After a bit," he assured readers, "you become quite used to seeing everything official done by the negro. There is an ebony policeman on guard at the corner—a most gorgeous policeman in a hot-looking uniform of blue"[66]—tropical beauty safely constrained by an English suit.

The overt racism of Starr's reaction to the absence of U.S.-style segregation is more offensive today than Marden's patronizing but ultimately accepting attitude. Neither egalitarian nor color-blind, he nevertheless did not flinch from sharing a pew with fellow Christians of complexions darker than his own. And yet it was Starr whose Caribbean visit unsettled her racial convictions: "it was all so strange,—the feeling I had about that word 'we.' There was a slow dawning in my soul that never before had the word 'humanity' meant anything but a white humanity to me."[67] Her fearful queries about the status of whites in Jamaica immediately foreclosed on this reluctant realization that her faith made her part of a community with dark-skinned people. Nevertheless, her momentary self-questioning hints at the work that culture would do. By offering every people a separate, distinctive existence regardless of their environmental circumstances, it simultaneously asserted the humanity of all of them and relieved racists like Starr—and Marden—of the need to integrate themselves into a civilized "we" that was not lily white. Things were different there; but you could get used to it, and it had no necessary implications for racial integrity.

The cruise helped to generalize this separation, and thus the emergence of the idea of culture, by weakening the older model of travel in which long stays tended to overlap with settlement and investment. Unlike earlier Caribbean travelers who voyaged on freight liners, cruise passengers were not bound by the mundane necessities of the islands, whether climatic or social, and they socialized with each other, not local people. Moreover, the floating resorts offered a very modern, safe, sanitary way to visit the Caribbean, a region whose bona fides in these regards were still suspect. "Culture" was something that one could enjoy in small doses, short visits, and symbolic souvenirs, while consolidating separate meanings of "we."

CHAPTER 3

Fountain of Youth

The climate of Southern California "is described as semi-tropical," Charles Dudley Warner noted, and that fact raised a serious question: "Will these mild qualities of climate and condition in any injurious degree undermine and deteriorate the Anglo-Saxon energy and thrift?" Although the settlement of the region by whites constituted a worrisome racial experiment of vast scale, Warner nevertheless found reason for hope, for the climate "is not enervating, and is more stimulating than any other semi-tropical climate I am acquainted with." He and many others "have a hope, almost amounting to a belief, that the Anglo-Saxon energy and spirit in the setting of the peculiar climate of Southern California will produce a new sort of community, in which the vital forces of modern life are not enervated, but have added to them something of the charm of a less anxious and more contented spirit."[1]

This hope—that the Southland might rejuvenate white bodies and white civilization without fundamentally altering either—was critical to the promotion of this transnational region for both tourists and settlers. It relied on selling a new opposition between culture (a historical accretion unique to distinct peoples) and race (an inherited biological condition). This relatively stable duality diminished fears of racial degeneration by downplaying the role of the natural world in shaping human minds, bodies, and communities. In this new way of thinking, people could enter into new environments and alter their homes and lifeways to suit without becoming fundamentally unlike themselves. In other words, like germ theory and steamships and with their assistance, Southland promoters rearticulated the relationship between humans and nature by insisting that the former could enjoy the latter without losing control over themselves or their destiny.

Nature dethroned made a lovely playmate. Forty-two years after Warner published his anxieties about the white settlement of California, Florida boosters boldly claimed that his hopes had been realized there: "Man and Nature have conspired to make [the state] the healthiest, happiest place in all the world," in the popular view a "land of perpetual youth" whose real attraction was "the easy, comfortable living which the climate makes possible." And there was no need to worry about racial degeneration, because "human nature does not change, even when it goes to Florida. Wonderful as the Florida climate is, it has not the power to alter the instincts, tastes and habits of those who come under its influence. It can only rejuvenate their bodies."[2]

It all started with the weather. Deploying temperature, humidity, and precipitation data to prove, against the popular wisdom, that tropical climates were really mild and healthful, promoters soon began to boast that the Southland offered a better way to live precisely because warm weather enabled people to be outside, close to nature, much of the time. Inhabiting the architecture and emulating the festivals typical of tropical peoples promised to endow whites with the joyous youthfulness of those native to the Southland. And yet the acceptance of such racial gifts in the climate that had fostered them would not amount to racial degeneration because the tourist industry made climate into a commodity, something that well-heeled travelers could enjoy according to their whims and always in safe, sanitary luxury. As a result, under U.S. management, the tropics would become not the site of civilization's senescence but its fountain of youth.

It's Got Climate

"I was so amazed at Los Angeles at some people who were talking so loud I could not help hearing," Massachusetts resident Amy Bridges wrote in her diary in February 1887. "One was asking the attractions of San Diego—'Oh— it has got the shipping and the climate,' 'it's got climate.' As if climate was a commodity. But it is spoken of so, frequently out here."[3] The process of commodification began with physicians and soon included a wide range of boosters drawing on weather and epidemiological data to insist on not only the healthfulness of tropical places but also the benign influence of their lack of seasons. These arguments blurred the distinction between temperate and tropical to the profit of the latter areas and encouraged whites to believe they could inhabit the tropics without fear of death or degeneration.

At the simplest level, to combat the popular view of the tropics as cess-pools of disease, Southland boosters and medical climatologists (often the same people) harped on the salubriousness of the local climate. No one doubted that winters were warmer and milder in the tropics than in northern places; the question was whether that unseasonal heat was healthy. Highlight-ing that anxiety about hot weather, when physician and recovered consump-tive patient Charles J. Kenworthy gave an acclaimed speech to the Florida Medical Association in 1881 countering negative judgments of that state, he cast northerly Minnesota as its chief rival.[4] The comparison seems absurd in the early twenty-first century, not because Minnesota's cool lakes and snowy winters do not attract tourists but because Florida's broad beaches and blaz-ing sunshine have become icons of the ideal vacation, even if individual tour-ists would rather go skiing.

Kenworthy argued that, contrary to its reputation for swampy stickiness, Florida offered both the dry, bracing climate best for most invalids and the warm, moist one that a few required. He amassed weather data to show that the humidity thought to catalyze disease was actually higher in Minnesota than in Florida. His statistics also proved that British soldiers suffered higher mortality rates in Nova Scotia than in Jamaica, and that people in the north-eastern part of the United States were more likely to die than those in the southeastern—all because of the variable weather and their inability to get outside: "Residents of cold and changeable climates are subjected to great and sudden atmospheric changes, deprived of sunlight, fresh air, sufficient exer-cise, and are daily poisoned by heaters." Florida, on the other hand, provided "the necessary relaxation from 'brain fag,' opportunities to take out-door ex-ercise, plenty of sunshine, pure and bracing air, and other necessary adjuncts" to health, and its residents were notably healthy.[5]

Prescriptions for sunshine and fresh air were hardly new (nor have they gone out of fashion), but in the context of Florida and Southern California boosterism they became an argument about lifestyle. California and Florida boosters promoted their states as places where people could live healthier lives in closer contact with "the quiet of Nature, the blooming of flowers, the singing of birds, the babbling of brooks"[6] than could people in colder climates. Thus medicine laid the foundation for what would soon become a broadly cultural argument that people lived differently—better—in the Southland. That "better" entailed the adoption of traits and activities once taken as evidence of the childish backwardness of tropical peoples.

Arguing for the region on the grounds that it had no winter or very mild winters reflected the fact that initially most tourists visited during that season, when temperatures were at their lowest and insects and disease less prevalent. Whereas northeastern and midwestern resorts served primarily a summer trade, travelers going south for health or pleasure mostly went between January and March, avoiding both the supposedly unbearable tropical summers and the harsh winters at home. "It is the custom," the most comprehensive early guide to Mexico noted, "for travellers to regard Mexico as purely a winter resort, and the greatest influx of visitors is between November and March." The Florida Excursion Company's 1884 tour ran from January 7 to April 8; Raymond-Whitcomb's 1907 journeys to Florida and the Bahamas departed on January 21 and February 4, 11, and 25, returning February 23 and March 9, 16, and 30. The Hamburg American steamship company offered several Caribbean cruises in 1912, departing New York City on January 23, February 10, February 24, March 7, and March 26. Whereas the Palm Beach, Florida, hotels were so full during the 1899 season that guests were sleeping on cots in the parlors in late March, by March 30 John and Emma Gilpin succeeded in getting a room in the most prestigious, Flagler's Royal Poinciana, and noted that the dining room was so empty that they had a waiter to themselves. All the hotels were preparing to close in the first or second week of April.[7]

During the winter, promoters promised, the weather would be sublime: "Nowhere Else on Earth can the seeker after Health and Happiness find such rich reward; California land of sunshine, fruit and flowers, where there are no sudden changes in temperature but a bracing, tonic, balsamic air the year round." Agreeing heartily, the Los Angeles Chamber of Commerce declared, "It is only in Southern California that true atmospheric perfection can be found." Although climate-based advertising was particularly popular among Southern Californians—a brochure compiled for the 1893 World's Columbian Exposition admitted that "the climate has been the main feature upon which the writers have dilated"—other places hoping to attract winter visitors made similar claims. The Florida Excursion Company urged 1884 travelers to join its tours to "enjoy the genial, health-giving climate of the 'Italy of America'" and assured them that, at least in the town of Orange Heights, there was no malaria. A Florida hotelkeeper told nature writer Bradford Torrey, "'Yes, we've got a climate'" (but this Yankee transplant added dryly, "'and that's about all we have got,—climate and sand'"). Getting straight to the point, Puerto Rico boosters insisted that "there is no climate in the world which surpasses that of Puerto Rico for the establishment of winter resorts." "The climate of the Mexican tableland is one of the finest in the world," a partisan of that country insisted, because its "dry, warm, unvarying air" and "the absence of brusque climatic changes" made it an ideal health resort. One visitor to Cuba remarked, "In Havana, one thing is certain—you can luxuriate in the climate; it is soft, and yet, from the propinquity of the sea, it is fresh," at least in January.[8]

Demurrals from the assertion of climatic perfection were not welcome; as "Silvia Sunshine" wrote of Florida in 1880, "Persons here from Northern climes are expected to spend the winter in breathing the balmy air . . . and praising every thing they see. If they have any doubt . . . , let them lock it in secret, and keep silent until they leave." With the air of a determined Cassandra, another writer reported that although ailing visitors to Los Angeles "usually picture to themselves an entire winter here out of doors, in the enjoyment of genial sunshine," in 1884 fog, rain, floods, and cold left winter visitors "confined to their rooms nearly one-half the time, and every day in need of fire." "Once upon a time a stranger went to Southern California," according to Irvin Cobb, "and when he was asked the customary question—to wit: 'How do you like the climate?' he said: 'No, I don't like it!' So they destroyed him on the spot . . . and hid his bones in an unmarked grave."[9]

In describing the climates of the Southland, travel writers and travelers often resorted to seasonal comparisons based on the annual cycle typical of the northeastern and midwestern United States. Given the moral weight attributed to the seasons (see Chapter 1), comparisons with springtime, a season of new growth and vigor, were particularly appealing. Clarence Edwards gave the invocation of spring more fully than most in a 1909 *Travel* magazine article: "Here is respite from summer's fierce heat, that Moloch demanding human sacrifice of annual thousands. . . . Here is surcease from the biting cold, for the blooming flower and singing bird bring delight to the senses while other lands lie wrapped in winter's mantle. . . . All seasons seem but a continuation of an eternal spring." The symbol and season of rebirth, eternal spring banished the irritations and deadly diseases associated with the chill of winter and the sultriness of summer. Spring promised the mild, equable temperatures so highly recommended by medical climatologists without the racial risks or personal discomforts of tropical summers. Travel writers endowed Mexico, especially its high central plateau, with the attribute of eternal springtime most often. The Mexican National Railroad mentioned the salubriousness of Mexico's "glorious climate of perpetual spring-time" several times in an 1892 flyer, and Gates Tours assured its travelers that "although the country lies near and partly within the tropics, the high altitude of a greater portion, where the lines of pleasure travel run, is such that a perpetual spring-time is the average of the weather."[10]

But promoters did not long remain content to clothe winter in the new green of spring. They soon began to insist that Southland summers were also pleasant, temperate seasons. Tireless California booster George Wharton James acknowledged that "there are those, unfamiliar with California's climate, who assumed that because it is warm and congenial in the so-called winter months, it must be fearfully hot in the summer," but he insisted, "nothing can be further from the truth." A travel writer similarly pooh-poohed northerners' prejudices against Florida summers: "In summer a perpetual breeze blowing from coast to gulf neutralizes the heat along with a refreshing daily shower." Nassau, in the Bahamas, enjoyed perfect temperatures, "varying little between sixty-seven and seventy-five degrees" so that the island "never becomes oppressively warm." And the United Fruit Company advertised its resort in Jamaica as having "a climate that is all you expect—balmy, salubrious, sunny, but not hot."[11]

As evidence that, in addition to never being cold, tropical places were not really hot in any season, many guidebooks included temperature charts, typically showing monthly average temperatures year round and sometimes including information on rainfall, humidity, and average days of sunshine per year. In 1899 the Los Angeles Chamber of Commerce compiled U.S. Weather Bureau data over twenty-two years to show that area temperatures averaged 55°F (13°C) in winter, 60°F (16°C) in spring, 70°F (21°C) in summer, and 65°F (18°C) in autumn, for a yearly average of 62°F (17°C). The chamber failed to highlight the July and August days when temperatures edged over 100°F (38°C), although it did hang a note on the table reminding readers that the area's dry atmosphere made heat much easier to bear. "The climate of Puerto Rico," one flyer claimed, "is warm but is not uncomfortable at any time. It is considered to be the coolest place in the tropics," for its average temperatures ranged from 73°F (23°C) in winter to 76°F (24°C) in summer. Havana enjoyed a mean temperature of 77°F (25°C) year round, with a high of 82°F (28°C) in August and a low of 71°F (22°C) in January. The fact that the humidity never descended below 82 percent the author buried in the tables.[12]

Such charts also often compared the average temperatures of the southern place in question with those of other, perhaps better-known southern resorts. The Coronado Hotel Company, for example, included in its promotional brochure a table comparing Coronado Beach's average monthly temperatures with those of the French Mediterranean resorts of Mentone and Nice, as well as the Italian cities of Naples, Rome, and Florence, all popular tourist destinations. Indeed, the California town was warmer in winter and cooler in summer than the European cities, although not by much. "The climate is as near perfection as it is possible to find," Ratcliffe Hicks declared from his vantage in Pasadena, California. "It is far better than in Nice or Cannes, for there it is often very cold in Winter, and always very hot in Summer." In a 1903 book based on a lecture tour in the United Kingdom, the United States, and Canada, James Johnson touted Jamaica: "The clear, rare atmosphere of our higher elevations, I venture to affirm, will do more for the invalid than Egypt, Mentone, Nice, or the Riviera for Europeans, and California, Nassau, Bermuda, or Florida for the American." Kenworthy compared temperatures in the Florida towns of Key West, Punta Rassa, and Jacksonville between November and March to those in Cannes, Nice, and Mentone, France; Nervi, Italy; Nassau, the Bahamas; and in the United States, to the famous resort of Atlantic City, New Jersey; towns in the southeastern states of Georgia and South Carolina; three towns in Minnesota (his personal bête noire); and Los Angeles.[13] Even as such statistical braggadocio touted the climatic excellence of a particular place, it also outlined the emerging global archipelago of hot-weather resorts, the Southland on a global scale.

Another common comparison stacked the summertime temperatures of southern resorts next to those of northeastern and midwestern U.S. cities. By turning the charge of excessive heat back on the North, these comparisons blurred the qualitative distinctions dividing temperate from tropical. "Frequently when northern cities are sweltering with the mercury at 98 [37°C] and 100 [38°C]," one guidebook author wrote, "Floridians are comfortable at 88 [31°C] and sleeping under cover at night." Another crowed, "Cooled by the Gulf breezes, Tampa [Florida] laughs at the languor of the plains and pities the distress of cities gasping with heat." Quoting a U.S. Weather Bureau meteorologist, Puerto Rican promoters declared, "'There is not a State in the United States in which higher temperatures do not occur every year.'" Acknowledging that Havana had suffered days when the mercury surged over 100°F (38°C), one guidebook author insisted that this was, at least, no worse than summer scorchers in northern U.S. cities. Mexican promoters, holding a much stronger hand, pointed out that "even at midday it is never as hot in Mexico City as it becomes all over the United States in the summer." Health writers William Edwards and Beatrice Harraden compared July and August temperatures in Boston, Baltimore, and Atlantic City with those in Coronado Beach and Los Angeles, showing that the two California sites were sometimes quite a bit cooler than their eastern counterparts. As Los Angeles transplant Selena Ingram wrote smugly in her diary one fine June day, "Our weather is simply perfect—such a contrast to the heat in Chicago!"[14]

Some sources, of course, admitted that the climate in the tropics was hot, especially in summer, but then denied that the heat was enervating—thus denying that it would produce the racial degeneration or laziness so typically attributed to it in popular climatic determinism: "the air hasn't that breathless, enervating quality which 'takes the sap out of a fellow,'" as Ralph Henry Barbour put it in a guide to Florida. Another author made the connection to—and disconnection from—the tropics explicit: "Here [in Fort Myers, Florida] the winter tourist finds himself on the borderland of the tropics, enjoying all that the tropics can offer for his pleasure, yet with the noticeable absence of that enervating influence which the zone of the equator exerts, sapping out life and ambition. Here in Fort Myers a man is alive every moment of his time."[15] Like Charles Dudley Warner in Southern California, these Florida partisans believed that whites could thrive and exercise their ambitions in a warm climate, contrary to the prevailing wisdom. But in doing so, they might find themselves changing—becoming tropical whites, the same breed but with a new sensibility.

Luxuriously Hot

Although the temperatures themselves probably did not change substantially between the 1880s and the 1930s, attitudes toward them seem to have done so. Whereas the constant claims that the Southland featured eternal spring seem to have been quite important to turn-of-the-twentieth-century travelers, later travelers increasingly embraced hot weather. "I am told that the summer weather as a whole is more pleasant than the winter but how that can be I cant [sic] imagine," Samuel Dexter wrote to his children from San Diego in 1901, "for if you will just imagine the finest day you ever saw in the month of May when its [sic] neither hot or cold one such as if riding you would put on a light overcoat and if walking the overcoat would be unnecessary and you will have a fair conception of what we have had since our arrival here." Overcoat ambivalence fairly well defined this Rhode Island businessman's infatuation with wintertime Southern California, and he was not alone. Marie Robinson Wright marveled over the climate of Mexico's *tierra templada* or temperate lands: "There is not a day, and scarcely an hour, in the year when one could say, 'I wish it were a little warmer, or a little cooler.' It is never warm enough to make you pull off your coat, and rarely cool enough to button it."[16]

"From the first of October until the middle of June, warm shawls, New-markets, fur-lined cloaks, and heavy overcoats are in brisk demand, except, perhaps, at midday," Emma H. Adams advised invalids planning to stay in Los Angeles. Having suffered through one of the region's occasional rainy years, she found that "light clothing, made of linen, cambrics, and similar fabrics, is never needed except on a few days in Midsummer, and even that can be dispensed with." "It can be accepted as a safe axiom that summer clothing is always out of place in Mexico City," T. Philip Terry assured readers, describing that metropolis's climate as "usually mild, but exhilarating" with a mean temperature of 65°F (18°C). For cities lower in altitude, he recommended "the summer outfit" supplemented with "a light overcoat and medium weight underwear"—an apt reminder of how many more layers of clothing people used to wear. These layers, in combination with the head-to-toe, long-sleeved, hatted and gloved, stockinged and booted attire typical of the well-to-do in this era, make a preference for mild temperatures seem only natural—the more so given that air conditioning was still in its infancy and limited to a few factories and mansions. One has to sympathize with Selena Ingram, living corseted, petticoated, and gowned on a private railroad car in northern Mexico in the autumn of 1908: "It is pretty hot in this country—94 [34°C] now in this car—but cars are always hot."[17]

Yet the idea that a place could be "luxuriously hot"—a sensual indulgence—was not unknown, and by the 1920s heat was the primary reason why people went to tropical resorts: "The principal thing that most tourists do," declared two Florida partisans, "is to loaf in the sun, usually with as few clothes on as the law permits." (More about clothing and the sun in Chapter 4.) Indeed, the evidence for a changing attitude toward heat lies more in the clothes that vacationers shed and what they did in the Southland than in what they—or the travel writers who shaped the field of play—said about why they went south. Only a few people actively praised the temperatures. William Corlett wrote of the fourth day out from New York City to the Caribbean, "It was so warm at eleven o'clock that the mere exertion of writing made one perspire," but he was far from distressed: "The whole environment was soothing, sensuous, delightful." Nancy Johnstone, a British radical fleeing the wreckage of her hopes in Spain to Mexico in the late 1930s, wrote, "Nearing Havana the weather became gloriously hot," leading her and some of her fellow steerage passengers to sleep on deck at night.[18] Individuals may differ in delighting in the heat or rejoicing in an optional overcoat, and in these cases Corlett and Dexter chose destinations well suited to their preferences, while Johnstone soon fell in love with the warm, flowery valleys of Mexico's tierra templada.

Nonetheless, the diminishing attention to the perils of heat in my sources—combined with the growing tendency of U.S. travelers to choose tropical destinations—suggests that idiosyncrasy is not a sufficient explanation. Although the industry advertising and travel writing that provide the bulk of my evidence had a vested interest in presenting a positive view of warm weather, their evident success in attracting hundreds of thousands of tourists to resorts in Florida, Southern California, Mexico, and the Caribbean suggests a widespread transformation in attitudes toward hot weather. The usual story of the French Riviera credits people from the United States with establishing it as a summer resort in the 1920s; until then, only its mild winters had attracted visitors. By the late 1930s, as Puerto Rican business leaders undertook a concerted effort to make the island a major destination for U.S. tourists, authors of a new guidebook abandoned the older claim that Puerto Rico's climate was the coolest in the tropics to boast that its winter temperatures were significantly higher than those on the Riviera or in Los Angeles. In the city of San Juan, they wrote, average winter temperatures exceeded those of Miami by 7°F (4°C) and those of Honolulu—another rising star in the tourist firmament—by 4°F (2°C). Temperatures had dipped below freezing in both Los Angeles and Miami in recent decades; it had been cold enough to snow on the Riviera and even in North Africa; but San Juan's lowest temperature in thirty-nine years was 62°F (17°C). By 1937, Hamburg American, that veteran of the Caribbean cruise industry, was selling not only "opportune escapes from the rigors of a northern Winter" but also refuge from "the billowy blasts of Spring. Instead of ice and snow and sleet and slush and penetrating cold . . . radiant, tropical sunshine" (though it promised "cool breezes," too). Such "hotter than thou" boasting suggests that the change in attitudes toward hot weather was well under way in the 1920s and 1930s, *before* the widespread adoption of air conditioning in commercial buildings, railroads, and ships.[19]

This cultural shift, like all its brethren, is difficult to trace; its signs are suggestive rather than definitive and must not be taken as evidence of unanimity. John Gilpin's sister Sue withstood more than twenty-five years of entreaties to winter with him in Florida, preferring her snowy Pennsylvania home for reasons not recorded in his letters. New ski resorts and winter festivals competed with Florida fishing trips and Caribbean cruises for customers, and the Rocky Mountains and Swiss Alps attracted growing numbers of winter visitors in the same decades. In other words, climate itself became a tourist attraction in this period: "The visitor in Mexico can choose his climate as one selects a meal a la carte. . . . Simply by going up or down it is possible to adjust the temperature to the individual taste."[20] Given modern rapid transportation and enough money, one could choose which season to enjoy and partake only of its pleasures.

In such circumstances, well-to-do people could evade the climate's ability to mold human beings. But in addition to the waning power of nature, the new attitude toward summertime heat derived in part from a revalorization of seasonality and its underlying rationale, climatic determinism. This reversal of values transformed the danger of racial degeneration via tropical heat into the promise that a tropical vacation would heal the wounds of civilization. The constant promises that the Southland offered either "eternal spring" or "perpetual summer" signaled the absence of the God-given round of seasons that climatic determinists and Christians alike credited with proper racial and moral development. "California is the land of perpetual summer, where every month is June. Roses bloom outdoors there in midwinter," burbled one Santa Fe Railroad brochure. Bermuda enjoyed "eternal springtime" according to the Furness Withy Steamship Company. Florida's "climate is a continual summer." "You do not need to wait six months for summer," the Florida East Coast Railway insisted. "Springtime and the golden days along the Gulf Stream, lie just over the southern horizon." Or en route to California, one might be grateful that "generous nature has so ordained that, without leaving Uncle Sam's broad domain, and in only four days time, we can be luxuriously and speedily transported . . . away from the frost-blighted foliage of the north, into the land of perpetual verdure and perennial bloom."[21]

Travel advertising and writing naturally cast the absence of winter and the eternal reign of spring or summer as a good thing, and especially in the late nineteenth century they cited physicians' recommendations that the sick and weary seek mild, equable climates. But evading the cycle of seasons was not natural, and it implied certain other unnatural changes, such as the reversal of time. "It was February in New York; it was a bright June morning when, four days later, we dropped anchor" in the Caribbean. The very act of going south was portrayed as a trip back in time: "The calendar seems literally reversed when the ship sliced through the ocean."[22] Although the journey could have just as logically represented a move forward (the seasons are, after all, cyclical), in the context of white supremacist beliefs in the backwardness of tropical people, the journey southward into summer was associated with a return to childhood and a retreat from the burdens of adulthood and civilization.

But in the romantic mode, it could simultaneously signal a return to Eden, that time before sin, shame, and self-denial—that time of a perfect correspondence between humans and nature. "Haven't you sometimes dreamed of those Elysian Fields where cares might be forgotten and life would be in blissful harmony with nature?" the Florida East Coast Railway murmured. "Just beyond the southern horizon lies the land of your heart's desire where climate and nature have conspired to produce a well-nigh perfect environment for the life ideal." For one traveler, the approach to Havana revealed "the promised land—the land of the cocoa and the palm, of my childhood's dreams of tropic fruits and gorgeous flowers . . . !" As the Illinois Central Railroad and Standard Fruit and Steamship Company urged, "Forsake the frets and cares of the humdrum workaday world . . . and be off to a land of gaiety where spring reigns throughout the year." In more fanciful language, another writer promised that "in but two days' time from New York," the traveler "can reach the enchanted isles . . . where the Frost King may not follow, or claim [the traveler] for his own."[23] The Frost King—winter itself, but also time and time's inevitable consorts, aging and death.

This promise of an escape from cold, dull industrial civilization and the burdens of mature responsibilities entailed the very same eternal youth and absence of privation that racial ideologues labeled racial degeneration. Travel advertisers redeemed it by associating it with a return to bodily health and vigor—not the indolence and indifference predicted by the climatologists. The Atlantic and Gulf Railroad proclaimed of Florida that "instead of the debilitating effects of a warm southern climate, so often spoken of by writers, we here see and feel only an invigorating effect." Southern California's climate, George Wharton James claimed, offered "freedom from enervating heat in summer, and benumbing cold in winter." In addition to a renewed youthful vigor, residents in these areas would live longer: "The health of the inhabitants of Florida is proverbial; many can now be seen who are ninety years old and upwards." Sixty years later, St. Petersburg, Florida, "has made its good fortune by realizing that people over twenty can have a good time," George Seaton wrote, and "many a twenty-year-old boy has gotten a new respect for Grandma after trailing her" through her busy recreational schedule. San Diego's Peter C. Remondino was one of the most insistent on this point, arguing that people moving to Southern California gained "ten years more with the additional benefit of feeling ten years younger during the time, for there is a rejuvenating influence about the atmosphere that is remarked upon and felt by all newcomers after a residence of several months." "In a certain city out on the [Pacific] Coast," humorist Cobb claimed, "there is one paper that refuses even to admit that a human being can actually expire while breathing the air of Southern California."[24]

The rhetoric culminated in the revival of the old legend of the fountain of youth. In this Florida had a bit of an edge, thanks to the sixteenth-century Spanish explorer Ponce de Leon's legendary search for it there. "As I gazed on the marvelous spring," a zookeeper wrote of his expedition to capture an alligator, "the spirit of the Fountain possessed me and I dreamed that I had found what Ponce de Leon so long and so vainly sought. . . . Perpetual Youth of the spirit is one of the Florida Enchantments." Although apparently the conquistador had not realized it during his two years as Puerto Rico's governor (thus the necessity of sailing to Florida), the island's promoters claimed that he had "felt that San Juan was really the garden or fountain of perpetual youth and after 400 years it still seems to have that same quality for you never saw such happiness as is displayed by visitors to the beautiful romantic and historical island."[25]

However fanciful the claims, the widespread emphasis on the tropics as a site of rejuvenation for weary, ailing whites highlights the extent to which the cult of youth for which the twentieth century is famous had both geographic and racial sources and implications. As one enthusiastic son of California proclaimed, "The Californian is unfettered by conventions; his spirit is free. The naturalness of childhood holds on into age. . . . The true Californian plays at living, and perhaps, nay, no doubt, this is the better way to live!" Hamburg American made a similar claim for its Caribbean cruises in a 1937 brochure: "Life begins anew for the cruise passenger in search of health and pleasure. . . . With renewed vigor, one wants to play again, to feel young again, and every opportunity to satisfy this desire is available."[26] The economic and political expansion of the United States into the tropics, both within and beyond its borders, entailed the incorporation of lands where youthfulness was natural, and those natural youths were originally nonwhite. The ability—and the growing desire—of temperate-zone whites to rejuvenate themselves in such climates marked a growing desire to absorb tropical influences and the nature of tropical peoples.

In other words, the development of Florida and Southern California by U.S. whites and their travels there and in Mexico and the Caribbean meant something in addition to the spread of U.S.-style white supremacy and economic dominance. Consuming the tropics forwarded a popular romantic racialism that far exceeded in reach the better known literary and artistic primitivism of the early twentieth century. And that romantic racialism offered its consumers an alternative tropical whiteness that evaded the evils of both excessive civilization and excessive primitiveness. The evidence of this alternative lies in the promise that life itself was better in the Southland. Quite aside from those who arrived in hopes of recovering from deadly illnesses, many of the people who moved to or simply moved through these landscapes of plenty believed themselves to have changed or wanted to be changed because they did so. Life in "our East, with its impossible climate, its conventions born of a life rigidly circumscribed by nature" produced neurasthenia and bodily frailty. The solution was California, where, as George Wharton James enthused, "there is that in the climate of California . . . that makes one feel *different*. The primness, the stiffness, the formality, the reserves of life seem to fall from one." The result was a "Festival Spirit . . . in many respects, equalling that found among the Latin races of Europe"—a carefully circumscribed comparison to the peoples of Western civilization rather than their dismayingly mixed American descendants. Still, James praised the relaxing effects of warm weather and bright sunshine, rebutting critics who called them the first symptoms of degeneration. "The climate of Southern California," he wrote, "makes the people buoyant, volatile, pleasure-loving and free. . . . The feeling in the air is, there is no fierce summer, no harsh winter, so 'On with the dance, let joy be unconfined.' "[27]

Although this minister turned culture huckster was sui generis, his climate claims drew on a venerable tradition and echoed everywhere. The Panama Mail steamship line told its New York–bound passengers that "though Los Angeles teems with business, and Progress is shouted on every side in headline type, there is nevertheless a permanent holiday spirit in its sunbathed streets." Living in California, such arguments implied, entailed the absorption of "Latin" traits—without losing that essential temperate gift for progress. As is well known, Californians of U.S. origin were quick to claim the fabled warmth and hospitality of the Spanish missionaries as regional traits by the turn of the century. As a character in a didactic pro-California novel declared, " 'I'm a Californian. I was born here and even if I haven't Spanish blood in my veins, I have the spirit of the old padres.' . . . The open-hearted hospitality of the Spaniards is canonical law throughout the West."[28]

One did not have to settle permanently in California to enjoy these happy effects, as both warm climates and nonwhites were widespread in the Western Hemisphere. Havana's Hotel Cecil promised guests ideal accommodations "where land, tradition, and climate give life a sense of ease and happiness known only in the tropics. . . . Come into a new life full of color, gaiety and sunshine." American Express Travel Services assured travelers on its 1939 West Indies cruises that the mountain air and "the carnival spirit of the colorful native life up there [above La Guayra, Venezuela] make you feel absurdly young and happy." In the Bahamas, "no shrieking motor horns are heard to shatter the peace and contentment of your rediscovered Eden. The 'natives' smiling disregard of the rush and bustle that characterize our large cities will give you a clearer viewpoint from which to estimate the value of worry and work"—that is, of the value of adulthood and civilization. Mexico visitor Elise Haas wrote to a friend, "What a lesson we hurrying, scurrying Americans can learn from the leisurely Mexican and how many tired, strained faces could be smoothed into serenity by the calm, unhurried manner of living of these people." Wells Fargo assured its travelers to Mexico that "the very Indian village of Yautepec . . . will tempt you to 'go native' and spend the afternoon lounging under its splendid trees and listening to the unending song of wild birds that crow in the leafy branches."[29]

No one will be surprised to learn that few U.S. tourists actually "went native" in any socially or politically meaningful sense (partial exceptions might include the artists who participated in Mexico's folk arts renaissance in the 1930s and the African Americans who sought out their counterparts in other nations).[30] The romantic stereotypes constantly reprised in travel writing constituted racial gifts for the weary white person, not demands for racial, class, or national equality. Advertising short, rapid journeys through a tropical bazaar, tourist brochures offered healing drafts for overcivilized, hardworking whites, not encounters with people with politics or places with histories. Nevertheless, the commercial repetition of this theme suggests the broad appeal of the idea that whites would benefit from incorporating a bit of the tropics into their lives. The loosening of the bond between race and nature, captured in the idea of culture, diminished the danger of that incorporation; it no longer entailed degeneration but rather rejuvenation.

A key element in this portrayal of the natives as a natural resource for whites was the supposedly natural hospitality of southern people, long thought to be an effect of the tropical climate and also a characteristic of preindustrial societies. The people of Tampa had "that spirit which welcomes every newcomer with true Southern hospitality," one traveler claimed, and the residents of Key West "are about the most friendly, pleasant, hospitable, accommodating and altogether delightful people one could wish to meet," in the opinion of a writer who otherwise found the islanders shabby, un-American, and inappropriately dependent on the federal dole in the late 1930s. A Panama Mail line passenger wrote of the denizens of the West Indies, "In this land of the marimba, where the air [is] heavy laden with rich odors of spices, the perfumed banana and other tropical fruits . . . , the people are loving and loved, and hospitable almost to a fault." The Mexican National Railroad proclaimed in 1892 that "the people [of Mexico] are a hospitable, pleasure-loving set, and very kind and courteous to strangers within their gates." A later generation of proudly nationalist promoters agreed: "Mexicans are notorious for their gentle manners, they are regarded as well educated people and their hospitableness is widely acknowledge [sic] by all." A visitor riding horseback in Puerto Rico would find a welcome at the humblest farmer's hut because of "that true hospitality for which the Puertoricans [sic] are noted."[31]

Although this trait was attributed to many varieties of southerner, U.S. whites believed it to be especially characteristic of Latins and nonwhite peoples precisely because of their backwardness: "It has been said that hospitality wanes as civilization advances." By the time the American Automobile Association's Elmer Jenkins told delegates to a 1931 Pan American Union meeting that "your people are innately courteous and hospitable," the sentiment was thoroughly clichéd. It was also highly politicized: Latin Americans generally considered people from the United States rude and inhospitable, suggesting ways in which this banality might serve the hosts as much as the guests.[32]

The emphasis on southern peoples' natural hospitality cast leisure—which imperial moralists preferred to call laziness—as a major natural resource, just like bananas but better suited to tourism. Advertisers often portrayed the Southland, especially the Caribbean islands, as a "land of leisure"; in those places "under the Southern Cross . . . life moves leisurely" because "there is a tranquilizing influence in this warm sea air of the South, which tends to mental repose and an idle and dreamy existence." Alternatively, it constituted a playground for northern workers let out on recess. The American Line grandly declared the entire Caribbean region a "winter playground of surpassing loveliness," whereas the Furness, Withy and Company steamship line more modestly branded Bermuda as the "Playground of Eternal Springtime," and Holland America labeled Nassau "the playground of the carefree Bahamas." "It would seem to some presumptuous to call Florida the greatest winter playground of the world," the editor of the *Miami Tribune* conceded, before proceeding to argue that it truly was. Hinting at less childish pleasures, travel writer Sidney Clark declared, "Cuba, the estranged daughter of Spain . . . inherited just enough of her mother's indolence to inject a sense of sweet leisure into the veins of a rushing world."[33] Whereas North Americans and Europeans had long believed that labor in the tropics would kill or at least brutalize whites, increasingly they believed that leisure there would restore them to youthful vigor.

Compounding the effects of this innate hospitality was the natural joy that the locals exuded, relieving U.S. visitors of their cares. "Cubans," Clark insisted amid the political violence of the 1930s, "are among the most buoyant, happy, hopeful people on earth," and this trait made for "a wonderful feeling of freedom" among tourists because it allowed them simply to enjoy themselves. ("For tourists, the sunshine cannot be serious," Derek Walcott said in accepting the Nobel Prize for Literature in 1992; the Caribbean was for them "a place to flee not only winter but that seriousness that comes only out of a culture with four seasons.") From this point of view, leisure flowed from tropical places and peoples rather than the privilege of being a tourist. The playfulness that sprang naturally from the generosity of tropical nature and discouraged the natives from applying themselves to the project of civilization now became a gift enhancing the civilization so laboriously constructed by temperate peoples. Journalist Harry Foster rehearsed all the usual stereotypes in characterizing "the Latin-American": he "lived completely in the present, with scarcely a thought of the morrow" and, "being indolent, he has infinite leisure for entertainment. At all times he is friendly, agreeable, and courteous." But unlike the theorists of racial degeneration, Foster rather liked this approach to life: "There was something pleasant and carefree about this Mexico that proved infectious," a fever he had no wish to avoid.[34]

As another travel writer put it, "Everyone ought to go to Mexico, for in that Republic you will find all the time there is, and if our share thereof is not enough almost anyone there will have some to spare which he will gladly give away. To those people whose time is money, therefore, a trip into Mexico is a bargain." Trinidad offered "pot of golden hours for any voyager." The traveler in the Caribbean, Jean Lane promised, could "spend uncounted time, for time is cheap in that world."[35] Civilization, racing toward the future, had no time; the backward tropics, neglecting the contest, contained all the time in the world. The realized power of age might here regain the unrealized possibility of youth.

The threadbare cliché that the tropics were lands of "mañana—to-morrow, by-and-by" rested on the venerable European and North American belief that people in the tropics neither needed nor wanted to work for their subsistence, much less any loftier goal—"the care-free mode of life of the inhabitants is so different from our complex existence,"[36] as the Raymond-Whitcomb tour company put it in a brochure for a 1927 Caribbean cruise. The fantasy that the residents of the tropics lived in a world unaffected by industrialization and capitalism—that they neither worked nor worried—did not so much mask the ongoing incorporation of the labor and resources of the Southland into a U.S.-dominated hemispheric economy as naturalize it. The tourist industry made the availability of the tropics for the pleasure of U.S. visitors seem like a gift readily offered by the locals, a reflex of the natural difference between temperate and tropical peoples. Once given as a gift, the tropics ceased to be racially dangerous and became instead culturally pleasurable.

The social results of U.S. economic dominance were not invisible to tourists, even those who did not visit sugar or banana plantations. Most travelers encountered swarms of vendors and beggars at every port and railroad station they passed through—"the land army of the predatory poor is always mobilized and waiting"—but few recognized the extent to which their own privileged wealth compelled boys, and sometimes grown men, to dive for coins that passengers tossed over the ship's railing. Instead, these activities seemed to be an expression of the nature of the place: "THE CARIBBEAN: Swarms of laughing and shouting black boys row out to the ship at nearly every Caribbean port and dive for the coins that are thrown in abundance into the water for them. A sight like this is a real part of the West Indian scene." Colorful markets and casual labor appeared to most travelers as the *opposite* of work—in fact, they appeared as the culture of people who had, thanks to their tropical circumstances, failed to achieve capitalist civilization because they had too few wants. An interviewer who surveyed U.S. residents about their attitudes toward Latin Americans in 1940 reported, "Most people are very, very ignorant. . . . By replies I received I know that they have the idea that all South Americans are part Indian and sleep all afternoon. . . . I imagine here most people think of them as doing the rhumba rather than working for a living."[37]

Such stereotypes produced a characteristic developmental narrative: although tropical lands and their peoples were natural hosts, without U.S. commercial acumen and industrial prowess they would never be able to extend the gift of their graciousness to the world. Many accounts of the rise of these popular tourist destinations emphasized that U.S. entrepreneurs discovered and put to their highest use the natural attributes of soil, climate, and race through agribusiness and resort development. "Once [the Spanish] had [Florida], no one seemed to know what to do with the place . . . , a sandy, apparently worthless waste," wrote one author. "Juan Ponce de Leon might well be termed the patron saint of winter tourists. . . . Unfortunately for him, however, he was born too soon. The world was not yet ready to make use of what he had discovered." Readiness arrived with a "shrewd, hard-headed, practical businessman"—Henry Flagler.[38]

Similarly, the Spanish colonists of Southern California, their U.S. usurpers declared, had failed to take advantage of the rich opportunities the region offered. An ardent advocate of Latin gaiety and the climate that produced it, George Wharton James claimed that "a few Americans took a leaf of wisdom from the books of the Mexicans, though they read into it far more golden profit than the natives ever dreamed of." Southern California did not develop after the U.S. takeover in 1849, the Automobile Club of Southern California claimed. "Rather, it idled along, satisfied with life, holding its fiestas and rodeos, with such commercial activities as were evidenced being more or less in the hands of a few Americans" until the Southern Pacific Railroad arrived in town. The same story could be told of sites outside the United States. "In any European country there would be a funicular (two in Switzerland) to this glory spot," Sidney Clark wrote of a peak offering a good view of the city of Santiago, Cuba. "There would be a huge resort hotel, a number of chalets, a casino. . . . Being in Cuba, there is absolutely nothing here except a couple of negro huts."[39]

In the Caribbean and Latin America, the Panama Canal was the ultimate such argument: U.S. know-how and good sanitation opened the whole world to whites by making the pestilential tropics safe for travelers. Advertising its 1935 cruises, the Grace Line proclaimed, "Here you have the spic-and-spanness of American enterprise. . . . Where fever and death once convinced the French that no canal would ever be built . . . [is] now one of the most healthful spots in all the world." Panama Mail's marketers agreed: "Since American authorities assumed administration of the canal zone, it has changed from one of the most malarial to one of the most healthful spots in the world." But even before the canal, U.S. sanitation campaigns in Cuba and Puerto Rico after the 1898 war and in Veracruz, Mexico, in 1916, proved (at least to U.S. citizens) that the United States was conquering tropical nature for universal benefit—unlike any of the region's past masters. The Raymond-Whitcomb tour company invoked the black legend to highlight the beneficence of the

Pax Americana: "Only the imagination can picture the greed and the cruelty by means of which Pizarro and his fellow-Conquistadores transported untold wealth in gold to their King in Spain [across the Isthmus of Panama]. The smooth banks of today resemble little the pestilential road that served the avarice and the treachery of those long-gone roisterers of the days of the Gold Road." The bright white light of engineering and sanitation cast into shadow the bitter struggles that enabled the founding of Panama and the construction of the canal. Similarly deaf to politics, Canadian Agnes Laut congratulated the U.S. military and U.S.-owned oil companies for cleaning up the Mexican cities of Veracruz and Tampico and urged Mexico's revolutionary leaders to welcome foreign investors: "When this is done Vera Cruz and San Juan Ulua and the beautiful tropical country inland will come into their own as one of the most delightful winter playgrounds in the world. . . . Tourists to Vera Cruz would bring more money into Mexico than the country's national revenue."[40]

The increasing circulation of romantic stereotypes combined with this narrative of a beneficent U.S. hegemony to convert the nightmares of racial ideologues into tourist daydreams. One need not credit the tourist industry or individual tourists with antiracist ideals or cross-cultural solidarity to recognize that the highly successful promotion of tourism in the Southland offered a way to transform civilization—to "go native"—that did not challenge white supremacy but nevertheless suggested that it was inadequate, even inimical, to living a happy life. The romantic critique that motivated much early twentieth-century criticism of civilization pervaded the travel industry's promotional materials and made the Southland a potent, if deeply flawed, means of prying apart climate and race so that white visitors might benefit from the former without losing their health and social dominance. In this sense, the tourist industry acted much as did germ theory, reducing nature's awesome power to create races and impose death sentences to the graciousness of the hostess of a garden party, proffering racial gifts sanitized by modern engineering.

In Southern California and Florida, developers catered to these ideas by sponsoring public festivals and encouraging the use of architectural and decorative styles that signified the tropics to the average well-to-do white traveler. Both places appropriated and gentrified the styles of their Spanish colonial pasts, notably by encouraging residential architecture in supposedly "Spanish" or "Mediterranean" styles and colors—creams, turquoises, and ochers painted on stucco—that evoked warm climates and bright sunshine.

Although Henry Flagler's Florida East Coast Company abandoned quasi-Spanish architecture and names for its hotels as it moved southward, from St. Augustine's fancifully "Moorish" Ponce de Leon, Cordoba, and Alcazar to the U.S.-colonial-style Royal Poinciana and Breakers in Palm Beach, developers like George Merrick in Coral Gables continued to favor styles that evoked the Mediterranean and the Middle East (Plate 3). Celebrity architect Addison Mizner built several Palm Beach villas with Spanish names like Amado, Sin Cuidado, Collado Hueco, Casa Bendita, and El Solano for wealthy clients who clearly found the Spanish conceit appealing. Carl Fisher's Miami Beach represented the culmination of this trend in its development of a tropical art deco style that referred simultaneously to the whitewashed, brightly accented homes characteristic of some Caribbean islands and the massive white cruise ships that dominated pleasure travel through the region by the 1930s.[41]

Whereas early Southern California developers such as the Coronado Company imitated common eastern architectural styles, a heavily modified "Spanish colonial" or "mission" style dominated in the area after 1915, especially in upscale residential construction. Even when such features were no more than decorative flourishes that did not alter the structure or spatial organization of buildings (most mission-style structures are made of wood and stucco, not the traditional adobe, and they feature front and back yards instead of central patios), cumulatively and symbolically they constructed landscapes of tropical fantasy that millions of U.S. whites found attractive. In the instances when such structures were built in planned communities like Coral Gables (Plate 3) or Rancho Santa Fe, they inhabited suburban landscapes built for year-round outdoor leisure—including golf courses and swimming pools—that exemplified the lifestyle that Florida and Southern California claimed to provide.[42]

The many festivals organized by Florida and Southern California developers showcased their warm winters and horticultural wealth—thus the endless flower and orange festivals scheduled for midwinter, most famously Pasadena's New Year's Day Rose Parade. Herself a recent arrival to Los Angeles, Eleanor F. Bennett took some visiting cousins to see it in 1905: "So many flowers in the middle winter is what is so wonderful and the extravagant use of the same seems almost incredible if it were possible for our eyes to deceive us. Perhaps the best was the steamer, rolling down the street embowered in roses & smilax"—a whimsical example of the new balance between civilization and tropical bounty that Southland promoters advertised. A calendar of Florida events compiled by the Federal Writers' Project for the state's entry in the American Guide Series listed orange, strawberry, tomato, azalea, camellia, and tobacco festivals and dozens of sports competitions, from the Orange and Kumquat Bowls in football to regattas, air shows, trap shooting, fishing, and golf—most scheduled between January and March.[43]

Such parades and fairs were as close kin to industrial and agricultural expositions as they were to tourist promotion and the community-building pageantry popular at the time. But they also deliberately sought to recreate a "Latin" festive tradition that evoked the area's Spanish colonial heritage. As New Orleans's Mardi Gras became a major tourist attraction by the turn of the twentieth century, other cities in the Southland set out to revive or establish similar festivals. Although Los Angeles's short-lived Fiesta de los Flores struck many as too "Latin" to be appropriate for U.S. whites, promoters in California and elsewhere enjoyed considerable success in exploiting Spanish colonial and tropical themes in community pageantry. For instance, Tampa's Gasparilla Carnival featured the arrival of a band of Spanish pirates: "Each year in February . . . the pseudo-pirate, Gasparilla, and his motley 'crewe' descend upon the city from the Plant Park docks amid popping guns and corks. . . . Based on the life and alleged depredations of Captain José Gaspar, the celebration includes parades, pageants and balls." Even as events like these assimilated to the United States the idea of the festival, a tradition largely associated with Catholic folk religion and long marginalized in the predominantly Protestant United States, they also highlighted the growing economic and social importance of the tourist industry. Thus with the advent of the horse racing season, "Miami is 100 days of perpetual carnival"[44]—Latin festival spirit and Yankee materialism profitably blended.

Of course, such festivals had long been regular features of public life and the Catholic religious calendar in Mexico and the current or former French and Spanish colonies of the Caribbean. There the problem was adapting a venerable and politically labile tradition to the demands of the tourism industry. In many places, including Mexico and Cuba, the authorities had repressed or banned these events because they represented the power of the church and often acted as vehicles for collective action and social critique by poor, African-descended, and indigenous peoples. In the early twentieth century, however, the highly developed social machinery of community pageantry in the United States offered a model for using public parties to bolster local authorities and advertise local businesses. By the 1920s and 1930s, elites were reconsidering the bans in light of the possibility of turning such troublesome events into displays of national beauty and distinctiveness for an international audience through tourism. As a 1941 report for the U.S. coordinator of commercial and cultural relations between the American republics remarked, "They have rich color, action, and traditional significance. They can be used directly to dramatize the costumes and customs of the various countries" and would serve as a good basis for publicity "designed to promote international goodwill and as a means of stimulating tourist travel." Guillermo Andreve, writing a report on tourism for Panama's government in 1929, asserted that his country's annual carnival only needed advertising to overmatch its rivals in Cannes, Havana, Madrid, Nice, Paris, San José de Costa Rica, and San Sebastián, Spain—a list demonstrating the extent to which the revival or invention of a festival tradition and the reorientation of religious celebrations toward tourism overlapped with the development of the Southland as a global playground.[45] Carnival's potential subversiveness, like that of tropical fecundity, would be tamed by being made over as culture.

The combination of the romantic tropics and U.S. initiative produced the possibility of a new kind of whiteness, one adapted to the tropics without being absorbed by it. This adaptation made what ideologues called racial degeneration into a pleasure readily, commercially available for well-to-do travelers—and also available in fantasy form through advertisements, travel writing, films, cabarets, and songs to those who could not afford a trip to the Southland. The romantic racialism popular in the early twentieth century was grounded to some degree in the absorption—political and cultural—of the world's tropical regions into North American and European empires; geography, climate, and race were all intertwined. And metropolitan whites imagined this absorption as a transformative prescription for some of the ills caused by civilization. The tourist industry played a key role in formulating and popularizing this idea by literally and figuratively mapping a world full of resources for the bodily and the psychic comfort of weary or troubled northerners. In the process, what had been racial traits springing from the constraints of nature became cultural practices reflecting the benefits of human variety.

Among the chief signs of this new tropical whiteness were a transformation in dress and the growing importance of the beach to tourism in the Southland. The amazing shrinking bathing suit and the two activities it encouraged—swimming and, above all, tanning—signaled the very personal absorption of the same "tropical color" so long feared and despised by racial ideologues.

CHAPTER 4

Dressing for the Tropics

In 1900, *Cosmopolitan* published a didactic little essay entitled "What Is a Gentleman?—A Lady?" on the importance of dressing appropriately. The four conversationalists agree that Adam—the original Adam—was a gentleman in his time despite his lack of clothing, but " 'we have to conform to the habits of our class, whatever that class may be. We should not be pleased if Alice had come down to dinner in a golf-skirt or tennis shoes, should we?' " This belief that dressing for dinner was a critical expression of both the progress of civilization and a person's elevated status within it was not just another of the melodramas of etiquette commonly dispensed by magazine advice columns. After a bridge game at the summer resort on Santa Catalina Island near Los Angeles, Selena Ingram wrote in her diary, "It was too late to dress for dinner when we got home—& we had to go in the [hotel] dining room as we were,—& as a good many new people had arrived—I was sorry not to be dressed appropriately."[1]

But increasingly, U.S. whites in the Southland were not sorry to cast aside formal wear, and they did not mind anyone coming to dinner in her golf skirt. The rapidity with which respectable attire—especially the bathing suit—shrank and became less formal was key evidence of the impact of the tropics on white civilization. Heightening the social implications of scanty and casual clothing was a radically new aesthetic practice: tanning. Suddenly after the turn of the twentieth century, white people began deliberately to darken their skins by lying out in the sun with as little clothing covering their bodies as the law permitted. The transformation in clothing and the rise of tanning represented an assertion of a new intimacy between U.S. whites and nature, especially tropical nature. Although neither the new fashions nor tanning were limited to the Southland, by the 1930s it was the source—imaginatively and often literally—of the new styles and the ideal toward which all municipal beaches and backyard sunbathers strove.

Southernwear

As is well known, respectable people wore a great deal of clothing when they appeared in public in the late nineteenth century. The quantity, formality, and detailing of public wear represented wealth, leisure, and class status (or aspiration), and its variations enabled the proper performance (or bungling) of gender, age, occupation, and marital eligibility. Photographs of early well-to-do tourists in the Southland show men in long trousers, collared shirts, waistcoats, and suit jackets and women in ankle-length skirts, long-sleeved blouses, hats, and gloves. For a hike and picnic in San Gabriel Canyon near Los Angeles in the early twentieth century, the members of one party wore long sleeves and either long pants or floor-length skirts; two of the male excursionists wore suit jackets, and most wore hats—though one woman's was no larger than a skullcap and another's was a large, shady bonnet.[2]

The minimal clothing of poor people in Mexico and the Caribbean frequently made travelers uneasy, if not openly disapproving. Describing the men rowing small boats out to meet the steamer at Fort de France, Martinique, William Corlett noted that "negro blood predominates" among the island's mixed-race inhabitants, and "few had even a suggestion of clothing, an abandon not tolerated in most communities." (These men were about to dive into the water after coins thrown by tourists, a pursuit unlikely to be enhanced by shirts and trousers.) Upon seeing men and women bathing and doing laundry in the waters flowing from the eponymous hot springs of Aguas Calientes, Mexico, Charles Dudley Warner wrote, "the stream from the springs, in which there is promiscuous bathing for a mile, is said to give one a fair idea of the Mexican disregard for conventionalities"—rather than, for example, an alternative etiquette prizing cleanliness above bodily concealment or the bathers' dispossession from the spring by the commercial spa established there. A sign of poverty, the paucity or lack of clothing revealed, along with bare skin, the lack of self-disciplined enterprise to which most white travelers credited their privilege. All the Cuban peasant needed to overcome tropical indolence was a vision of a better life, one analyst imagined, "and his pride will cause him to exert himself laboriously so that [his children] may be clothed with more garments than has been the custom in the tropics." From this point of view, to abandon multiple layers of clothing during a stay in the Southland was not a rational response to warm temperatures but a sign that the tropics were exercising their dreadful powers of racial degeneration. Indeed, physicians had long recommended that whites wear not less but more clothing to protect them from the tropical climate, such as woolen bands around their stomachs to prevent dysentery and special hats and underwear to ward off the evil effects of strong sunshine.[3]

Or in the era of germ theory, shedding clothing might be—and in fact was increasingly portrayed to be—a blow for freedom against the foolish fetters of social convention. Aiming at one of his favorite targets, Kenneth Roberts noted in 1922 that Palm Beach's owners were "frightened for the first time in years—frightened that the wealthy tourists will desert . . . the continuous clothes-changing and the eternal chatter and twaddle of society" for Miami, "where people go in to dinner in golf clothes without getting a hard look from the head waiter." But even in the staid confines of Palm Beach, things were changing. In the old days, Roberts claimed, the society ladies at this famously exclusive resort "spent at least forty per cent. of their waking hours changing their clothes. . . . Their menfolk were kept constantly busy hooking them up the back." But by the 1920s, "dresses are safely attached to the human frame by as few as three hooks, all of which can be reached without dislocating an arm" and even more radical, many "dresses are merely slid on over the head and worn just as they fall." Less sarcastic observers noted, "The Florida summer dweller wears the minimum of clothing, light in weight, light in color and loose in texture," and sartorial prophylactics earlier believed necessary were being discarded: "the habit of going hatless in Summer—the year around, for that matter—appears to the observer from outside to be more prevalent among Florida men than it is anywhere in the North." In these tamed tropics, the disorders traditionally associated with hatlessness in hot climates were rare; "Sunstroke or heat prostration is unknown in Florida."[4]

These scanty new garments had a name: "sports clothes"—but also "Southernwear" and "resortwear," so closely were they associated with winter visits to the Southland by the 1920s. Not coincidentally, a good deal of this clothing was also designed and produced in Florida and Southern California, and its connection to those places featured prominently in the marketing materials. Originating on the golf course and tennis court, sports clothes were made of lighter fabrics and required much less underclothing than normal attire, especially for women, and increasingly also dispensed with overclothing, such as jackets, gloves, and hats. It featured short sleeves, casual necklines, higher hemlines, and slimmer silhouettes, as well as fewer buttons in more convenient places. Gender differentiation also lessened to some extent, with women's sporting outfits modeled after men's to the point that women began to wear pants and even shorts in public by the 1930s, while men enjoyed a wider range of colors and the privilege of baring their knees. "We come into the Tropics this afternoon," Madeline Allen wrote to her family from a steamer southbound from San Francisco to the Panama Canal on March 31, 1931, and "that is when we will begin stripping down." Alas, she had not brought the right clothes: "I wish I had brought my shorts and backless shirt. . . . How do you think Dan's [her husband's] shorts would look on me?" The development of new fabrics, the spread of readymade clothing, and the participation of growing numbers of women in athletics and employment all contributed to the transformation in dress in the United States, but the change was most visible in its association with a leisured, outdoors lifestyle that was in turn strongly associated with—although certainly not limited to—the Southland.[5]

Informality of dress increasingly became one of the luxuries associated with life at a tropical resort, and especially cruises: "I see that we could wear absolutely anything we wanted," Allen reported. The United Fruit Company's Great White Fleet, which long boasted of its luxury accommodations and exclusive passenger lists, reported in the 1930s that on board its cruise ships, "informality prevails—whether it's for a dance or a swim or an exchange of opinion on the sun deck." And a later brochure for the notably named "Vagabond Cruises" emphasized, "Informality is the rule. You dress as you please and do as you please." The Panama Mail Steamship Company advised that "Sports Clothes the Order of the Day: Summer sports clothes, with wraps for cool evenings on deck, will be most comfortable and suitable throughout the cruise, except for the first and last days in northern waters." Not all cruises were so casual; Eleanor Early recommended bringing at least six dinner gowns because "you will dress, by the way, every night for dinner," but she immediately qualified her advice: "I mean other people will, and you will do as you please."[6] Formal attire had become optional even among the wealthy by the late 1930s.

The new options in clothing surely made the heat of the tropics easier to bear, but they were a symbolic as much as a practical form of acclimatization. When F. P. Garretson remarked grumpily on a hot day during a turn-of-the-twentieth-century visit to St. Croix (then one of the Danish Virgin Islands), "we ourselves were ready to throw off all conventionality, and envied the little naked darkies in their cool attire,"[7] he dramatized the centrality of etiquette to racial distinction and the threat that tropical heat posed to it—as well as the association of informality and undress with youth. In abandoning the comprehensive, opaque clothing recommended by an earlier generation of imperial physicians, tourists increasingly opened themselves to the tropical climate, emulated the locals, and regarded both as sources of well-being and rejuvenation. Once in the North only little boys wore shorts in public; now grown men and even women would don them.

Nowhere was tourists' increasing tendency to emulate the "little naked darkies" more evident than in the growing popularity of going to the beach (the topic of the rest of this section) and the rapidly shrinking bodily coverage of the typical bathing suit (the subject of the next section). Although it may be hard to believe today, the beach was not particularly important in early Southland tourism. True, seaside resorts became popular in Britain at the end of the eighteenth century, and people in the United States flocked to Atlantic Ocean and lakeside resorts decades before and throughout the development of Florida and Southern California. By 1900 beaches in or near major cities attracted huge crowds every summer weekend, as much for the rides, shows, and dance halls on their amusement piers as the surf and sand. Nevertheless, the Raymond-Whitcomb tour company chose inland Pasadena as the site of its huge tourist hotel in the mid-1880s, not Long Beach or Redondo Beach, though entrepreneurs would build successful hostelries, bathhouses, and amusement piers on those beaches and many others within a few decades.[8]

An 1880s essay on Bermuda, although it mentioned good ocean bathing, spent more time on the "delightful drives" on the good coral roads to caves, grottoes, and lakes, as well as boating and promenading on the stone-paved waterfront. For visitors to Jamaica in 1906, Hamburg American emphasized "the riotous luxuriance of the tropical foliage" and recommended a carriage ride to the "Bog Walk" near Kingston and the Castleton Botanical Garden. Although it suggested that visitors might enjoy sitting on the broad verandas of the Hotel Titchfield to look at the sea, the line arranged no beach visits for passengers to indulge in the surf bathing praised as "the finest in the world." Ida Starr, visiting Kingston around 1900, was dismayed to find that the Myrtle Bank Hotel was not "embowered in myrtle green and magnolia" but located on "an arid sand beach." Steamship excursions on northern Florida's rivers and visits to its inland freshwater springs attracted far more tourists than its white sand beaches in the 1880s and 1890s. When the Florida Excursion Company urged its customers, "in packing, do not forget your bathing suit; you will need it at Green Cove," this destination was not a saltwater beach but a hot spring south of Jacksonville where "the waters are health-giving . . . ; a prominent physician writes of surprising cures in cases of neuralgia, nervous prostration, rheumatism, liver and kidney complaints having been effected by them."[9]

When early visitors to Southern California and Florida went to the beach, they, like many nineteenth-century visitors to English and Mediterranean resorts, strolled and botanized rather than swam—and they certainly did not sunbathe. Sea air, as much as seawater, bolstered health and did not require donning a special costume or risking one's life in chilly waters and dangerous currents. The beach in La Jolla, California, Samuel Dexter told his children, was "a great place to gather the pretty abalone shells," if the visitor had thought to bring a chisel to pry them out of the rock. "Oh how I did enjoy the time on the beach," Eleanor F. Bennett rhapsodized of a visit to San Diego, "lieing [sic] in the sand, eating my lunch and scrambling over rocks, climbing up & down steep places ladders etc." The Florida Excursion Company glossed its customers' stay in St. Augustine, Florida, as "wanderings through the quaint old streets, sailing down the bay to the light house and the coquina quarries, gathering shells by the sea shore, strolling along the sea-wall."[10]

Of his first visit to St. Augustine's beach with his wife and son, John Gilpin wrote, "[we] wandered for hours, drinking in the refreshing breezes, and gathering shells, of which we found considerable variety." But even though the Gilpins had just spent three months fishing, hunting, camping, boating, and generally living a vigorous outdoor life, they had not come to the beach prepared to swim. Still, "Vincent was eager to paddle" in the surf, John told his sister, "so we arranged his clothing to allow him to do so, and you never saw a happier boy. The water was so tempting, I went up the beach some distance with him, and as we had the whole ground to ourselves, I disrobed him & myself, and we had a glorious bath." In later years, John and Vincent made ocean dips central to their Florida experience (Emma hardly ever swam). During an 1888 stay in Manatee County, the Gilpin men went surf bathing nearly every day, and John remarked that their landlord "says he recognizes, through our experience, the great value of this feature of his place," which he had not even built near the beach. It could be "reached by a sail of ¾ of a mile, with winds always always favoring—and all the conditions for pleasant bathing always to be found. He says he has decided to build a bath house or two on the beach, and I suggest the addition of a palmetto thatch awning, under which visitors would pass hours, even in the middle of the day."[11]

Pleasant for walking, beaches were also good places to drive—first carriages and later automobiles—in the years before the construction and paving of an extensive road network. The beach at Daytona, Florida, was renowned precisely for this; some of the earliest automobile speed records were set on its marvelously flat, hard beach, better than any pavement then invented. The Hotel del Coronado's management boasted of its "magnificent crescent-shaped beach" and claimed that "when the tide is out, there is no such carriage boulevard in the world." Illustrations in the 1886 and 1887 promotional brochures depict people driving and strolling on the beach; a few swimmers are tucked away in the background of the 1887 images, and the brochures give just one paragraph of text to the topic of surf bathing.[12]

Ocean swimming was so far from being a major attraction that even travelers expecting to have free time at the beach failed to bring bathing suits, and women in particular rarely knew how to swim. Traveling in western Mexico in 1909 with a party of U.S. railroad executives and their wives, Selena Ingram wrote of a stop near Mazatlán, "We spent the entire afternoon on the beach which is beautiful beyond description! We were all enraptured with it & wandered up & down the beautiful stretch of sand . . . until the sun set in a blaze of glory." Overcome by beauty (or perhaps heat and boredom), the next day the ladies of the party abandoned some of their clothes and all of their decorum for a romp in the water: "This morning I followed the others to the beach as soon as I finished breakfast," Ingram noted, "—& such a time as they were having! They had started in to wade, & getting their skirts wet, had decided to enjoy the water thoroughly." Their lone male escort "was assisting each lady to get a bath & enjoy the breakers. He was out—up to his waist in the water, in all his clothes, & the ladies all (except Mrs. Randolph & myself)—went in just as they were—only removing their silk skirts." Although Ingram, like Emma Gilpin, almost never swam, she enjoyed the event: "It was a funny sight—& they were all wild with excitement over it. Occasionally they would fall flat in the water—& such a scramble as they had to get up!"[13]

For those less willing to immerse themselves in the ocean swell, turn-of-the-twentieth-century beach resorts offered carefully regulated "plunges" and "baths": enclosed, roofed tanks that separated bathers from ocean, beach, and sky and regulated the temperature of the water. Ingram wrote of a family trip from Los Angeles, "We left for Long Beach at 5 o'clock—& had a nice walk on the beach. . . . The boys and Selena Pope had a swim in the 'plunge' & we had dinner on the car just before we got into Los Angeles at 7.30." The overlap between such early swimming pools and public bathhouses (and correspondingly between swimming and bathing) was still considerable. Writing home of a visit to Santa Monica, California, Samuel Dexter reported, "At the beach one can take a bath in the surf or by paying a quarter have a plunge bath in the swimming pool in the house or have a cold or hot salt-water bath in a bath tub. Grandpa took the latter. The rest of the party did not seem to feel the need of a bath so took none." This situation also prevailed in Florida: "As a matter of fact, most of the swimming done in Florida is done in tanks or pools, which are as often filled with fresh water as with salt."[14]

Although urban beaches in the Northeast and Midwest probably hosted more people on any given summer weekend, locals in Southern California and Florida seem to have taken the lead in developing a beach culture centered on ocean body surfing rather than strolling and picnicking. The experience of midwesterner C. W. Johnston during his first visit to Southern California may exemplify both the novelty of surf bathing to many and its prevalence on the coast. He reported that "I came here with a fine new black bathing suit, in due regulation and form, to enjoy as best I could a new sport to me, bathing in the sea." Daunted by the huge waves, he nevertheless "pushed on and on in an effort to submerge that part of my body exposed for the first time to the elements." Swept off his feet, he struggled up to find "a woman at my side, smiling and offering me any assistance I needed. This I enjoyed so much." His humiliation was complete when "she afterwards started out for deep water and swam like a duck. . . . She floated on the top crest or dived underneath and arose beyond, happy and confident." Ingram's five children went swimming nearly every day during family summers on Santa Catalina Island, though she and her husband rarely did so—she preferred bridge, he, golf. Although many people still enjoyed driving or motorcycling on the beach at Daytona in the late 1930s, "a large part of the life of Daytona Beach is lived in bathing suits, in or out of the water." White U.S. children in Panama, J. T. Boumphrey wrote, began swimming at an age when their bathing suits hung off "the little rounded forms."[15]

A curious item in the *Los Angeles Times* highlighted the racial implications—or lack thereof—of the new vogue for swimming, particularly for women. Praising the beauty and vigor of native Hawaiian women, the anonymous writer remarked, "This physical splendor is due to the mode of living rather than to the inherent qualities of the race." A white girl who adopted the Hawaiian custom of frequent swimming soon ceased to be "slender, almost attenuate[d]" and "developed her frame, filling up the hollows, increasing the muscles and beautifying the lines." Except for her skin color, "she could have passed for a full-blooded Kanaka of noble blood." Thus tropical life could be transformative without risking the really important things. Probably because beachgoing and swimming entailed whites' becoming more like tropical people—baring their bodies and subjecting them to the forces of nature—the many beaches and swimming pools opened in this era, in Southern California and Florida as elsewhere in the United States, were strictly segregated. By law, custom, and violence, African Americans and other nonwhite people were barred from using public facilities or restricted to limited hours or undesirable areas. Wherever possible, U.S.-owned or managed resorts sought to extend segregation throughout the Caribbean, often with the tacit support of local white elites.[16]

Even though beachgoing and ocean swimming grew increasingly important to Southland tourism from the 1910s, as late as the 1930s the facilities for it were limited where today they are extensive, especially in the Caribbean and Mexico. Ocean swimming was limited in Puerto Rico because of a lack of protection against sharks and a shortage of capital to build beach and hotel facilities that would attract the wealthy Americans who were the only ones who could afford such a trip. A 1944 analysis of the potential for tourism in the Caribbean islands noted that many had not even built roads to their beaches, suggesting how unimportant they were to the local economy. Although the towns of Mazatlán and Acapulco on Mexico's Pacific coast drew some traffic from passing steamers in the 1920s, the latter's development into a world-famous resort only really accelerated with the completion of a road between Mexico City and Acapulco in 1927, and for a variety of reasons the central government did not put its weight behind beach tourism until the 1940s.[17]

Bathing Beauties

The significance of the beach in the generation of tropical whites emerges most clearly in considering what people wore there. The transformation of the bathing suit—and its migration into social situations far from pool or beach—is perhaps the most startling change in the respectable wardrobe in this era and the most overt sign of new ideas about the proper relationship between white bodies and the natural and social worlds. Men and boys had long swum naked, but when middle-class and upper-class women joined the ranks of health-seeking bathers in the early nineteenth century, a century of conflict over the necessity of bathing costumes and how much flesh they should cover ensued. Some U.S., English, Australian, and Mediterranean beach towns segregated male from female bathers, but the impossibility of preventing spectatorship made a mockery of this solution to the problem of bodily exposure, and the growing importance of family togetherness in the mid-nineteenth century marshaled a growing number of opponents to the policy. The result was the advent of the bathing suit. Male swimmers were forced to don knee-length drawers and short-sleeved shirts, whereas female bathers entered the water clad in voluminous wool sacks covering them from neck to toe and often including stockings, slippers, gloves, and caps. The absence of these garments from fashion advertisements and pattern books suggested that they were ad hoc, utilitarian garments until the later part of the nineteenth century.[18]

The wool gown failed to solve the problem posed by women's public bathing, however. The likelihood of such a gown becoming transparent when wet, washing up around the wearer's armpits, or causing her to drown with its sopping weight exercised many moralists, satirists, and fashion writers in varying degrees. Just the sight of women combing their wet hair apparently excited some onlookers inappropriately. As the bathing suit made an appearance in pattern books and then advertisements, it gained in tailoring and adornment and lost in comprehensiveness. By 1900, it had shrunk to a short-sleeved, belted, calf-length gown over loose bloomers and stockings; slippers, gloves, and caps remained common accessories, and some women also wore corsets.[19]

But the shrinkage had only just begun. At the turn of the twentieth century, many beach towns fought protracted battles with eager beachgoers about how small a bathing suit a woman could wear or whether she might dispense with stockings. By the mid-1910s, the controversial "one-piece" suit made its appearance. This garment was most often a loose-fitting, hip-length tunic with short attached bloomers and no skirt or sleeves; fashionables wore it in taffeta, ordinary people in cotton jersey or wool. The suit's abbreviation made women's legs the cynosure of all eyes and rendered the question of stockings urgent by the early 1920s. "A prude can feel more at ease on the beach at Palm Beach than at any other resort in Florida," Kenneth Roberts reported, because "women are not allowed to appear on the beach with any portion of the leg uncovered"—and the stockings covering those shameful limbs had to be black. Things were different at the racy new resort in Miami Beach, where "the one-piece bathing suit is heavily displayed by engaging young women, and there are also large numbers of bathing suits which appear to be one-half-piece or even two-fifths piece"—so small that no stockings were long enough to reach up to them.[20] The rapid change was remarkable enough that in 1931 Underwood & Underwood, one of the major U.S. manufacturers of stereographs and postcards, produced a photograph of five women modeling the styles of the past half-century (Fig. 3).

Nor were women alone in baring more of their flesh to the elements on the beach; the shirts and drawers that male swimmers had reluctantly donned in the mid-nineteenth century were dwindling again by the early twentieth, as the hemlines of drawers rose, shirts lost their sleeves, and some beaches allowed men to go bare chested. In 1938, George Seaton advised novice male cruise ship passengers that "some of the more conservative ships still require tops to be worn in the outdoor pool, so take a detachable one along, or make sure in advance you won't need it." The Italian liner Madeline Allen traveled to Europe on was not a conservative one. One of her fellow passengers,

Figure 3. Women's bathing suits shrank so rapidly from the late nineteenth century to the early twentieth that contemporaries remarked on it. "Half Century of Bathing Suits Shown at Quota Club Convention," Underwood & Underwood, 1931. Library of Congress reproduction no. LC-USZ62-116423; digital ID cph 3c16423.

"a beautiful young man . . . has dark wavy hair and big dark eyes and very tanned skin, and lies all day in the sun in short bathing trunks, and obviously enjoys his figure."[21]

Women—and one supposes, men—in California and Florida seem to have led the way in shrinking the costume. At least, the 1916 Sears, Roebuck catalog advertised its more daring women's swimsuits as "California Style" and the more conservative towns—including some in California—specified that such suits were not acceptable. On his maiden swim in the same year, Johnston was shocked to see that many women on Southern California beaches flaunted bare legs (well before they did so at Miami Beach, but perhaps because the town only came into official existence in 1915): "In the afternoons, the bathing suits, short above and below, are the popular attractions. Women with corns, ingrowing toe nails, and possibly some modesty, wear stockings, while the others do not." In the mouths of proponents, such an attitude reduced modesty to an aesthetic issue; only those with something to hide would veil their bodies. Cartoonist Adolph Fera's protagonist, "Mr. 'Skinny' East," was mortified to have to walk from his vacation rental to the beach in his new bathing suit—while locals clearly felt no embarrassment at such public undress (Fig. 4). Marcella Seiden, a Chicagoan enrolled at the University of Miami in the mid-1920s, pasted into her scrapbook several photographs of her female friends in stylish one-piece bathing suits on the beach, including one in which they kick their bare legs up like chorus girls and another in which a bare-chested young man and a woman in a brief one-piece suit embrace.[22]

A sign of the importance of both the beach and the shrinking bathing suit, the bathing beauty was relatively rare in early Southland promotional materials but ubiquitous in those of the 1920s and 1930s.[23] Brochures from the 1880s and 1890s on California and Florida featured orange groves and massive hotels; Mexico and the islands in the Caribbean promoted their imposing Spanish fortifications, cathedrals, and colonial monuments. When women did appear, they tended to be "types"—national, racial, or occupational—and, in any case, fully dressed. That these places could be represented by nearly naked young women playing on the beach clearly did not occur to boosters at this time; that such images are now so iconic as to be banal is an artifact of the profound changes of the twentieth century, not the least of which was the emergence of the tropical resort.

None of the older attractions disappeared, but in many cases they were squeezed to the side by images of women in bathing suits. One of the earliest such advertisements appeared on a brochure for Redondo Beach, California,

Figure 4. Newly arrived in Southern California, "Mr. 'Skinny' East" is embarrassed to be seen in his fashionable new bathing suit, but the locals think nothing of it, suggesting the emergence of a beach culture in which scanty and casual clothing grew increasingly acceptable. Adolph Christian Fera, *Post Cards of a Tourist (Mr. "Skinny" East): Cartoons of Southern California* (Los Angeles: Henry J. Pauly, 1910): 43, call no. 351476. Reproduced by permission of The Huntington Library, San Marino, California.

about 1910 (Plate 4). Already by 1922, Floridians expanding on "the ever-sunny skies and the perfect-thirty-four bathing girls" inspired skepticism in some hearers. By the mid-1930s, a visiting Brit interpreted the phenomenon as a crass advertising ploy. "A live publicity agent" brought in to promote the new resort at Miami Beach had reduced the entire project to this: "You could bathe in winter on Miami Beach, which meant you could see girls' legs galore. So Miami Beach poured out to the newspapers and the newsreels 'girlies' with lovely legs, girlies in slips, girlies in bathing 'creations.' . . . Girls' bare legs in winter are Florida's unique assets." Indeed, this visitor was taken to see a civic water show that amounted to little more than a parade of beautiful young women in bathing suits. St. Petersburg's focus on older tourists meant that its advertising never featured "'a cutie' posed in the foreground," Seaton remarked, "for which blessed relief many thanks."[24]

By the 1930s, the bathing beauty was a staple of tourism promotions for the Southland. On Pan American Airline's cartoon maps of the Western Hemisphere, slim young white women in one-piece suits represented beach resorts, in stark contrast to the stout black woman in a long skirt and blouse with a basket on her head who stood in for the local people. Cruise lines pictured the pleasures they offered with pretty girls in scanty bathing suits dashing into the waves (Fig. 5). In 1939, when the Mexican artist Miguel Covarrubias painted six murals representing the Pacific world for the San Francisco Exposition, he used a blonde in a white two-piece bathing suit and sunglasses to embody Southern California (Plate 5). Whereas in the 1880s Charles Dudley Warner had frowned at the sight of Mexicans washing their bodies and clothing in the streams near Aguas Calientes, in the 1930s the U.S. artists Heath Bowman and Stirling Dickinson sunbathed nude on the beach near Iguala, Mexico, in sight of fully clad local women passing by to scrub their laundry in a more secluded spot. Once the scant clothing of dusky tropical peoples signaled their improvidence and immodesty, but now the nearly naked white body—especially when young, slender, and female—symbolized the best and most modern human interaction with the tropics.[25] (I address the implications of the bathing beauty for heterosexual liberalism in Chapter 5.)

As women in swimsuits became the most prominent human symbol of tropical resort life, they also appeared in a widening range of social situations. In the 1920s and 1930s, the United Fruit Company brochures featured what are most likely staged publicity photos portraying attractive young men and women splashing in the new shipboard swimming pools and playing modified forms of golf and tennis. Both men and women, but especially the latter, frequently appeared in thoroughly modern shorts and single-piece bathing suits even when they were not swimming (Fig. 6). The Florida Hotel Commission's 1930 guide to the state featured photographs of people in swimsuits playing miniature golf and picnicking in a West Palm Beach park.[26] Their attire represented the culmination of the erosion of earlier sartorial standards that had been a critical boundary between white and nonwhite, temperate and tropical, civilized and backward. But perhaps the most striking sign of racial degeneration remade as white rejuvenation at the tropical resort was the rise of a new aesthetic practice: suntanning.

Figure 5. By the 1930s, the cruise lines were advertising the Caribbean not with its Spanish colonial fortifications and cathedrals but with bathing beauties and beaches, as in this image. *1937 West Indies Cruises, Hamburg-American Line/North German Lloyd* (October 1936): 2, Hamburg American folder 8, KMEC, HL. Reproduced by permission of The Huntington Library, San Marino, California.

A Coat of Tan

European and North American whites had long prized their pale skin as the insignia of superior virtue and natural mastery, so the new fashion for skin darkening in the 1910s and 1920s was a startling departure. Although the usual story credits either industrialization or Coco Chanel with inspiring millions of pale-skinned Europeans and North Americans to sunbathe, the

Figure 6. By the 1920s, advertising for Caribbean cruises typically featured handsome young models enjoying each other's company while wearing sports clothes or bathing suits, even when far from the pool, embodying the casual, sexualized experience on offer. *Ships and Ports of the Great White Fleet* (United Fruit, 1930): 10, United Fruit Company folder 3, KMEC, HL. Reproduced by permission of The Huntington Library, San Marino, California.

evidence suggests a far more complex accounting. Research on British tanners links the practice to the naturist, camping, and Scouting movements, the growing availability of paid vacations, the popularization of Mediterranean resorts, and the changes in medicine that I outlined in Chapter 1. The role of the beach cultures emerging in the Americas, Australia, and New Zealand at the turn of the twentieth century and the development of the global tourist south to which such cultures contributed in promoting tanning have surprisingly received almost no attention.[27]

Incorporating the Americas into the history of tanning forces a substantial revision, because here (as in New Zealand and Australia) skin color had long been a major dynamic in producing and practicing social inequality. The era in which U.S. whites began to tan, the early twentieth century, was one of virulent racism and intensifying anxieties around racial-national integrity. The segregation and disfranchisement of African Americans, the allotment of Native lands and the removal of Native children from their families, anti-Asian land and citizenship laws, race-based immigration restriction, and the exercise of military and political power in the Caribbean, Central America, and the Pacific were the U.S. elements of a global white supremacist movement that cast the scramble for empire—and resistance to European conquests—as a war among the races for world domination. Although anticolonial and antiracist movements were gaining traction by the 1920s and romantic racialism was in vogue, few U.S. whites would have questioned the rightness of their race's dominance or the vast apparatus of custom, law, and force that maintained it.[28]

Why, then, would they choose to darken their skins under these circumstances? Pale-skinned people's suntanning constituted a kind of "brownface," a playful experiment in becoming nonwhite that stemmed from, encouraged, and literally embodied a renovated relationship between civilization and nature. Like the closely allied practice of "playing Indian," turning brown gave whites privileged access to traits otherwise lost to civilization's triumph—and yet, crucially, it was transient, the underlying whiteness always liable to reappear. Although tanning overlapped with the naturist or nudist movement—a tanned skin signaled its bearer's close contact with nature—it was a much less radical and more commercial practice.[29] It required no rationale beyond adherence to fashion, and it flirted with public nudity without going all the way. From the new intimacy between whites and nature, tanning advocates promised, would come more youthful, sexy, and healthy white people—and this was especially true for white women, whose remaking would modernize U.S. society.

The centrality of white women in matters of skin color is hardly surprising, since their fair cheeks had been symbols of the race's supposed superior beauty and sexual virtue at least since the late eighteenth century, an association heightened in the United States amid the struggle over slavery during the antebellum period. This link held true at the turn of the twentieth century, as whites justified the subordination of African Americans and other nonwhite people, including lynching and rape, on the grounds that they were excessively, dangerously sexual. Thus it is hardly surprising that throughout the nineteenth century many socially white women tried to be as pale as possible. Recipes and advertisements for skin whiteners and freckle removers appeared regularly in dermatology textbooks, women's magazines, and newspapers, and the most commonly used cosmetic was white powder.[30]

When tanned skins began to attract notice in the late nineteenth century, they were typically those of the growing number of well-to-do women who were participating in outdoor sports like camping and hiking or visiting seaside resorts. (That elite men sometimes got tans in the course of riding, hunting, or fishing notably excited no one's interest.) Women who traveled to the Southland were among them. In April 1880, at the end of her first winter in Florida, Emma Gilpin wrote home, "I will be glad to get back although we have had such a splendid winter—You will hardly know us we are burned so brown." Samuel Dexter reported to his children from Southern California in late February 1901, "Mama is doing very well. . . . She is as brown as though she had spent a season at Chatham and is feeling quite well"[31]—"Chatham" probably referring to the town on Cape Cod, Massachusetts, and signaling the importance of seaside resorts in well-to-do women's access to outdoor recreation.

U.S. doctors and beauty counselors began protesting deliberate skin darkening by the early twentieth century. In 1907, the *Chicago Daily Tribune*'s anonymous beauty advisor pointed "the finger of scorn . . . at the score of reckless sun bathers who . . . cherish an ambition to acquire a certain bronze color on neck, arms, and face"—note the scant extent of skin that could then be respectably exposed to the sun. Four years later, a writer for the fashion magazine *The Delineator* reported: "A few years ago women strove to get themselves as sunburned, tanned, and freckled as possible." But now, she sighed with relief, they were "coming to have more sense" and the fashion in complexions was once again for "the fair-as-a-lily kind." And by 1912, physician W. A. Evans was using his health advice column, which appeared in the *Chicago Daily Tribune* and at times in the *Washington Post*, to inveigh against deliberate tanning.[32] Clearly, some U.S. whites had begun to darken their skins on purpose as early as 1900 or thereabouts.

At the same time that Southland developers began to solicit the attention of wealthy visitors with claims of their region's mild, healthful climate, physicians and scientists began to revise existing understandings of light, including sunshine, while inventors produced increasingly functional forms of electric illumination. After a brief and quickly discredited fad for the use of "blue light" in healing in the 1860s and 1870s, the first recommendations for the therapeutic use of light, including sunshine, came from physicians in the 1880s and 1890s. In presenting an 811-page summation of her medical school lectures on the topic in 1904, Dr. Margaret Cleaves wrote, "While light energy is as old as the sun, and so almost are its therapeutic uses, never in the history of medicine was it as fully appreciated as now."[33]

She was right that the idea that sunshine was a good general tonic was not new, and it was not necessarily connected to the beach or sunbathing. On a hike in the mountains near Los Angeles, the unhappy, ailing Eleanor F. Bennett rejoiced in "feeling the wonderful sunshine penetrate to the innermost depths of ones [sic] physical being cleansing out every weary ache & pain." Moreover, medical climatologists certainly did not endorse the profligate use of sunlight for beautification: "don't lie, like a Strasbourg goose, broiling your liver in a 'sun bath,'" physician and Southern California booster Peter C. Remondino scolded, recommending instead immersion in sunshine only on a cool, breezy day. Sunbathing for the purpose of getting a tan, W. A. Evans declared, was wasteful: "If a person has gained his tan by out of doors work or play he has acquired physical capital. The same cannot be said for tans acquired by lying quietly on the beach exposed to the sun or wind. That is the counterfeit article."[34] Whites who tanned on purpose, in Evans's view, were portraying themselves as healthy, vigorous people when they were not in fact so—they deceived nature into giving them the appearance of health without doing the work necessary to build a strong body. Sunbathing was a tropical cheat, something for nothing.

As the idea of travel as a medicine in its own right declined after 1900, regional boosters and tourist industry entrepreneurs put increasing emphasis on the plentiful sunlight their locations enjoyed, in contrast to the places where a majority of U.S. whites lived. "Sunshine is the best medicine. It has a healthy effect on the mind," declared a California partisan, and insisted that in his state sunlight was nearly constant. Cleaves, for one, favored sunbathing at the seashore because reflections off the water increased the power of the sun's rays, and local boosters were eager to promote such claims, listing the number of sunny days per year in their favored locale alongside the usual temperature charts. The Los Angeles Chamber of Commerce touted an average of 316 and provided a detailed table showing the percentage of sunny days each month between 1896 and 1898. A St. Petersburg, Florida, newspaper editor earned reams of free publicity for decades after promising to give away the entire daily edition of the paper on every day that was not predominantly sunny, and the town's leaders reportedly had spent a million dollars by the late 1930s advertising it as the "Sunshine City." Touting Florida's constant sunshine, Frank Parker Stockbridge and John Holliday Perry claimed that there was "something almost spiritual in its power to instill that sense of general well-being, the feeling that all's right with the world and with one's soul."[35]

And the case for sunshine was more than spiritual in the early twentieth century. In the absence of effective cures for diseases (notably tuberculosis) based on germ theory, doctors continued to prescribe climatological treatments, including carefully regulated "heliotherapy" and "phototherapy," well into the twentieth century. A growing body of clinical and experimental evidence confirmed the belief that exposure to sunlight could kill bacteria, hasten healing, heighten disease resistance, and make tuberculosis patients feel more cheerful and vigorous. The attention to sunlight in the treatment of tuberculosis was only one aspect of a broad range of experimentation concerned with the therapeutic usefulness of radiation, both visible and invisible. The development of new forms of artificial light represented a step toward bringing light itself under human control and the exciting possibilities of doing so. Physician J. H. Kellogg claimed to have invented the first incandescent light bath in 1891 and used it to treat a wide range of ailments, and the array of devices available for the therapeutic application of light only multiplied after 1900. By 1905 he had a sanitarium in Southern California, while others made similar claims for the health effects of Florida sunshine. In the late 1920s, a Cuban tourism promoter called for a study of the island's geographic and climatic advantages, "as for example, the strength of our sunshine. . . . The rapid rise of the sun cure and what it means for the preservation of health are well known."[36]

Among other things, research into light encouraged physicians treating urban children to aggregate and add to previously scattered evidence on the relationship between sunshine and rickets, a crippling, sometimes fatal failure of the bones to harden properly during infancy and childhood. By the 1920s, it was clear that sunshine was a sovereign cure for rickets and related adult diseases. Still uncertain of the mechanism of this miraculous cure, researchers classified the unknown substance that human skin produced when exposed to the sun as one of a new class of nutrients—vitamins. Vitamins A, B, and C had already been discovered, so this new substance was labeled D.[37]

The discovery of vitamin D and its source in sunshine simultaneously gave new life to the idea that humans had to have a closer relationship with nature to thrive and challenged the holism typical of medical climatology. Like germs, vitamins—or nutrients more generally—were tiny, hitherto unknown entities with vast power to affect human health. Like germs, vitamins helped to reduce a complex, individualized system of checks and balances between bodies and environments to a matter of seeking or avoiding discrete substances. No longer would people be at the mercy of nature; science had the keys to perfect health and long life. Although vitamin D (unlike its three predecessors) turned out to be extremely scarce in the food supply, researchers quickly figured out that irradiating common items like milk and bread imbued them with the precious substance, and food, cosmetics, and supplement makers eagerly adopted the process. The other, even more common solution was daily doses of cod liver oil, one of the few substances naturally high in the vitamin.[38] It was far easier—and much more pleasant—to sunbathe to get one's required dose of the vitamin.

The discovery of vitamin D reinforced the existing practice of phototherapy and gave the sheen of science to the movement to bring whites back into closer contact with nature: "Our ancestors lived in the open under the beneficent rays of the sun," declared one physician; but now "the human race, mainly through the development of great cities, has cooped itself up in box-like rooms, shutting itself off from the health-giving properties of nature. We must learn to live again in the open." And that new intimacy promised greater vitality—including youthfulness and sexual potency. Tanning, like tropical travel, would give overcivilized whites a touch of the adolescent vigor supposedly typical of people of color. A tanning advocate argued, "We have become sundodgers as a by-product of our civilization. We hide under roofs and behind walls. . . . When we go outside, we shield ourselves in an armor of clothes." The result was mental, physical, and sensual deterioration: "Here, out of his house, comes a dull and listless fellow. He is tired without being able to rest. His muscles are flabby. He has no appetite. He is the typical nerve-fagged indoor worker." But driven by instinct, he lies down in the sun: "An hour or two later, he awakens, stretches comfortably, springs to his feet. Somehow the day has become brighter, his nerves calmer, his step springier than before. He hums; he feels energetic, perhaps even a bit romantic."[39]

Such revitalization meant even more for women; fashion writer Juliet Dixon hailed "this new freedom" and exulted that "the sun and the wind are our friends again, as they were when the world was young." Like Dixon, most popular writers presented tanning as a critical sign of women's liberation from old-fashioned prudery by returning to an earlier, more "natural" relationship with the sun. The modern girl wore a tan (Plate 6). And that golden-hued modernity, another fashion writer enthused, is "something a little rakish and yet very sweet, like a girl from a South Sea isle who knows the wind and the sun and the sea and what life is for, and nothing about the ugliness of sin and bored living: enchanting and free." Among a group of female movie stars—the epitome of modern girls—in 1930, the majority who chose to tan "say it makes them feel husky, self-confident, jolly and athletic." Actress Joan Crawford, one gossip column confided, "has banished make-up altogether and wears a lovely natural brown skin." And so clad in nature's grace, "she permits herself a bit of lipstick, and one can be more generous with it, with a tanned skin."[40] As it had for centuries, brown skin signaled a more vivid, expressive sexuality.

A key element of women's new freedom derived from the fact that tanning well required wearing as little clothing as possible—it contributed to the era's characteristic decrease in the quantity and coverage of respectable clothing. "The vogue right now is a coat of tan," the *Los Angeles Times* declared, and the result was a public striptease: "In order that this coat may be displayed to better advantage, various pieces of personal wear are being cast off. The stockings are being shucked and hats are flung to the winds."[41] That the ability to tan played a role in this transformation of the U.S. wardrobe highlights the extent to which it was about a new relationship between white bodies and nature, not just a practical desire for clothing suited to the climate or adapted for swinging a golf club or tennis racket.

The amazing shrinking bathing suit had an important role in the rearticulation of the relationship between whites and nature because, although it certainly made swimming easier, it also facilitated tanning. By the 1930s women's swimming costumes had become what one fashion writer called "nice, tight, eye filling suits . . . that are going to fit and stick closer than your skin," one-piece garments covering the body only from breasts to upper thighs and cut low in back. Along with the once mandatory black stockings, gloves, sleeves, and bloomers had vanished. The public baring of women's bodies, especially their hips and legs (which had for so long been rigorously concealed) could not but be sexualized. For a woman, sunbathing was a sexual act: "clad in one of those cut low in front, on the sides, behind and at the bottom bathing suits, she begins consorting with Old Sol"—as if with a lover. Evoking the respectable woman's duty to curb male sexual advances, the J. W. Robinson Co. department store advertised suntan lotions with the assertion that "most women use the right sort of preparations and let the sun go jut as far as they please—and not a bit farther." A beauty columnist, reporting approvingly on the rejection of bronze for golden tans, reported that "Even the brunettes . . . are inclined to be indifferent to the sun's advances" in 1933.[42]

The role of medicine, particularly the discovery of vitamin D, in the transformation of respectable clothing is hard to evaluate, but tanning advocates thought it was substantial. In 1904, before the change, Cleaves insisted that "the custom of many individuals of spending hours of the day during their sojourn at the seashore clad only in scanty bathing attire is a commendable one, from the point of hygiene," no matter how "a critical and perverted mind may regard it from a point of taste. Less cumbersome and light-excluding attire at all times and seasons would redound to better health." Over thirty years later, another doctor and longtime *Good Housekeeping* columnist wrote: "More than anything else, that discovery [of vitamin D] made possible your going about in public with an amount of bare skin that would have put you jail a few years ago." Another writer acknowledged that "it has taken some time to come around to the present acceptance of abbreviated bathing suits on the beaches, and in the increased use of street garments." But sunbathing partisans could trust that "the time is doubtless coming when even those who have no easy access to a beach or river bank will be freely permitted to wear bathing suits while engaged in informal pursuits on dry land."[43]

The change was far more evident in women's clothing than men's, and tanning had a somewhat different meaning for the male of the species. "They [are] . . . more upholstered than chairs, harnessed like beasts of burden—all buckles and buttons, with necks confined by halters, legs encased in flapping cloth tubes," tanning advocates lamented. But this imprisonment would surely soon end: "They . . . will thrust the fashion-makers on a pyre of discarded coats and waistcoats; and they will start all over again where Adam left off." This freedom, like women's, harked back to a mythical time before original sin and rehabilitated overt sexuality. As one unusually gender-neutral paean to tanning put it: "Yes, the styles in human hides are changing materially as we sever barbarous Puritanical repressions and borrow more and more from the earlier, morally and physically wholesomer [*sic*] ages not too far removed from Eden's fig-leafed bathing beaches."⁴⁴

But advice aimed at men emphasized that tanning would sustain white men's traditional power. Indeed, a few commentators urged men to throw off their chains as soon as possible, because women's scantier clothing might be a direct threat to men's dominance. J. W. Sturmer noted that, because "all woolen clothing is an effective ultra-violet filter . . . , the modern male promenading on the boardwalk receives practically no such radiation through his clothing." Women were more fortunate: "The most transparent textile is a loosely-woven rayon or artificial silk, which explains why the sex known during the Victorian era as the weaker sex is on the way to becoming the robust sex. The girls are getting more solar radiation, hence more vitamin D." Edwin E. Slosson put it more directly: "The summer girl has carried the bathing suit inland and now appears upon the street in all seasons in a costume that meets the requirements of heliotherapist [*sic*]. . . . This raises a question demanding masculine consideration. Will not these sunkist [*sic*] flappers . . . be too big to beat and too smart for the unenlightened wits of men?"⁴⁵ No doubt both comments elicited a little chuckle from readers, but the link they drew between vitamin D, sun exposure, and women's empowerment circulated widely in the popular press.

For white men, therefore, a tan promised more than enhanced vitality and sexuality; it promised continued mastery over white women and nonwhites, precisely by endowing the masculine sunbather with some of the youthful potency associated with the latter. Although "nobody sympathizes with a sunburned elderly bachelor," one writer declared with a wink, everyone would admire the new man who emerged from the peeling, blistering white skin: "What a husky dog he is, and quite young-looking! Brown as an Indian." In the story "A Son of the Sun," author Jack London's erotic description of the protagonist, David Grief, earnestly conveys the same message: "Heavy muscled he was, but he was not lumped and hummocked by muscles. They were softly rounded, and, when they did move, slid softly and silkily under the smooth, tanned skin. Ardent suns had likewise tanned his face till it was swarthy as a Spaniard's. . . . It was difficult to realize that the skin of this man had once been fair" but his blue eyes and blond hair asserted that crucial fact. Whereas the blazing South Pacific sun destroyed other white men—"ripping and smashing tissues and nerves, till they became sick in mind and body, tossed most of the Decalogue overboard, descended to beastliness, drank themselves into quick graves"—Grief was impervious to its power and "merely became browner with the passing of the years. . . . Yet his blue eyes retained their blue, his mustache its yellow, and the lines of his face were those which had persisted through centuries in his English race." As a result, he was the commercial master of the South Pacific: "As the golden tint burned into his face it poured molten out of the ends of his fingers."[46]

But not everyone believed that tanning had a beneficial effect; talk of racial degeneration circulated alongside praise for sunbathing. In 1907 the *Chicago Daily Tribune* conceded grudgingly that "to say that there was any-thing demoralizing in such protracted sunbaths perhaps would be going too far, but they certainly have their influence." As evidence, the unnamed writer protested, "Take the seacoast or summer resort trains which are met by bands of savages, their faces tanned to a deep mahogany, their collars turned in, and their sleeves rolled up; they are not unlike the natives of some tropical island. There is a deal of whooping when the astonished pale face descends from the train and is carried away by the indecorous South Sea Islanders." And when these ersatz natives returned home after the summer vacation season, an-other writer noted in 1929, "A tribe of swarthy foreigners seems to have taken possession of the banks and office buildings. Apparently the predictions of certain pessimistic sociologists have come true, and the rising tide of color is threatening Nordic supremacy."[47] Like the comments about the threat that tanning would make women stronger than men, these passages were satirical, not serious—but the success of such jokes rested on the common belief that skin color and behavior were intimately linked.

Moreover, some commentators were serious when they portrayed whites with tans as less than fully civilized. Stuart Chase, writing in *The Nation*, argued that true sun worshipers like himself had to have traits long associ-ated with backward, nonwhite peoples: "Freedom . . . , a pagan regard for the comeliness and well-being of one's body . . . , a sound belief in the important function of laziness in life, a hatred of the round, silly face of a clock, an understanding of the irrelevancy of clothes—who shall say of what strange and primitive juices . . . the true sun-worshiper is made?" And he believed that tanning could transform U.S. society for the better precisely by making it less civilized: "If the republic wants to go native and can hold to it with any fidelity, it will probably do more than any other conceivable action to balance the inhibitions and pathological cripplings induced by the machine age and the monstrous cities in which we live."[48] The phrase "go native" underscored the monumental racial consequences Chase attributed to tanning: it would not only bring civilized people back into balance with nature but also root

U.S. citizens in the land they had conquered. This was the deepest meaning attributed to tanning and the romantic racialism in which it participated. By turning brown, U.S. whites might legitimize their dominance of their own nation and even the entire hemisphere, at least in a metaphysical sense. They might be at home everywhere.

Although I suspect that Florida's high government officials did not share Chase's radical naturism, the state's hotel commission nevertheless endorsed the idea that tanning—and the whole beachgoing, outdoors lifestyle of which it was a part—made contemporary U.S. whites the proper heirs of an ancient indigenous history. "The native Floridians called themselves 'Children of the Sun,'" the commission's state guide asserted, and they understood the "therapeutic value of the actinic [ultraviolet] rays of the sun . . . centuries before the advent of the white man." The foolish Spaniards, however, "failed to learn that the secret of health could be found in the beneficent sunshine" rather than its waters or the mythical fountain of youth, and "considering the scanty attire of the Indians a menace to health, continued to wear the heavy clothing" suited to chilly Europe. Later English settlers were more perspicacious but soon fled renewed Spanish control, the true realization of Florida's wealth only arriving with a new generation of Children of the Sun, the U.S. settlers who recognized the peninsula as "a gigantic amusement pier . . . , a natural year-round playground for the nation." Most tanning advocates constructed a similar genealogy of the practice, beginning with ancient sun worship and ending in some form of the plea that modern residents of the United States must "recover the full heritage of health, energy, and high spirits rightfully ours as 'children of light.'"[49]

Such lineages and London's brown white man indicate both the latitude and the limits of the racial blurring that tanning embodied. Most tanning advocates intended whites to regain the bond with nature characteristic of primitives, but they did not intend them to relinquish the benefits of civilization: "To get all the ultraviolet radiation we need, we do not have to exist like savages, nor put on weird costumes, nor give up a single boon of civilized life." Suggestively, the phrase typically used to describe skin darkening in the 1920s and 1930s was "a coat of tan"—a coy veiling of the newly bared white body. A coat of tan would ensure not mere primitive nakedness, but a civilized and powerful nudity. Of his maiden attempt at tanning in the L Street Bathhouse in South Boston, Stuart Chase wrote of beholding "a hundred naked men, nine out of ten of them colored like South Sea Islanders. . . . But how naked I felt, creeping out to lie among them, a pale white wraith in

a field of bronzes." Soon, however, he had "the most just and timeless covering of homo sapiens"—a tan. Chase's embarrassment was not unique; among
Chicago's weekend sunbathers "white limbs are as scarce as white birches at
the shore and are considered more or less indecent."[50] A coat of tan was just
the thing to wear to the reconciliation of civilization with nature.

The news that tanned skin blocks the ultraviolet rays that stimulate vitamin D production gave scientific credibility to the idea of a "coat of tan."
Too much sun was not healthy, and the white body had natural means of
preventing excess. "Remember," Walter H. Eddy wrote in his regular *Good
Housekeeping* column, "a quickly acquired brown pigmentation is not proof
of having used sunlight healthfully. . . . [A] too tanned skin may prevent sun
benefits. The disease of rickets is far more prevalent in infants of the dark-
skinned races." The implication was that whites benefited from the sun *more*
than people of color because, whereas people of color could never adjust
their skins to admit more sun, whites could regulate theirs: "Darkening of
the skin . . . is not considered a benefit, rather a detriment, as it undoubtedly
makes it more difficult for the light to penetrate. . . . Therefore one tries for
a light or golden-brown tone of the skin."[51] By moderating their skin darkening, whites avoided the danger into which people of color had heedlessly
fallen—that of becoming so dark that the sun could not do its health-giving
work. Whites could have both nature and civilization; nonwhites remained
trapped by nature.

The ability to don and doff a tan quickly was especially important for
white women, for whom a tan was strictly a seasonal accessory. What was
beautiful in the summer—or on one's return from a winter resort—was not so
desirable in the fall. "The better the sport she is in the summer," warned Hazel
Rawson Cades, "the bigger the wallflower she'll be in the fall." She continued: "Be careful of sunburning your hands and arms if you want to use them
again socially. A monotone effect to the shoulder is considered better looking with evening gowns than a half-and-half brown-and-white combination."
The mismatch between sports clothes and bathing suits, on the one hand, and
evening gowns, on the other, was more than simply aesthetic (after all, today
the response to this beauty problem is to tan topless or nude). It marked a
transition from a time—or place, as in the eternal summer of the tropics—in
which flirting with racial difference and sexual boldness was acceptable, and
a time and activities in which it was not. "All spring and summer, practically
every living woman of you has tried to sun-tan as black as your hat. Now,
suddenly, every woman wants to look a white and fragile as a lily," wrote one

beauty advisor, who offered some tips in response to her readers' "sudden yearning for a new face, all innocent and fair." According to one columnist, the fashion for more feminine evening gowns had led to a rejection of tanning among debutantes; as one young woman said, "It would be rather queer to wear one of those ruffly light things with a face like an Indian." The writer associated the change with a "new maidenly reserve."[52] Whatever happened on the beach, in high society whiteness, femininity, and sexual restraint remained tightly bound together.

This point underscores the strong tie between tanning and the emerging archipelago of tropical beach resorts in the early twentieth century. Although most white people would acquire their tans at beaches—and rooftops and backyards—close to home, the tan still murmured of the Southland, that fantasy island where life is all leisure and no obligation, the sun always shines, people are always young and beautiful, and overt sexuality carries no social stigma. The travel industry circulated this kind of imagery with ever-greater frequency from the 1920s, perpetuating the ideas that had long structured Euro-American ideas about the tropics and their dark-skinned residents, but now associating them with white people's physical and emotional well-being. The very distance between these fabled places and home and the fact that most whites visited there on a brief vacation safeguarded civilization while stretching its limits. One could have all the self-indulgent leisure of fabled primitives along with the perfect health guaranteed by modern medicine—all in two weeks on the beach or the deck of a cruise ship. The tan was the visible sign that both white men and white women could profit from the tropics without risking their civilized birthright.

CHAPTER 5

Lands of Romance

In 1936, the white U.S. travel writer Sidney Clark took a walk through Havana's red-light district—but instead of perpetrating the prostitution of a nation, he staged a fable of modern marriage. Accompanied by his wife and another white U.S. couple, the writer sought the "'star-eyed, radiant-faced señoritas'" who danced and drank in the popular *Terry's Guide to Cuba* and often decorated advertisements for Southland destinations. To their dismay, the visitors found instead that many of the sex workers were "so old and ugly that they sear the eyes of the beholder." The ladies, Clark declared, "discovered that they did not like this quarter, not-at-all," so the party moved on to the nightclub district, where the four encountered what Clark deemed "the handsomest, friendliest lot of [police] officers" that he had ever seen. His wife "fell in love with Pedro and each successive officer she saw" (Fig. 7).[1]

This coy little morality tale, in which the modern husband gives up his traditional sexual prerogatives and the modern wife her traditional prudishness in order to achieve mutual marital felicity in the clubs of Havana, suggests that tourist encounters—both real and imagined—between U.S. whites and Latin American and Afro-Caribbean people played a role in the emergence of heterosexual liberalism in the twentieth century. As I showed in Chapter 1, the tropics and their nonwhite residents had long represented for European and U.S. whites the exuberant bodily passions that they believed themselves to have mastered in service to civilization. At the turn of the twentieth century, many wondered whether civilization had dampened those natural urges too much, effeminizing men and neutering or masculinizing women, thus endangering the reproduction of white supremacy. Some believed that imperial adventures would rejuvenate civilized men, but at the risk of moral and physical illness—including perhaps the transgression of the color line, as in

Figure 7. Behind the backs of two middle-aged U.S. couples (the men smugly porcine, the women not at all sure they like what they see), a sleek modern girl and a dapper Mexican policeman make eyes at each other, intimating the role of the Southland in the liberalization of heterosexuality. René d'Harnoncourt, *Mexicana: A Book of Pictures* (New York: Alfred A. Knopf, 1931): "The Tourists." Courtesy of the Braun Research Library, Autry National Center of the American West, Los Angeles; 917.2 H.

the story with which Chapter 1 opened. One response, amply documented by historians of imperialism, was policing colonized peoples in an effort to make them safe for their colonizers.[2]

Another response was to change directions, like Clark and his wife in Havana, and find ways in which the tropics could spark white *women's* desires, thus making them more suitable and willing partners for imperially virile white men. This was the approach of tourist businesses whose fortunes relied on attracting growing numbers of wealthy white North Americans and Europeans to the tropics. Frequently fascinated by the gender and sexual practices of the Southland's peoples, especially those of white Latin Americans, U.S. travel writers typically presented them as foils for changing ideals back home. Through such writings and the corresponding itineraries, tourist industry publicists reversed the long tradition of casting hot weather and nonwhites as threats to white health and racial integrity. Instead, they portrayed the cultures and peoples of Latin America and the Caribbean as natural resources that could revitalize U.S. whites' passions for each other. As in Sidney Clark's fable, white men could avoid tropical risks if white women became their full partners in tropical adventures, for it was precisely this equality of opportunity that would prevent either one from crossing the color line. In short, tropical tourism participated in the liberalization of heterosexuality while promising to bolster white racial integrity.

The role of tourism in the Southland in this significant change in sexual mores underscores the extent to which the latter was an integral part of the upsurge in romantic racialism in the early twentieth century. Both heterosexual liberalism and romantic racialism developed in a global imperial geography in which sex and race were mutually implicated, bitterly contested measures of humanity and progress. Both ways of thinking questioned the social restrictions imposed in the name of white civilization by invoking human nature as the ground for a more capacious freedom. Rather than only reinforcing conservative gender and sexual ideologies, racism also, in these circumstances, forwarded the process of heterosexual liberalization.[3] The interweaving of romantic racialism and heterosexual liberalism yielded Mr. and Mrs. Clark, hand in hand, shuddering at Havana's female prostitutes—repellant embodiments of the old-fashioned double standard—and ogling its male police officers—attractive, eager donors of the gift of tropical sensuality and racial harmony.

Plate 1. Designed to sell oranges, this image of the sexy señorita (see Chapter 5) and the palm-flanked adobe mansion in the background conveys the social dimension of recasting the tropics as a place of healthful luxury.

La Reina brand, California Fruit Labels Collection, courtesy of the Department of Special Collections, Charles E. Young Research Library, UCLA.

Plate 2. This classic Southern California landscape foregrounds the red-roofed adobe mansion associated with a lost Spanish colonial aristocracy and surrounds it with orderly orange groves, the tropics tamed by the gentleman farmer. Above rise snowcapped mountains, proof that Southern California enjoyed the full range of seasons.

Courtesy of the Autry National Center of the American West, Los Angeles; 91.170.464.

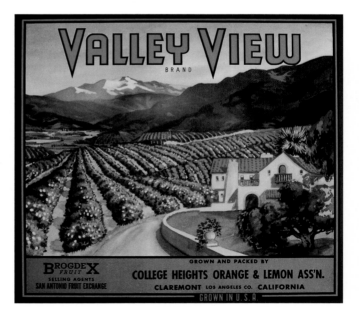

"Rich and Full of Pleasantries"

Plate 3. The tropical fantasy architecture of the Southland, shaded by palms and lapped in flowers. This image appeared in a promotional piece for George Merrick's Coral Gables, Florida, development. Rex Beach, *The Miracle of Coral Gables,* illustrated by Edward A. Wilson (Coral Gables, Fla.: 1926): 54, call no. 374298.

Plate 4. One of the earliest "bathing beauties" used to advertise a Southland destination. Note she wears the black stockings whose rapid abandonment from the mid-1910s scandalized many outside the emerging beach cultures in Southern California and Florida. Los Angeles & Redondo Beach Railway Co., *Redondo Beach and the Pleasures You May Have There* (ca. 1910): cover, call no. 323207.

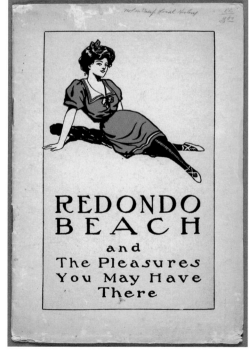

REDONDO
BEACH
and
The Pleasures
You May Have
There

Plate 5. This is how the painter Miguel Covarrubias elected to represent Southern California on a mural for the 1939 Golden Gate International Exposition. Detail, "Peoples of the Pacific," from Miguel Covarrubias, *Pageant of the Pacific* (1940): plate 1, call no. 239209.

Plate 6. The modern girl wears a tan. *Year Round Vacation Trips* (Panama Pacific, ca. 1920s), Panama Pacific folder 2, KMEC, HL.

Plate 7. The sexy señorita as the Southland's winsome hostess. This modernized version has lost her comb and fan (compare Plate 1). *West Indies 1927 Raymond-Whitcomb Cruises* (1926), Norddeutscher Lloyd folder 42, KMEC, HL.

Reproduced by permission of The Huntington Library, San Marino, California.

Plate 8. An updated version of the seductive mulatta, the black female dancer converted the passions of the tropics into a thoroughly modern sophistication that white U.S. tourists were eager to experience. Detail, "Peoples of the Pacific," from Miguel Covarrubias, *Pageant of the Pacific* (1940): plate 1, call no. 239209.

Reproduced by permission of The Huntington Library, San Marino, California.

Plate 9. How one Florida college student imagined herself in the late 1920s. Green and orange are the University of Miami's colors.

"Kid Hot," Marcella Seiden Scrapbook, HistoryMiami.

Warm, Voluptuous Scenes of Tropic Lands

For centuries, Europeans and North Americans had perceived the tropics, as well as the people who lived there, to be alluringly sensual. "If we painted her"—and when it had a sex this climatic zone was always female—"we should not represent her as a neat, trim damsel, with starched linen cuffs and collar," Harriet Beecher Stowe wrote of Florida in 1873. "She would be a brunette, dark but comely, with gorgeous tissues, a general disarray and dazzle, and with a sort of jolly untidiness, free, easy, and joyous." Draining and ditching, Stowe mused in later pages, might turn this dusky bacchante into an orderly citizen, and indeed throughout the region the reduction of exuberant tropical landscapes to plantations growing sugar, bananas, pineapples, and coffee for metropolitan consumption went hand in hand with the growth of tourism. But even tamed, the tropics remained highly sexualized, a region where "Nature cannot but feel intensely the advent of Flora," spring cast as the first flush of arousal. One poet pictured Southern California as "blossom-crowned, fruit-laden, and replete . . . / Her marvelous sweet mouth, and warm as sweet, / The smiling South uplifts for us to kiss." Another poet sighed for a land where "Tall fronded palms with eager arms / Commune with a tropic moon. . . . Tired hearts find balm in flowered alms / Near the shore of a blue lagoon." Not one to veil her double entendres in landscape imagery, Amy Oakley titled two of the chapters in her 1941 Caribbean travelogue "Tempestuous Jamaica" and "Uncle Sam's Virgins." And a Panama Pacific Line brochure of the 1930s whispered huskily, "the spell of the South is hailing you down to warm, voluptuous scenes of tropic lands."[4]

The image that most ubiquitously embodied the perpetually youthful, ardent nature of Latin American—and its availability to well-to-do travelers from the United States—was the sexy señorita (Plates 1 and 7). Classically, she wore the high comb, mantilla, and ruffled gown of a previous century's high fashion, and she almost always fluttered a fan in a flirtatious dance. Her extraordinary sexual appeal stemmed in large part from the racial ambiguity that most U.S. whites attributed to Latin Americans. Marie Robinson Wright wrote of the elite women she met in Mexico: "The slender oval of the face, the rich olive of the cheek, the long, sweeping dark lashes over super eyes, glowing at once with passion and tenderness, the low forehead with its rippling mass of dusky hair, the slender neck, the lithe form, the springing step, and the dainty foot make them like a poet's dream of darkly brilliant loveliness." Evoking the age of dashing caballeros and swashbuckling pirates, the sexy señorita had no secular ambitions; she wanted only to dance and attract her man, whom she adored unreservedly. In political cartoons, she represented all of Latin America as longing for Uncle Sam's embrace, or at least the aid of his strong arm in rescuing her from quarrelsome Latin American or European men.[5]

The sexy señorita was only the most common of several female figures used to symbolize Latin America and the Caribbean, following—but tidying up—the long tradition of portraying both dark-skinned women and the tropics as sexually promiscuous. One Hamburg American flyer described Trinidad as populated by "dark-eyed senoritas from Venezuela, pantalooned Chinese women, buxom negresses, statuesque quadroons," in the next phrase conceding that there were some men on the island as well ("swarthy Portuguese and turbaned Hindus"). The popularization of African music and dance throughout the world in the 1920s and 1930s recostumed a venerable figure, the beautiful and sexually available mulatta, as the rumba dancer. The granddaughter of the fabled quadroon or octoroon courtesan, she embodied whites' prurient fantasies about slavery, Latins, Africans, and tropical immorality—and their new global availability in the figure of the black professional dancer. "St. Pierre," one cruise brochure recalled nostalgically of that town on the island of Martinique, "was once the Caribbean Paris where the high and colorful gaiety of its dusky notables—beautiful, statuesque creatures with eyes of fire—held their revels and their court"—before being destroyed by a volcanic eruption in 1902.[6] To personify Cuba, the Mexican painter Miguel Covarrubias chose a beautiful brown-skinned dancer in a sexy slit skirt (Plate 8).

The representation of Latin America and the Caribbean as beautiful, willing, dark-skinned women exemplified the profoundly gendered and sexualized iconography of empire and race. The prevalence of such imagery in political cartoons and advertising confirms that U.S. men liked to think that the rest of the Western Hemisphere was courting their attentions and longing for whatever favors they doled out. But this figure did not only mirror men's desires; it also served as a foil for and ingredient in the formulation of modern liberal heterosexuality.[7] In travel writing and advertising, the sexy señorita represented ideal heterosexual romance because she embodied the two things that modern civilization seemed to threaten: gender difference and its supposed natural consequence, heterosexual passion.

Many travel writers made a point of writing about Latin American gender relations, most often focusing on courtship, to explore the relationship between customary constraints, romantic love, and personal fulfillment. Implicitly or explicitly, all such accounts asked which society (the modern Anglo-Saxon or the traditional Latin American) better assured both individual happiness and social morality. Not surprisingly, the answers varied—but all portrayed women's status and the conventions producing heterosexual marriage as critical points in evaluating a society's success. These narratives usually began with architecture and then remarked on three elements: women's seclusion and gender segregation, the evening promenade, and men serenading women, or "playing the bear."

The very built environment of Latin American cities made them seem like coy maidens to many U.S. visitors. Many writers remarked on the custom of building houses with blank walls to the street and a garden or courtyard inside, in contrast to the U.S. custom of setting houses back from the road behind grassy lawns. "The first permanent structure here was a fortress," Charles B. Reynolds wrote of Havana, "and the city appears to have taken its architectural pattern from the bastions and embrasures of La Fuerza," that original fortification. "There are no front yards; the houses are built flush with the street and close together. . . . Havana doors are a study; they are often double, 10 to 15 feet high . . . , heavily barred and studded, and furnished with ponderous bolts and ornamental locks and knockers." If "in Havana every man's house is his castle," Reynolds gave his readers the fortress of tradition, closed tight against the modern Yankee.[8]

Yet although houses were walled and girt with iron, the huge barred but unglazed windows common in many tropical mansions negated the privacy promised by the thick stone walls and lack of front yards. Reynolds breached the fortresses of Havana in a few sentences: "The grilled windows affording full view of the interior of the house give a measure of domestic publicity which is strange to the northern eye. . . . In warm, sunny, open air Havana, people live in their homes in the public view, eat and drink and visit in the public view; and even do their courting where they may be seen of all men." In Matanzas, Cuba, William Seymour Edwards wrote, "We could look right into the courtyards, and even into the living rooms of the houses, so close did our *cocha* wheel come to the open doorways and to the wide-lifted curtains of the glassless windows," revealing a mother presiding at the breakfast table while smoking a cigar larger than that of her husband. For Philip Marden, the lack of privacy worked the other way: the large windows in his hotel room in San Juan, Puerto Rico, forced him to shower in view of a black woman (described as "an opulent black mammy," surely to deny the erotic potential of her gaze) living nearby, "who signified her good-humor by waving her hand. There was nothing to do but wave back."[9] The fortress of Latin American tradition, it seemed, provided neither the privacy nor the old-fashioned gender relations that it promised. Instead it seemed to violate all the architectural and spatial norms upon which U.S. gender and familial ideals rested—at once too closed and too open.

Longing to penetrate the secrets behind the stone walls encircling Latin American domestic life, travel writers—and perhaps amateur visitors as well—often engaged in patio peeping, strolling along the sidewalks peering through window grilles or open doorways, hoping to catch a glimpse of the lavish gardens and secluded women thought to be therein. The practice echoed the long tradition of Westerners fantasizing about the secrets of the oriental harem. Reynolds imagined a tropical oasis: "lemon and palm and banana, orchids and roses and other flowers, and ferns and vines, with caged birds, a fountain plashing in the center, and perhaps a piece of statuary. It is all very cool and inviting as one catches a glimpse of it from the hot street." In the central courtyards of homes in Chihuahua, Mexico, Cora Hayward Crawford glimpsed "dancing fountains and brightly blooming flowers, and, occasionally, . . . a fair-faced, black-eyed beauty" in the central courtyards of homes.[10] At the center of rock-ribbed tradition was the sexy señorita, the princess in her tower, the heart and source of tropical society, its sweetest fruit and prettiest flower.

Women's seclusion and the rigid segregation of unrelated young men and women represented the practices least like those of most U.S. residents and almost always earned their fascinated criticism. Like the house-fortresses that put their inmates on display, these practices, critics believed, failed to produce the faithful, loving marriages they were intended to assure; they led not to monogamous chastity but betrayal and unhappiness. The poet Langston Hughes, who spent a year in Mexico in 1920–1921, noted that "good girls, in Toluca, as is the custom in very Catholic and very Latin countries, were kept sheltered indeed, both before and after marriage. They did not go into the street alone. They did not come near a man unchaperoned." Crawford commented, "That a union from such an acquaintance, giving neither party an opportunity to learn the inner life of the other, should result unhappily is not surprising."[11]

The evening promenade around the town plaza was the main opportunity of youths to interact. As every writer agreed, at dusk in villages throughout Latin America, everyone gathered in the plaza to walk, men in one direction and women in the other. In cities, this event turned into a parade of carriages and riders along a central boulevard and tended to involve mainly the wealthiest residents. Young men and women seized this opportunity to flirt—demonstrating, in critics' eyes, the irrepressibility of heterosexual desire, so cruelly imprisoned by convention. Crawford, riding in a carriage in the grand promenade along Mexico City's Paseo de la Reforma, breathlessly noted that "smiles and swift glances flash like electric currents from carriage to caballero" and admitted that "the excitement communicates itself to our cooler natures." Hughes remembered that "in Toluca, the evening promenade was an established institution for the young people of the town." His friend Tomás brought him along "at the hour when all the girls were out walking, too. But not walking with young men. Oh, no! Not at all. That was unheard of in Toluca. The girls of the better Mexican families merely strolled slowly up and down with their mothers or married sisters, or old aunts, or the family servant, but never unchaperoned or alone."[12] The boys, Hughes discovered, traveled in packs of three or four, slowing down to stare at the girls who interested them, while the girls giggled and looked away.

After the promenade came "playing the bear," when the suitor visited his beloved at her house and courted her through an iron-barred window—surely many a tourist imagined Romeo suing for Juliet's favor. Despite prophesying doom for marriages in which the spouses had never gotten to know each other, Crawford allowed her eyes to mist over at this style of courtship: "The picturesque balconies with their gay awnings must be tempting places for the Mexican style of courtship," she sighed, describing the wooing as "serenades and notes passed through the barred windows, happily replied to if a rose is thrown down by the fair hand of the adored señorita, perhaps the sweeter for a dainty kiss from the red, smiling lips." Although "a far-away sort of loving hardly to be appreciated in our freer country," it was also "the poetry of courtship and the sweeter for being stolen." Hughes, traveling among the boys in Toluca, remarked that frustrated swains had two brothels to choose from, not to mention fair game among the working-class girls of the city. Journalist Harry Foster denied the possibility of genuine marital love in Latin America.[13]

Despite such critiques of the inequality and injustice embedded in traditional courtship practices and marriages, to many people from the United States, Latin American courtship seemed very much more romantic than their own—"the sweeter for being stolen." To them, it must have seemed as if Latin Americans deliberately arranged their lives so as to stage the plot of innumerable nineteenth-century romantic novels—true love rebelling against social convention—every day. The modern freeing of young women from conventional restraints might be a sensible acknowledgment of human nature, but it was not romantic. As Javier Troncoso y Gama wrote in the short-lived U.S. travel magazine *Lands of Romance*, "The time is fast passing when the 'reja' (or balcony rail) is the scene of tete-a-tete between the Mexican girl and her 'novio' (sweetheart)." Instead "courtships among the majority of people are carried out in the dark seats of cinemas. . . . In other words, Mexico is reaching the stage of advancement—if one may call it this—where, in matters of courtship and of love, romance is being judged a superfluous nuisance."[14] The guitar-strumming swain and the girl behind the iron bars represented the melodrama at the center of Latin American gender relations, in contrast to the grubby, lustful functionalism at the center of U.S. gender relations. South of the border, true love found itself caged by convention; north of it, romance died as the cage's bars were broken.

In short, travel writers' discussions of courtship debated the emergence of "modern" courtship practices, suggesting how modern freedoms might best be limited to preserve the possibility of heterosexual romance. Echoing a common lament for the losses inflicted by modernity, J. T. Boumphrey compared the "dark-skinned black-eyed women" of Panama, "soft-voiced, charming girls with unconscious dignity," with the "quick movements, loud voices and quantity production" of the United States. Showing a decided soft spot for cabaret dancers, he condemned both wealthy men's efforts to seduce them into prostitution and respectable women's blaming the girls for the men's evil intentions. Although he acknowledged the truism that prohibitions only inspired people to desire what was forbidden, in his view modern freedoms were debasing, especially to women. Yet his conservatism was of a rather bohemian flavor; he approved of an interracial marriage between a Swiss trader and an indigenous woman founded on the local custom that either partner could sever the partnership at will. But such willfulness should be limited. The modern white girl, exemplified by "Gertrude Kingston, only daughter of the Colonel of the Tenth," earned his greatest opprobrium, for "she drank, smoked, danced, and flirted," and unlike the cabaret dancers she didn't have to be coerced into spending the night with a man—even worse, she took the initiative. Boumphrey, like some U.S. feminists and (as we shall see) female travelers, preferred the indigenous woman, content in her traditional role when endowed with the privilege of choice usually associated with heterosexual liberalization.[15]

Not everyone was nostalgic for the romantic old days, of course. Modernity had its own joys. "The rules of social behavior, even in the most sophisticated dancing places of Havana," Sidney Clark noted, "must be decidedly irksome to young people." Having taken his wife through the city's red-light district and watched indulgently as she flirted with handsome policemen, he was undismayed when she accepted an invitation to dance from the man seated next to him at a party. Clark promptly asked the man's wife for the same favor, but she turned him down, declaring that she would only dance with her husband. When another man began to harangue her in Spanish, Clark imagined that he was saying, "Good heavens, girl, get up and dance with him. You're not an old heirloom to be laid away on the shelf just because you got tied up with [your husband]. Snap out of it. Be human."[16] In this passage, human means heterosexually liberal; it means Mrs. Clark—white but imbued with enough tropical passion to dance and flirt, respectable but unbound by stifling tradition, married but youthfully sexy. And it means interpretation in the absence of knowledge, the deployment of a supposed Latinness by U.S. visitors privileged to assume that what they wanted was what Latins and Caribbean residents were saying.

A Little Innocent Wickedness

The risk that modern tropical whites like the Clarks ran in warming themselves at the fires of southern passion was, of course, racial degeneration. In the eyes of white supremacists, the loss of sexual morality in the climate's warm embrace would ruin not just one generation but several, since once whites' racial-sexual fastidiousness was sufficiently eroded, reproduction (and even more shockingly, marriage) across the color line became possible. This danger was especially acute when white men ventured to the tropics on their own—far from both white women in the flesh and white women as symbols and arbiters of civilization. The promise of renewed virility through imperialism threatened white supremacy even as it was realized. At the same time and in addition to the threat posed by beautiful tropical maidens, nice white girls at home were abandoning husbands and children for education, waged work, and politics. Demanding a greater public role, women in the United States and throughout the industrialized world were also marrying later and bearing fewer children—a phenomenon the sociologist E. A. Ross dubbed "race suicide." To many, it seemed that advanced civilization was as dangerous to the reproduction of white supremacy as was tropical backward-ness.[17] What was to be done?

One obvious solution was to send battalions of white women to the tropics to defend their men, and indeed many colonial powers did so. Such women often proved themselves able imperialists, but their achievements did not silence pundits such as the prominent U.S. geographers Ellsworth Huntington and Ellen Churchill Semple, who warned that living in the tropics undermined white women's health. "The women of Florida—I heard them say it themselves—are pale and wan compared with their northern sisters," Huntington claimed ominously. Semple stated flatly that "the severity of the climate [in the tropics] excludes the white woman."[18] These enervated women would fail to bear strong children, and those children would grow up without the vigor that was their racial birthright.

The contrast between wilting wives and reinvigorated husbands consti-tuted a serious obstacle to white imperialism in the tropics, at least (and one suspects mainly) in scholarship and fiction. As symbols and sources of civi-lization, white women were the reasons why men went adventuring and why they returned, and so women's inability to be fruitful in the tropics marked the inability of civilization itself to put down roots there. One of the solutions to this conundrum that circulated in writing, advertising, and films about the Southland was that absorbing a bit of the sensuous tropics would both pre-vent white women from losing their femininity and rekindle passion between white men and white women.[19] A little cultural inoculation would cure the tropical pathology afflicting imperial whites.

Two stories, one published in 1912 and the other in 1925, sketch the way that such fears and hopes circulated and were resolved in romance, a genre often deployed in imagining national and imperial relationships. The first, *Cabbages and Kings*, is a satirical account by O. Henry of life and politics among U.S. expatriates in an imaginary small Central American port town, Coralio, in the equally imaginary country of Anchuria. Each major plot line focuses on a couple whose relationship represents one of the problems posed by U.S. involvement in the tropics. Willard Geddie, the young U.S. consul stationed there, has fled the United States after a romance ended in a "mis-understanding and quarrel"—rejecting civilization in the shape of a woman. "Happy and content in this land of perpetual afternoon," he courts Paula Brannigan, the daughter of a local Irish-born magnate and his mestiza wife. But then Geddie receives a message in a bottle, written in the hand of his lost love and thrown from "the beautiful white yacht" of a U.S. millionaire that is cruising off the coast of Anchuria. Civilization, on a tour of the tropics, has extended her hand. Unconvinced of his fickle white love's worth, Geddie proposes to Paula: "Here was surely a heart made for love and steadfastness. Here was no caprice or questionings or captious standards of convention. . . . He had attained a Paradise without a serpent. His Eve would be indeed a part of him, unbeguiled, and therefore more beguiling."[20]

Affirming his social as well as physical acclimatization, Geddie resigns from service to his country and moves into his in-laws' house to become heir to an Anchurian fortune. In contrast to the *Overland Monthly* story with which I began Chapter 1, this fable suggests that it is better for young men to go native than to suffer the slings and arrows of civilization, especially in romance. Rewriting the foundational fictions of many Latin American nations to legitimize U.S. imperialism, O. Henry's tale portrays the adoringly submissive, part-Indian Paula Brannigan as a symbol of the nation of Anchuria (and by extension all Latin American countries), available to the right (white) man because the local men are too foolish and lazy to compete.[21]

But not all exiles in the tropics are so willing to forgo their birthrights. When Geddie's replacement as U.S. consul plays a practical joke that brings a white U.S. merchant and his daughter to Coralio to sell shoes—an accoutrement of civilization for which the locals have no use—the daughter's honesty and refinement make it impossible for her to succeed there. Desperate to avoid losing her favor, the consul manufactures demand by sowing cockleburs in the previously smooth, soft dirt roads of Coralio. With this bit of capitalist legerdemain, he redeems himself and sails home, the daughter's hand in marriage shortly to be expected. The only U.S. woman (her whiteness qualified by French and Spanish heritage via New Orleans) well suited to Central America is an amoral adventuress who seduces and robs Anchuria's president, then meets her match in an equally amoral U.S. white man. Together, they successfully defraud both the nation and his former employer, a U.S. bank.[22] Going native, going home, or going rogue seem to be the only viable options for whites in Central America in O. Henry's satire—either way, the tropics win and upright U.S. citizens are better off staying home where people don't have to be deceived into needing shoes.

A second story, published in *Scribner's Magazine* in 1925 and titled "Tropical Heat and White Men," offers a different moral to the story of U.S. whites' negotiation of tropical dangers: a little personal ethical adjustment will eliminate the possibilities of either local marriage or a life of crime. An old white man, long resident in Manila, narrates the downfall of what should have been a happy young white couple. Arriving first, Harry is immediately corrupted by the "childish shameless tropical mating" all around him, in the shape of the Filipina prostitute Paquita. A few years later, the narrator is shocked to find a young white woman—"pretty as an angel she was, with her hair the color of first-quality hemp; her eyes like the skies" and named, of course, Lily—occupying the room next to his with only a screen between them. A thoroughly modern girl, she travels without escort or chaperone. Appalled, the Spanish landlady concludes that Lily is "not in the least suited to the tropics. She was of the North, inside her skin as well as out." She is no adventuress, though, but a wronged wife, seeking the husband who deserted her. Walking in on Harry forcing his attentions on Lily, the narrator learns that the villain is none other than this young man, long since married to Paquita and father of her child. Fleeing her perfidious husband, Lily throws herself from her bedroom window and dies on the patio below.[23]

A trite little racial melodrama rehearsing much the same dangers of the tropics as the story from the *Overland Monthly* fifty years before—yet "Tropical Heat and White Men" takes some unexpected turns, not least of which is that it is the white woman, not Paquita in the role of tragic mulatta, who kills herself after a white man's betrayal. Now that white women are modern enough to travel on their own, interracial imperial bigamy will no longer do (although the story's portrayal of Paquita as Harry's wife is surely a euphemism required for publication in a respectable magazine). If white mastery is to survive, whites themselves must change. Throughout the story the author hints that Lily's white modernity hinders her ability to keep a white man who has been seduced by the tropics. Although lovely, she has only the "straight gaze of straight youth" to compete with the Filipinas' expert swaying of ruffled skirts to reveal their legs. When Harry embraces the unwilling Lily, our narrator notes that "there was that about the young man a suggestion—a hint of an abandon which the girl could not have inspired"—but clearly Paquita could. An illustration accompanying the story contrasts the bold-eyed, full-breasted Paquita, holding her child in her arms, with a fashionably boyish Lily, her face hidden by a large hat (Fig. 8).[24]

The implication is that the white woman—the symbol of modern civilization—deserves her fate because she cannot meet her white husband's tropically heightened sexual desire. (In a political register, can the United States remain a virtuous republic while acquiring an overseas empire?) But allowing Harry and Paquita to live happily ever after makes for a troubling ending, because it means that the tropics won—white people will not survive there,

Figure 8. A boyish Lily confronts her bigamous husband and his womanly Filipina wife, who holds their child in her arm. Illustration by H. Van Buren Kline for Isa Urquhart Glenn, "Tropical Heat and White Men," *Scribner's Magazine* 77:4 (April 1925): 367.

and the United States will be undone as a white republic by its imperial adventures in the Caribbean and South Pacific. The narrator concludes that the best defense against such a tragedy is not adherence to conventional sexual ideals or even abiding by the color line but a " 'little innocent wickedness.' "[25] He means that white men experienced in the ways of the world might better resist the temptations of the tropics, yet Lily's failure makes clear that white women, too, needed a little innocent wickedness if they are to compete with the Paquitas so plentiful in the tropics.

Such advice was a variation on the popular wisdom of the 1920s that respectable wives needed to be sexy to keep their husbands interested in them. Usually credited to industrialization, a backlash against women's political activism and growing economic independence, and the emergence of a culture of consumption, the new feminine ideal—the slim, adventurous, sexually eager young wife—owed something to the incorporation of the tropics as well. Competing successfully with tropical maidens, as with chorus girls, meant taking a page from these brazen women's playbook.[26] If white supremacy was to survive, white women's modernization demanded both the underscoring of the color line and its blurring; only by absorbing a little innocent wickedness—a little of the youthful sensuality of tropical peoples—could white women keep their men and the United States uphold its standard as white republic.

At least one female travel writer took this advice to heart and demonstrated that the combination of a little wickedness and thoroughgoing modernity made for both a successful career and a happy intraracial marriage. Emma Lindsay Squier, a journalist who shocked her friends and family by traveling alone in the late 1920s or early 1930s aboard a Mexican steamer—"I was looked upon as a mild sort of heroine, 'going into a country like Mexico, all alone!' "—went south seeking not an errant husband but the flush of passion she had first felt as a ten-year-old reciting poetry before an appreciative Mexican audience. She was dismayed to find that in the event she did not attract any inappropriate attention from the Mexican crew and passengers: "I, who had been the envy of most of my feminine friends because of my slim figure . . . was looked upon as positively thin!" The modern woman, this anecdote suggested, might not be in any danger "down there" because she was too sexless to inspire any heated feelings.[27] Although the journalist later redeemed her pride by flirting with several appreciative Mexican men, her physical modernity redrew the color line in a way that protected her from the truly dangerous, primitive, dark-skinned men.

Another white U.S. woman traveling on the Mexican steamer, although just as adventuresome as Squier and like her a career woman, was not so lucky. She had legs that were "much too fat" in the United States but "the esthetic pride of the boat"—and consequently a real problem. Her old-fashioned shape-liness inspired the ardor of "the Yaqui General," member of an "inconceivably virile" indigenous tribe. The very model of the white supremacist's bogey-man, the general has decided to marry a white woman to affirm his high status among his people. Indifferent to rejection and unable to distinguish between courtship and companionship, he eventually murders a young man who accompanies this woman on a sightseeing jaunt.[28]

The moral of this fable is that white women had to modernize—especially their wayward female bodies—just enough to repel backward (nonwhite) men but not so much that they repelled modern (white) men. Because only the latter would respect women's new freedoms, white women had to direct their newly awakened desires toward white men, and their failure to do so risked modern progress itself. Harry Foster, a journalist traveling in western Mexico nearly a decade before Squier, underscored this point by condemn-ing Mexican marriages as unions motivated only by duty, not love; the men would philander and the neglected wives would allow themselves to get "fat and sloppy" while dedicating themselves to their children. The loveless tra-ditional match, in short, produced morally unattractive men and physically unattractive women. Similarly, in Clark's account at the opening of this chap-ter, the traditional form of extramarital sexuality, female prostitution, results in ugly, undesirable women. The pleasure Clark took in his wife's serial flirta-tions with Havana police officers also hints that a husband who indulges his wife's desires will have a lot more fun.[29]

Indeed, in the discourse of heterosexual liberalism white women's physi-cal and sexual modernization and growing independence, instead of endan-gering marriage or gender difference itself as conservatives feared, enabled a union of devoted, heterosexually fulfilled equals.[30] In narrating her own adventures, Squier insisted that whites like herself could appropriate Latin (and even Indian) passion while refusing the gendered inequities on which it was based. Thus she claimed the picaresque adventure story for women and, in publishing several of her Mexican sketches in major U.S. magazines, dem-onstrated professional success, too. Finally, she concluded her tale of modern female self-realization with a modern twist on the usual happily ever after by having her husband—a white man from the United States, of course—join her in the quest for tropical passion. While they were making a movie about Mexican fiestas, the journalist dressed up as a Tehuana, an indigenous woman renowned for her sexual and economic independence, and stepped into her husband's arms to dance.[31] For the modern white woman, as for the modern white man, the tropics offered rich resources that, properly deployed as culture (such as films of local festivals, made to be screened in the United States), could only enhance, not undermine white racial integrity.

One of the keys to understanding this paradoxical desire for Latin sensuality and rejection of its embodiments as adulterous and unattractive is to recognize that the desire focused on youth and courtship, whereas the rejection focused on adulthood, marriage, and parenting. When the denizens of the Southland exemplified the youthfulness attributed to them as a consequence of their residence in the tropics, they embodied the youth of humanity in all its joyous, beautiful promise. Hampered by the constitutional adolescence caused by life in the tropics, however, they squandered that promise upon marriage. White couples from the United States like the girlishly slender Squier and her supportive husband represented a thoroughly modern maturity in which youthful passion was affirmed instead of negated by the wedding vow and establishment of a household.[32] As with tanning, whites ended up with the best of both worlds.

Pleasure Pirates

Not all U.S. whites were as cosmopolitan—or as well connected—as Squier and her husband or Mr. and Mrs. Clark. Caribbean cruises offered a carefully sanitized opportunity to enjoy the ready sensuality and self-indulgence supposedly characteristic of the Caribbean, because except for brief, carefully arranged shore excursions, passengers lived on board the ship and consorted mainly with each other during the trip. The clean white ship moving through the Caribbean became a safe space for heterosexual play because of both its location and its careful management of passengers' contacts with the locals.

From the start, the "romance of the Caribbean" was a major theme in cruise advertising, but typically this phrase meant the region's history of swashbuckling pirates, helmeted conquistadores, and gold-freighted galleons. As the Panama Pacific Line put it in 1928, "On each voyage the Western World's chief sea of romance, the Caribbean, is crossed in the wake of Columbus, Drake, Morgan, the Spanish treasure fleets and the buccaneers." Identifying the era of Spanish colonization and European wars in the Caribbean as romantic located bold adventure, terrible villainy, and stirring tragedy in the past and in the south—a world apart from the modern, mundane north. As Raymond-Whitcomb put it in inviting customers to join its 1926 West Indies cruise, the Caribbean was suffused with "the glamour of romance—a quality with which unfortunately Americans none too often come into contact. Generally speaking our annals lack the blazing colors of veritable romance. . . . We have had little to do with towering galleons, armored soldiers of fortune, besieged white-walled towns, colossal heaps of golden booty, piratical forays from secret, palm-shaded lagoons."[33] In contrast, the clean streets, sanitary regulations, first-class hotels, golf courses, and good roads that the Pax Americana endowed the region with seemed worthy but dull. Coming from the pens of U.S. writers, this kind of complaint served to sharply distinguish the era of U.S. hegemony from that of the Spanish Empire, denying that in both the region's economy and governance were designed to profit people who lived elsewhere. It wrote the opposition between temperate and tropical into the historical record.

In contrast to the omnipresence of historical derring-do, romance among the passengers was not evident in cruise publicity initially, as the Southern Pacific Railroad's much-revised and reprinted promotional booklet *One Hundred Golden Hours at Sea* demonstrates. In its first two iterations in 1907 and 1910, a harried businessman recounted how his tyrannical wife and demanding or ailing children forced him to take a cruise from New York to New Orleans and then a rail trip to California. In response to the eternal question, "'Where shall we go for a vacation?'" he replied, "'I think a winter trip can be arranged and I believe such a vacation would result in permanent benefits, both physical and mental, for all of us'"—a thoroughly old-fashioned rationale for a southern voyage. Other early brochures confirm that cruises largely replicated the gender segregation typical of well-to-do U.S. people's daily lives and transatlantic steamship travel. Men met in the smoking room to smoke, drink, and play cards, while women gathered in the parlor or on deck to chat, read, and write letters. Illustrations featured mostly middle-aged and older people, probably actual passengers and not models.[34]

By the 1920s, however, the romance of ancient piracy began to shade into the romance of heterosexual liberalism via the rhetoric of tropical sensuality. As early as 1915, the narrator in the *One Hundred Golden Hours at Sea* series, for instance, was no longer "pater familias" but "little daughter," plotting to acquire several new dresses for the cruise, for "every night we dance—and the music is entrancing. . . . This is what I call modern traveling." By the 1930s,

the Holland America Line enjoined its passengers, "if the spirit of the Spanish Main moves you—enjoy a real tango" (exemplifying the disinclination of
most North Americans and Europeans to distinguish temperate Argentina,
source of the tango, from the tropical Caribbean). The Panama Pacific Line
assured its passengers that "the rhythm of romance [is] enhanced by a vacation journey on the largest and finest of American-built liners."[35]

This portrayal of the Southland as a place of sexual buccaneering—in
1929 Hamburg American advertised "Pleasure Pirate Pilgrimages"—was not
all in the minds of advertisers. In the scrapbook she kept of her years as a
University of Miami student (1926–1930), Marcella Seiden drew a picture
of a young woman in a daringly brief and exuberantly sexy pirate costume
adorned with a sash in orange and green, the university's colors. She labeled
it "Kid Hot" in large letters at right and "me" in faded pencil at the bottom
(Plate 9). For this woman, moving from Chicago to Miami to go to college
offered an opportunity to realize herself as a sexy modern girl. Yet she was
far from a social rebel. A member of the swim team and the glee and the-
ater clubs, Seiden participated in local women's organizations and eventually
served as president of her sorority.[36]

Although the Southern Pacific retreated to a reserved third-person narrator in later versions of its *One Hundred Golden Hours*, the trend toward
casting the cruise as romantic in the popular sense was increasingly realized
in the architecture and social organization of cruise ships. In the 1920s, a
new generation of purpose-built cruise ships offered spaces reflecting new
ideas about the interaction of the sexes: smoking rooms became cocktail bars,
and the pool and dance floor replaced the dining room as the center of social activities (Fig. 9). Needing less speed than transatlantic steamers, cruise
ships removed boilers and smokestacks and converted the space thus opened
up into sports and sun decks, reflecting the new ideas about recreation and
bodily display developed on the beaches of Florida and Southern California.
The conversion from coal to oil, a more compact fuel that could be piped in
rather than shoveled by men who had to be housed and fed on board, also enhanced this expansion of passenger space. Increasingly, cruise ships installed
pools—and not simply large tubs in the bowels of the ship or net enclosures
off the side, but deck-top facilities surrounded by space for sunbathing and
served by a nearby bar.[37]

By the 1920s the cruise experience was mainly about heterosexual play,
at least according to the marketing materials. They now featured attractive
young men and women in modern—and often scanty—sports and beach

Figure 9. Once only men could enjoy shipboard smoking rooms, but by the 1930s these had become cocktail bars open to both sexes. The woman sitting at the right is wearing her bathing suit, exemplifying the increasingly casual dress code. "Youth Steps Out," *Coast to Coast* (Panama Pacific, ca. 1930s): 6, Panama Pacific folder 2, KMEC, HL. Reproduced by permission of The Huntington Library, San Marino, California.

attire, posed to emphasize heterosexual interaction. Although "deck sports" typically meant shuffleboard, in one United Fruit Company brochure the phrase was placed suggestively above a cluster of scantily clad young people reclining on the deck and indulging in mutual admiration (Fig. 10). The typical day at sea, a Panama Pacific brochure claimed in 1934, ended dancing on deck "with a preferred partner. Later on, you stroll together toward the welcome coolness of the night air up forward. . . . The dance music floats up to you. Along the rail, two glowing cigarettes dance arabesques on the curtain of the night."[38]

The United Fruit Company's 1930s manual for its cruise director provides a revealing glimpse of onboard entertainments. The carefully structured games, contests, and social events detailed in the manual were all intended to promote opposite-sex sexual interaction. For example, there was the beauty contest, in

Figure 10. Even without the wonderfully suggestive "Deck Sports" title, this photograph of young men and women lounging on deck while chatting each other up conveys the centrality of heterosexual interaction to the Caribbean cruise by the 1930s. The predominance of women seems to have been as common on cruises as it was at terrestrial resorts. "Deck Sports," *Ships and Ports of the Great White Fleet* (United Fruit, 1930): 12, United Fruit Company folder 3, KMEC, HL. Reproduced by permission of The Huntington Library, San Marino, California.

which the male passengers "model comical and unique bathing beauty costumes" for the female judges. Parades of women in bathing suits, increasingly popular on land, seem to have been common on shipboard as well (Fig. 11). During evening dance parties—a staple of cruise life—the cruise conductor was to do everything possible "to see that all unattached ladies are given an opportunity to dance, either by an introduction to a partner or dancing with them yourself."[39] Dance-related games, such as the broom dance, in which an "unattached" lady had to dance with a broom until the music stopped, when she could take away another woman's partner, underscored the importance of heterosexual coupledom to the social experience of the cruise.

Whereas dancing was also a central feature of resort life on land, on board ship people played games they probably rarely encountered elsewhere, and these too were highly sexualized. The very first rule of the "beer-drinking" and the "ice-cream eating" contests on United Fruit cruises was that they

Figure 11. Like beach resorts, cruises often scheduled beauty contests or parades that underscored both the sexualization of the experience and its inward focus—passengers were encouraged to notice each others' pulchritude, not that of the locals at port calls. "Father Neptune Stages a Beauty Parade on Board the *California*," in *Coast to Coast* (Panama Pacific, 1928): 3, Panama Pacific folder 1, KMEC, HL. Reproduced by permission of The Huntington Library, San Marino, California.

should be played with "mixed doubles, ladies and gentlemen on each team." Both contests required team members to sit or stand in intimate contact with each other while one tried to feed the other, despite comic handicaps. The balloon-blowing contest was the most blatant: the male partner held a balloon to the lips of the female partner, who had to inflate the balloon until it burst. First to burst won. Such barely veiled simulations of sex play were not just the fantasies of some United Fruit Company flack who read too much Freud. A newspaper issued by passengers on a cruise on the Panama Mail's S.S. *Ecuador* in 1930 reported of the winners of an apple-eating contest that "Mr. and Mrs. Alvarez gave no one a chance, they evidently have eaten apples together before"[40]—a thoroughly modern Adam and Eve.

Thus, even though cruise ship publicity was predictably overwrought, it was not completely disconnected from the social experience on board. The passengers on the S.S. *Ecuador* really did engage in the entertainments that other promotional materials promised, from costume parties to a "cockfight" in which male passengers tried to throw each other off perches into the pool. A bemused Manuel Toussaint remarked, in a 1937 letter written on board the Panama Pacific's S.S. *Virginia*, that his fellow passengers "take the parties on board very seriously." In the Panama Mail newspaper, sexual innuendo pervaded the comic poetry and accounts of shore excursions. "Have you girls noticed how much more fascinating the MOON is when observed from the boat deck?" inquired an anonymous author. "Kindly choose your man and walk, do not run, to the nearest ladder. Room for all." British writer Clare Sheridan, fresh from lionizing the Bolsheviks and off to do the same for Mexico's revolutionary leaders, remarked that since departing New York City, the passengers "seem to have done the usual ship trick, which is to break up into couples and walk round the ship's angles at dusk, arm round waist. One looks on almost cynically, the thing is so inevitable."[41]

But whatever shenanigans passengers got up to, the demographics indicate that they were not usually the nubile young things featured in 1930s-era cruise publicity. Because passenger lists often included the titles—"Mr.," "Mrs.," "Miss," and "Master"—as well as surnames, they allow a sketch of the gender, age, and marital status typical of cruise travelers. On a 1928 Holland America Caribbean cruise, the majority of passengers were female—55 percent to the men's 45 percent. Of the 174 men and boys on board, 110 were married and traveling with their wives; two were definitely children, as they shared surnames with married couples and were listed as "Master." Most of the couples (92 of 110) did not have children traveling with them. Of the 216 women and girls, 110 were married and traveling with their husbands; 55 were married but traveling without their husbands. Of the 52 women listed as "Miss," 27 could not be positively associated with a family on board. Fifty-two men were traveling without identifiable family members.[42]

By comparison, a Grace Line ship running a regular route from New York City to San Francisco in 1936 carried 178 first-class passengers, 101 women (56 percent) and 77 men (43 percent). Sixty-six percent (118) of the passengers were married and accompanied by their spouses; of these couples, four had identifiable children traveling with them. Only 18 women were identified as unmarried and 18 men were traveling without wives; 23 women (married and single) were traveling without recognizable family members, while several women were traveling with their children but without a husband.[43] Thus, as with ethnicity, the gender ratio seems to have varied between cruises and regular liners, but not drastically.

The Panama Mail cruise passenger newspaper suggests that the preponderance of women was not unique to these two journeys, reporting that "according to authentic statistics, there are 2.3 females to each male aboard

this ship. Imagine entertaining .3 of a girl." Cruise ships, like many summer resorts, seem to have often hosted more women than men. Despite this
imbalance (or perhaps because of it), resorts were famous hothouses of flirtation, and cruises may have inherited (and cultivated) this reputation.[44] Even
though these demographics and the very considerable cost of a steamship
journey argue for a respectable and middle-aged clientele, the cruises' consis-
tent promotion of themselves as ideal spaces for youthful heterosexual play
made sense in large part because they were in but not of the tropics.

When cruise passengers did go ashore, by the 1920s they often went to
nightclubs and beaches that reinforced their sense of the Caribbean as a place
of sexual play and personal self-indulgence. In Havana, the brochures promised, "you may catch youthful inspiration from that fastest of all games, jai
alai, you may dance to the irresistible throb of a Cuban orchestra, or you may
just sit in some flowered patio and sip romance from a frosted glass to the
sound of a Spanish guitar under a tropic moon." It was not irrelevant that in
the 1920s, when alcohol was illegal in the United States, liquor was readily
available on board ships in international waters and in all the non-U.S. ports,
to the delight of many passengers. One opened a little doggerel about his
cruise along Mexico's Pacific coast this way:

> Boatload on boatload of sightseers gay
> Embarked from ship to Custom House quay,
> Music, dancing, drinking, which the law does not bar,
> We found awaiting at the Hotel Belmar.

Madeline Allen reported happily in 1931 that she and her husband "have
not needed our own supply at all" because the Italian ship on which they
were steaming to Europe served wine at dinner—"as much as we want"—and
sometimes the captain served liqueurs afterward. Traveler Elizabeth Buell
pasted a photograph of four women lounging in the ocean and lifting glasses
toward the photographer into her scrapbook chronicling a 1928 Holland
America cruise. The liquid in those glasses might have been lemonade, but
given the circumstances it seems likely that it was alcohol. Havana in particular U.S. tourists regarded as a giant nightclub. Promising that the city was "an
endless carnival of pleasure," an American Express tour offered its passengers
a thoroughly typical nighttime visit in 1928, involving an evening drive along
the waterfront boulevard, the Malecon, and through Chinatown, followed by

a stop at the stadium to see a jai alai game and a few hours at the Sans Souci nightclub and the Casino, returning to the ship at 2:30 A.M., all for six dollars (equivalent to about ninety dollars in 2010).[45]

The identification of Havana with exciting nightlife drew in large part on the overwhelming popularity of music and dance genres associated with people of African descent by the 1930s. From being a region backward because populated by people of color, the Caribbean had become the symbol and site of modern leisure practices—at least in the view of visiting whites, unaware of or indifferent to the extent to which their own preferences generated tourist services. The popularity of the rumba—a scandalous new dance—illustrates the point. Amy Oakley reported that U.S. tourists' interest in seeing the disreputable Afro-Cuban rumba performed disgusted elite (white) Cubans. Regardless, tourist visits to performances had become so common, according to Sidney Clark, that the habitués of a small Afro-Cuban "dance academy" took no interest in the arrival of a group of slumming whites. When a pair of professional dancers agreed to perform for the writer and his wife, he reported that "they prowled and strutted and wove their wicked hips. They sketched, in intricate steps, all the baser passions and infused them with savage beauty. . . . The rhythm became so hot that a primitive lust seemed to fill the dingy hall." Clinically, Clark pronounced that "the rumba acts as an intoxicant on all negroes of Cuba" and then admitted that "the frantic spirit of it caught and gripped even us *blancos*." Oakley, on a similar slumming excursion, feared for her "white serenity." Less prone to dramatics, George Seaton suggested that sensitive visitors limit themselves to the rumba danced at the popular San Souci nightclub, a performance "bowdlerized to the point where it is just improper enough to shock the visiting tourist." The real thing and its "voodoo" ancestor, available at the Afro-Cubano Club, "is fun if you like it, but *not* for the unsophisticated."[46] From a pit of degeneration, the Caribbean had become a school in sophistication for whites, and people of African descent once thought backward and eternally childlike now exemplified a thrilling adulthood.

Sidney Clark's account of his visit to Havana's red-light district indicates that tourists had ready access to prostitutes, if that was what they sought. But the romance that the cruises offered deliberately emphasized the capacity of the Caribbean climate and cultures to spark passengers' passion for each other, and nonwhites functioned mostly as catalysts, rather than objects or (most dangerously) as subjects of lust. One curious event recorded in the S.S. *Ecuador*'s passenger newspaper hints that the sexual dangers of the tropics remained, but mainly (as for Squier's unfortunate traveling companion) for those neither young nor modern. "One of our tourists, a man of liberal proportions, while sight seeing in Corinto [Nicaragua] had the annoying (?) experience of being made love to by one of the chocolate colored maidens," an anonymous author reported, "made love" in this context signifying flirtation rather than the act of intercourse. If the woman was a sex worker soliciting business, the stout tourist did not welcome her invitation. He "spurned her advances which caused her to employ drastic measures. Seizing his head gear she dashed into her domicile. He having long since been deprived of nature's covering for his dome was like a man in a dream who finds himself in a crowd minus his trousers." Distressed to find himself stripped of respectability by a wanton woman, he dashed into her house to regain his hat, a few moments later running breathless and sweating on board the ship to face the ridicule of his fellow passengers.[47] In the hands of a ribald author, the incident of the purloined hat highlights the diminishing danger that the tropics would divest white visitors of their dignity. Only the fat and foolish, determined to shield their aging bodies from nature and the designs of dark-skinned women, would suffer such humiliation; modern men and women would be flirting on the sun deck.

The story also suggests the cruel limits of the economy of tourism for the people of the Caribbean. Whatever this woman's purpose, she clearly felt she was being cheated of her just reward—and then the tourist was gone, aboard ship, out of reach—a pleasure pirate. In the 1920s and 1930s, the governments of the Southland took steps to ensure that rejuvenated and romantically inclined tourists would repay their hosts with a generous measure of both money and respect. Although these measures rarely benefited the smallest players in the tourist economy—the sex workers and street vendors—they did encourage tourists to regard their tropical destinations as bountiful sources of cultural pleasures instead of racial perils.

CHAPTER 6

Spontaneous Capital Invisibly Exported

In 1926, a leading Mexican statesman and philosopher, José Vasconcelos, announced to an audience in Chicago that "there exists a deep, important difference between the people of Latin America and the people of Anglo-Saxon America." He tactfully did not spell out that difference, typically rendered in Latin American literature as a contrast between gentlemen attuned to the finer things in life and money-grubbing merchants. Instead, he simply attributed it to the "Mediterranean" and "Baltic" roots of each population, that is, their supposed geographic origins. Vasconcelos then asserted that such differences were not, contrary to the common wisdom, the enemy of progress embodied in a singular ideal of civilization; no, "it is through differences—deeply inspired, sincere differences—that the human soul has made all of its conquests. . . . It is only material differences that create bitterness and rivalry among men. Spiritual differences on the contrary tend to the tightening of human bonds, because we find pleasure in every difference of the taste; and every peculiarity enriches the wealth of the species."[1] The possibility of advancing civilization and bringing its peoples together amicably rested entirely in the enjoyment of these spiritual distinctions.

In redefining the significance of human diversity, Vasconcelos—and many other anti-imperial nationalists of the time—downplayed the universal determining power of nature in favor of the eternal variety of culture.[2] His aim, like theirs, was to challenge the racial hierarchy rooted in climatic determinism while affirming his people's distinctiveness from the European or Anglo-Saxon ideal. This demotion of nature to humanity's handmaiden similarly characterized germ theory, tanning, and tourist promotions of the Southland. In each case, nature lost its determining power as humans gained the ability to manipulate it to their own benefit. Increasingly, it was not nature, the mere material world, that produced the differences that mattered. They occurred within the realm of human action—the realm of culture, or in Vasconcelos's terms, the spiritual—and in this realm, differences were gifts to civilization, not threats to it or failures to achieve it.

Probably only a few hundred people heard Vasconcelos speak at the 1926 lecture series, and probably even fewer understood his philosophical and political agenda. However, the ambition of his colleagues in the Mexican government to modernize their nation while celebrating its distinctive culture would circulate widely in the United States during the next decade, and in this less learned register the ideas he expressed fueled not just Mexico's involvement in tourism but the tourist industry around the world. Culture was already a politically and economically valuable commodity by the turn of the twentieth century, when many national governments recognized tourism as a vehicle of popular diplomacy as well as a luxury trade producing considerable revenue, and launched initiatives and rewrote laws and regulations to promote it.[3]

For poor nations with little international prestige, like many in Latin America and the Caribbean, attracting foreign tourists looked like an ideal means of both combating negative national and racial stereotypes and bankrolling domestic economic development. As one Bank of Mexico analyst put it, tourism required only the nation's "spontaneous capital," its history, folk arts and customs, and natural beauty, which could be exported "invisibly" in the minds and cameras of tourists without diminishing the quantity available at home. Colombia's foreign minister, Luis López de Mesa, asserted in the program for the First Inter-American Travel Congress in 1939, "Travel is, in fact, the only perfect international transaction since in exchange for money a country exports only the impressions it has made on the traveler."[4]

But of course invisibly exporting spontaneous capital wasn't really that simple. In examining the inevitable complications, I focus largely on Mexico because its leaders clearly articulated the nationalist aims and international significance of tourism promotion, and because its campaign exemplifies the implications of the Southland's emergence as a resort region for the popular understanding of human variation. Both the federal and some state governments dedicated considerable resources to cultivating the nation's spontaneous capital and promoting tourism in the 1920s and 1930s—especially to the hemisphere's and the world's wealthiest travelers, those from the United States. Moreover, Mexican leaders quickly saw the necessity of codifying a new distinction between tourists and other travelers to ensure that the nation earned U.S. dollars without ceding economic sovereignty.[5] Mexico was not alone, however, and I note similar efforts by other regional governments throughout. By the 1930s, even the United States joined the global competition for tourists.

Together, the legal and logistical framework of the tourist industry helped to make what an earlier generation had regarded as the exercise of tropical influence on human nature into a market in liquid culture, readily available to those willing to pay and yet ineradicably foreign to the visitor. One could visit the tropics for considerably less than the price of one's soul, because now the experience was not about race (the product of nature) but about culture (the product of humans)—something outsiders could enjoy but could not fully incorporate by definition. And by definition, tourists were those who did not put down roots, invest in, and grow up with the country. They could allow themselves to be temporarily seduced by tropical nature because, however much they might invisibly export, it would not enable them to spontaneously generate that particular form of capital. They would remain merely tropical whites, not tropical natives.

Cultivating Spontaneous Capital

A generation of scholars has shown the extent to which constructing landscapes as sights and fomenting the desire to go see them have long been critical elements in the formulation, assertion, and acclamation of nation-states—and as such, sources of pride, profit, and politicking. Tourism, like newspapers, vernacular languages, and political pageantry, helped to foster nationalism in the nineteenth and twentieth centuries. Iconic sights and fashionable itineraries grounded the imagined community of the nation in specific landscapes that embodied the ideals of national fraternity and territoriality. Travel books, even the most mundane railroad schedules, offered readers a sense of the scope of the nation, the character of its human and geographic components, and the relationships among those parts. Along with things like a national literature, music, and art, domestic tourism in North America and western Europe played an important role in attaching places to the nation and naturalizing nationality for citizens.[6]

By the turn of the twentieth century, tourism functioned as much as a ratification of the unique ethnicity or nationality of other peoples as it did an affirmation of one's own nationality. As the nation-state emerged as the global governmental ideal during the nineteenth century, cultural distinctiveness became an increasingly important ideological justification of or claim to national sovereignty. Culture expressed a wholeness, even rising to the level of a distinctive collective personality, that transcended the existence of a state. Cultural pluralism grew out of this circumstance as much as or more than it did out of challenges to civilized racism and colonialism. The process of officially identifying national heritage turned some vernacular customs and arts into important markers of a national culture. By 1900, autoethnographic works that characterized places and peoples in accord with emerging European conventions proliferated, as did national and colonial exhibits at expositions, folklore collecting, national historical and art museums, regionalist fiction, and many other ostentatiously modern technologies for constituting and displaying human difference. In these ways, nations simultaneously defined their distinctiveness and claimed their right to participate in modern civilization.[7]

In the context of an expanding global market economy and a burgeoning tourist industry, national differences came to be seen as a form of capital—"spontaneous capital" in the Bank of Mexico's happy phrase. Unlike every other form of that great desideratum, this one seemed to be both indelibly national and inexhaustible. It sprang from ineradicable human distinctions that, although previously thought to be the unavoidable—and perhaps undesirable—effects of the local environment, now comprised a transcendent national essence with none of the inconvenient limitations or fungibility of natural substances. Invisibly exporting spontaneous capital could very visibly benefit the nation both diplomatically and economically.

The salability of a nation's spontaneous capital on international markets corresponded with the global spread of the nation-state and the shift (at least rhetorical) toward representative forms of government. Travel enjoyed a favored status in the liberal political discourse that legitimized these developments. Since the republican revolutions of the late eighteenth century, individuals' freedom to travel had represented the success of the liberal, republican state in overcoming the limits to geographic mobility imposed by autocratic regimes. Giving social content to this abstract link between travel and political freedom, the pioneers of organized tourism advertised their services as the means to democratize what had been an aristocratic privilege and to overcome parochial prejudices. A sign of rational, liberal cosmopolitanism, the itinerant enjoyment of other people's customs would help to establish a global order of naturally unified nation-states organized by individuals' mutual respect. Voicing this sentiment in 1928, a Mexican official argued that one of the chief benefits of foreign tourism was "political and racial rapprochement with foreign countries."[8]

At the same time that the tourist industry underwrote this dream of a liberal utopia, it actively participated in both imperial initiatives (the management of subject peoples) and, especially in the Americas, colonial projects (the founding and extension of settler societies). On viewing the Hopi pueblo of Oraibi, one U.S. writer rhapsodized, "the thought sweeps over us—vast is this continent of ours, yet this is my country. My joy in all this beauty is my right." On the losing side of this assertion, the people of Oraibi fought bitterly with each other over whether to participate in U.S. assimilation efforts or resist them, even as whites flooded the high deserts of the Southwest to see them and other Puebloan peoples portrayed as peaceful, changeless models of a better world now lost to modernity—a trope common everywhere that indigenous peoples were defeated without being destroyed or assimilated into the conquering society.[9]

However, the Southland was a transnational region, and by the early twentieth century many of the several governments overseeing its parts grew increasingly interested in using tourism to oppose colonization—specifically colonization by the United States. When Florida and Southern California began to attract tourists in the 1880s, local promoters saw tourism as a loss leader for colonization to an even greater degree than had the several generations of U.S. land speculators who preceded them, and the strategy worked brilliantly. The same process seemed to be under way in Cuba and Mexico at the turn of the twentieth century, and the possibility that the United States might annex both (and other Caribbean dependencies) circulated in the U.S. press and occasionally in the halls of Congress.[10] But even as domestic U.S. politics diminished the likelihood that the colossus of the north would continue its centuries-long territorial expansion, increasingly nationalist Caribbean and Mexican authorities moved decisively in the 1920s to promote tourism while making colonization much more difficult. They did so by codifying the desire for culture—not land, business, or citizenship—as the only legitimate aim of pleasure travel, and hedging travel for other reasons around with restrictions.

This campaign to defend the nation through tourism centered on the assertion that to know a people was to respect it—the essence of the liberal argument in favor of the freedom to travel, and one distinctly at odds with colonization. As Mexican president Pascual Ortiz Rubio put it in 1932, Mexicans "are eager and anxious to have foreigners learn that truth about the nation, knowing full well that in that way—and in that way only—can Mexico gain in prestige and gain for itself its rightful place among the foremost nations of the world." In May 1937, the Puerto Rican legislature approved Act 174 with the intent "to encourage outside of Puerto Rico, in connection with the promotion of tourism, a good opinion of the culture and civilization of Puerto Rico." Luis Mendoza of the Cuban National Tourism Commission urged his fellow citizens to support the industry because it "has a double national interest: the economic, in that it provides the country with a considerable source of income, growing every year; and the political, because if the world doesn't yet appreciate the people of Cuba in the exact measure of their merits, it is because it isn't yet sufficiently acquainted with them."[11]

Culture in its nationalist guise was particularly attractive for the elites of nations ranked low in the hierarchy of race, like those in Latin America and the Caribbean, in an era of expansive white supremacist empires. The concept was compatible with the ameliorationist, assimilationist bent typical of many Latin American elites, who had long rejected the rhetoric of absolute racial difference associated with the United States. Pale-skinned leaders of nations with nonwhite majorities, including large African-descended and indigenous populations, elites in the Caribbean and Latin America long put their faith in social and physical improvement, claiming to exercise a tutelary racism in which their benighted peoples might, eventually, become civilized.[12] At the same time, the uncritical adoption of European standards of civilization contradicted these leaders' nationalism, their assertion of a distinctly American identity.

As a result, formulating a national culture here often entailed redeeming the tropical climate and its nonwhite natives and celebrating them—in combination with the European heritage—as the source of a unique new identity. In the Caribbean, anticolonial nationalists were especially emphatic about the existence of a unique, non-European culture in the islands by the turn of the twentieth century. Mexico's José Vasconcelos issued one of the most radical versions of this narrative, asserting in *The Cosmic Race* that the tropics would produce the next and transcendent stage of civilization in which all the races would combine to form a new, perfected one. Though his vision of a new master race never attracted widespread support, the integration of African and indigenous influences into the arts and their prominence in national symbolism throughout the region responded to the same impulse to reject or at least modify the implications of climatic determinism and the discourses of race and civilization that grew out of it. The celebration of mestizaje and indigenismo in Mexico or racial democracy in Brazil, although typically complicit with long-standing policies of "whitening" nonwhites and eliminating indigenous societies, functioned internationally as assertions of the cultural—not just material—value of the tropics to the world, the same claim that Southland tourism promoters made.[13]

Latin American and Caribbean states also sought to use tourism to mitigate U.S. economic dominance, hoping spontaneous capital would pay higher returns than foreign-controlled mines, plantations, and railroads. Such was the case in Mexico in the 1920s and 1930s. As the Mexican Revolution ground to a close, the new government badly needed capital to pay off wartime loans, repair the country's shattered infrastructure, revive its major industries, and develop its economy. The obvious source of funds was the United States, the world's wealthiest nation following World War I, but negotiations over reparations for U.S. property expropriated or damaged during the Mexican Revolution proceeded slowly and contentiously. U.S. opposition to the nationalist economic provisions in Mexico's 1917 constitution kept relations between the nations frosty for several years. A classic tourist-investor visiting Baja California Norte, Mexico, on a hunting trip in 1919, Ed Fletcher discovered several families and a troop of soldiers living on land that he and a friend had bought before the revolution. Complaining that the new leadership refused to defend the property rights of foreigners, he opined that "it is inevitable that the United States in the end must intervene and establish a responsible government and put this wonderful country on its feet." But he protested any charge of imperialism: "Before intervening we should make a solemn obligation to its people and to the world, that we will recognize the sovereignity [sic] of Mexico when it has a stable government. As we did in Cuba, so we can do in Mexico."[14]

Likewise regarding Cuba as an object lesson, Mexican officials were determined to avoid its fate. So they turned as early as the mid-1920s to the idea of using foreign tourism as a means of getting foreign money without foreign ownership. Tourism, advocates believed, "is an industry so organized that its principal tendency is to take advantage of all the foreign elements without allowing any of the nation's own to escape." The cities along the border with the United States, particularly Tijuana and Ciudad Juárez, offered one model—permitting the alcohol, prostitution, gambling, boxing, and horse racing banned or restricted in the United States, and taxing them heavily. Following this example as well as those of Monte Carlo and the French Riviera, Cuba legalized casino gambling for foreigners only and imposed steep taxes on it in its 1919 tourism promotion law. In Mexico's border cities, the tax revenues from these enterprises funded municipal and state infrastructure at the same time that they lined the pockets of local leaders, even though people from the United States owned and staffed most of the bars, casinos, and brothels and served their white countrymen almost exclusively until forced to integrate in the mid-1920s. But although acting as the United States' bartender and pimp might be lucrative, it confirmed stereotypes of tropical peoples as immoral and offended many Mexicans. It also bolstered the autonomy of northern leaders against the centralizing efforts of the new national government.[15]

Looking for an alternative and well aware of the profitability of tourism in Europe, Florida, and Southern California, in 1926 Mexico's secretary of foreign relations asked all of the consuls based in the Americas and Europe to report on tourism in their districts and evaluate its advantages and disadvantages. In the extant reports, nearly all the consuls assessed tourism favorably as a good means of enriching the nation, and all of them believed Mexico had the potential to be extraordinarily successful for two reasons: its proximity to the United States and its rich culture. "The American tourist, as the richest, is the most appreciated," wrote Manuel Tello, the consul in Hamburg, Germany. "That said, is it really necessary to insist that Mexico is a propitious field for tourism and that the only thing we need to do is to arrange for it, since we have at our doorstep the tourists par excellence?" From Havana, the most popular Caribbean tourist destination of the period, Consul Manuel Álvarez boasted that Mexico had extraordinary spontaneous capital: "Our country presents countless advantages in comparison with Cuba for attracting the American tourist because of its unsurpassable climate during all four seasons of the year; because of its notable architectural monuments; because of its incomparable panoramic beauty; because of its popular customs, which give it the stamp of its own original and unique nationality; because of the hospitality and refined manners characteristic of its people."[16]

So how were these advantages to be made to pay? As directed, the consuls closely examined tourist promotion programs in their localities, and their answers, by highlighting the differences between tourism in Europe and the United States, emphasized the need for Mexico to break with the hemispheric precedent that linked pleasure travel to colonization. Asked about the role of government, the consuls stationed in the United States focused on municipal and state authorities and identified things like good roads and irrigation systems as the key to success. Thus the consul in Hidalgo, Texas, reported that all

the towns in the region competed for tourists by paving their roads and improving their irrigation systems, which they advertised vigorously. Alejandro V.
Martínez in Phoenix, Arizona, noted that the most desirable tourists were
farmers, attracted by the availability of low-cost public lands, and wealthy
people intending to establish second homes somewhere with a warm winter
climate—just the types who had earlier flocked to Florida and Southern California. The consul in Chicago focused almost entirely on business travelers
and the increased volume of sales and business investment resulting from
their visits.[17]

Such examples underscore the extent to which tourism in the United
States remained embedded in colonization in concept and in fact. Only the
consuls in Chicago and St. Louis explicitly distinguished between the two
practices, pointing out that these cities were more interested in attracting
new residents than temporary visitors. But although Mexico's governments
had long welcomed immigrants, they did not welcome immigrants from the
United States after the secession of Texas in 1836, and the postrevolutionary
leadership invited U.S. investment only under tight restrictions. The consul in
Providence, Rhode Island, was alone in noticing that U.S. cities typically did
very little to advertise themselves to foreign tourists, focusing almost entirely
on domestic travelers. Indeed, the United States as a whole hosted few pleasure travelers from abroad; according to one U.S. Department of Commerce
analysis, whereas U.S. residents spent $5.4 billion abroad between 1919 and
1938, visitors to the country spent only $1 billion, largely because they were
comparatively few, first topping 100,000 per year in 1936.[18] Unfortunately, if
the Mexican consuls based in U.S. cities that received significant numbers of
foreign travelers, such as New York, New Orleans, and San Francisco, deliv-
ered reports as requested, they have not been preserved.

The consuls stationed in European cities wrote about a very different
set of circumstances. As the consul in Dallas noted, most foreigners entering the United States were immigrants looking for work, whereas in Europe
most travelers were looking for entertainment and education, not a new job
or home. Thus instead of farmers, cheap public land, and irrigation canals,
the consuls in Europe wrote about foreign visitors, tour buses, and souvenir
shops. Reporting from Germany, Tello noted that there were entire towns
that served as summer beach resorts and essentially closed down in winter,
and he estimated that Hamburg alone had thirty tour companies, twenty to
thirty souvenir shops, and a good number of tour buses. He even provided a
breakdown by destination city of the nearly 4.5 million domestic and foreign

tourists traveling in Germany in 1926. Although he does not cite a source, the existence of such numbers shows that some agency—governmental or private—was devoting resources to tracking the industry. Edmundo González Roa, stationed in Prague, categorized tourists by nationality (people from the United States were preferred, both because they spent the most and because former president Woodrow Wilson had championed Czechoslovakian nationhood) and found that the country had a good balance of summer beach resorts and centers of winter sports. Whole families lived off handicrafts made for the tourist trade, he reported, and these items "are very beautiful and of a grade similar to Mexican crafts."[19] These were good models for turning the nation's spontaneous capital into culture and selling it while avoiding the malign effects of foreign investment and vice tourism.

The accounts of European nations' management of tourism offered more useful advice for Mexican planners than did those in the United States precisely because tourism there was already, despite the rawness of national borders in the interwar period, distinct from colonization. As Mexico's central government proceeded to formulate plans for attracting U.S. tourists, it attended to many of the issues these reports raised.[20] The first task was to identify the nation's spontaneous capital and put it to work for the nation, which unsurprisingly required far more labor and capital than the hopeful adjective "spontaneous" acknowledged. Mexico did not have a well-developed domestic tourist industry in the 1920s, and foreign tourism had just made a promising start at the turn of the twentieth century before being snuffed out by the revolution. Although promoters glibly invoked the nation's wealth of colonial architecture and archaeological monuments, there were few canonical itineraries or guidebooks to tell people about them, and the infrastructure to transport and house visitors, where it existed at all, had been damaged by war or become dilapidated through neglect.

Travel writing about and guidebooks to Mexico published in the United States had proliferated between the 1880s, when the two nations were first connected by rail, and 1911. Predictably, most were accounts that combined garden-variety exoticism with smug complacency about the United States' superiority to its southern neighbor. After the profound transformation wrought by the revolution, such guides were badly out of date and decidedly at odds with the revolutionary agenda. The prolific T. Philip Terry, who succeeded in publishing an update of his 1911 guide by 1923, considered Porfirio Díaz's administration (1876–1911) "wise and foresighted," whereas the sacrifices of the revolutionary leaders "did not recompense Mexico for the terrific losses" incurred by the war. The Mexican Tourist Association retorted, "Mexico, under the Díaz dictatorship, was a feudal domain possessed by an opulent few and peopled by millions of paupers." The association's guide offered to tourists the "privilege" of witnessing a "new Mexico in the making," a "new, strong and prosperous democracy."[21]

To make its claim to a glorious future credible, Mexico had to redeem its past. Here as throughout the hemisphere, this redemption entailed laying claim to the ancient past and modifying, if not refuting, claims that civilization was born in Europe and had to be imported to the Americas. As a result, in the twentieth century the ruins of past civilizations became a particularly valuable source of spontaneous capital for invisible export. Elites in Mexico had long used the symbols and histories of native peoples to stake their own claim to the nation. In the late nineteenth century, the Díaz regime began to project such imagery on the international screen, using Aztec iconography on Mexican exhibits at expositions and erecting monuments to Cuauhtemoc, the last Aztec emperor. The massive ruins at Teotihuacán, near Mexico City, were excavated and refurbished to serve as the centerpiece of the centennial of national independence in 1910, and the site remains a major tourist attraction to this day.[22]

After the revolution, archaeology took a growing part in the government's campaigns to unify and market Mexico as the ancient home of highly civilized peoples. Eschewing mere argument, the bilingual *Mexico: Guia Ilustrado de Turismo* (ca. 1930s) bore an artist's vision of Teotihuacán as a bustling metropolis on its cover. The spectacular ruins in Yucatán and Oaxaca came to rival the attractions of the pyramids in the capital city's backyard despite being harder to get to. A writer for Pemex, the state-owned oil firm that was a major tourism promoter, declared that the nineteenth-century archaeologists "played down the advanced civilizations of Aztecs, Toltecs, and Mayans by referring to them and their activities with such derrogatory [*sic*] terminology as 'tribal council,' 'chiefs,' and 'warriors.' To them they were just more 'Injuns.' " But now the Mexican government had put an end to the theft of antiquities by foreign archaeologists and supported the serious, respectful study of these ancient civilizations, which were "in many aspects comparable to any in Europe during the same period."[23] More than simply denying the singularity of civilization, such claims asserted that civilization could and did arise in the tropics among people of color. Admiring Maya architecture and mathematics, like germ theory and tanning, conveyed humanity's ability to make nature meet its wishes, instead of the reverse.

Perhaps the best-known vehicle that the government adopted in its effort to remake Mexico's international image was the same one that it used to unify its diverse and often fractious regions and peoples: folk art. As an article in an official government tourist magazine declared, "Promoting tourism has to involve the parallel promotion of the popular arts." By endorsing the idea that all of Mexico's peoples had cultural gifts that enriched the nation and establishing programs that marketed some of the more easily commodified of those gifts, the postrevolutionary governments painted a picture of the nation that, like the soon-to-be-famous murals of Diego Rivera, overflowed with color and variety and yet also formed a carefully composed whole, a heroic national story. As did other nations' celebration of folkways, Mexico's had centralizing and modernizing purposes that reoriented craft traditions away from serving local needs and toward urban art and tourist markets, with decidedly mixed results for artisans' autonomy and prosperity. National and state agencies also sponsored performances of "traditional" dance and music, and revived (or ceased to suppress) traditional religious festivals that had long been anathema to Mexico's fiercely secular liberals. Seeking to attract tourists to a port renowned for disease and corruption, Veracruz's city fathers resuscitated the pre-Lenten carnival that had largely died out during the nineteenth century. Guidebooks produced in Mexico also increasingly featured folk and indigenous ritual dancers, presenting them as examples of culture in addition to or rather than faith: "Every day of the year, some place in Mexico, a fiesta is always going on . . . religious in origin though generally pagan in expression."[24]

The renewed celebration of religious festivals was not uncontroversial. Departing from the official list of questions about tourism issued in 1926, Consul González Roa in Prague urged that "the government should not support in the least those excursions of a religious character, such as pilgrimages to some shrine, that many foreigners attend from simple curiosity, because in such events what is unfortunately displayed to the tourist's eyes is human misery and the exploitation of the poor." This was not culture, in his opinion, but backwardness and oppression—a view shared by many U.S. Protestants, weaned on the evils of popery. Moreover, Mexico's cathedrals, convents, and shrines anchored conservative religious communities strongly opposed to the government's secular, nationalizing project. And yet these buildings also embodied the architectural grandeur of the Spanish colonial period, declared Mexico's European origins, and were tourist magnets here as in Europe. In a fraught and perpetually incomplete process that was nevertheless well under

way by the 1930s, the government sought to redefine Mexico's religious infrastructure and devotional practices as national heritage, simultaneously recognizing the power of Catholicism and turning it to the state's advantage. In
many official and privately printed guides of that decade, Mexico's churches
appeared chiefly as art objects. Acknowledging that the shrine to the Virgin
of Guadalupe outside Mexico City "has been for four hundred years the most
celebrated pilgrim place of Mexico," one guide urged tourists to "pay special
attention to the exquisite marbles, the fine pictures," and the solid gold and
silver rails enclosing the figure of the Virgin.[25]

U.S. visitors participated wholeheartedly in this celebration of indigenous
crafts and rituals in Mexico, as they did in the U.S. Southwest. As soon as
railroads linked the two countries in the 1880s, U.S. travelers began buying
baskets, pottery, serapes, leather goods, lace, and other handmade goods. In
Urupan in the mid-1880s, Charles Dudley Warner went looking for lacquer-
ware "famous the world over" but, to his cynical satisfaction, could not find
any high-quality goods at this, the center of its manufacture. The tiny souvenir booklet that Alice D. Perkins pasted into her scrapbook of an 1888 trip
to Mexico listed shops where visitors could find featherwork, grass pictures,
Indian wax, clay, and rag figures, lacquer and inlaid woodwork, pottery, ham-
mocks, and hats, among other "curiosities." By the 1930s, responding to con-
flicting, changeable government policies, high-end art stores served the few
wealthy collectors while souvenir shops offering cheaper goods proliferated
for the growing number of middle-class tourists. At the end of the decade,
folklorist and tourism entrepreneur Frances Toor, who played an important
role in merchandizing Mexican arts to buyers in the United States, could por-
tray Mexico solely in terms of the regional distribution of artisanal goods
(Fig. 12), while Erna Fergusson wrote a book solely on the country's festivals, for "Mexican fiestas offer a varied, unforgettable, poignant picture of the
people."[26]

The double aim of Mexican tourist promoters—to earn money from U.S.
tourists while eroding their racist beliefs about Mexico—appears most clearly
in programs such as the six-week summer school for foreigners at one of the
major universities in Mexico City. In addition to courses on language, literature, history, art, and social conditions, the students took courses on popular
dance and music and enjoyed weekend sightseeing excursions. Every Thursday at noon, students enjoyed performances of "the dances and music of the
various states of Mexico . . . often given by the natives themselves." To prove
that they had been good students, on the final Thursday the U.S. students

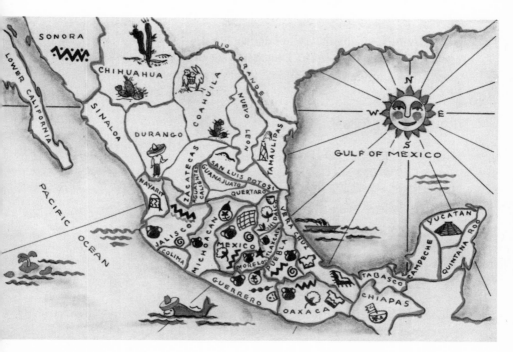

Figure 12. Mexico as a cornucopia of handmade goods. Representing everything from painted gourds to textiles and glass, the icons on this map also signal the popularization of culture in conceptualizing human variation and stimulating pleasure travel. Frances Toor, *Mexican Popular Arts*, illustrated by L. Alice Wilson (Mexico City: Frances Toor Studios, 1939): 23.

gave their own performance—not of U.S. folk dances or songs, but of Mexican ones. "On one occasion several American girls danced so well, and were so well disguised in their regional costumes," according to one writer, that a Mexican onlooker mistook them for professionals. In this context, "playing Mexican" was the sincerest form of flattery and evidence of the success of tourism promoters in making the nation's spontaneous capital liquid in international markets. Such performances participated in the increasingly

popular practice of having cultural groups enact "typical" customs as a means
of combating prejudice and encouraging pluralism.[27] In other words, making
spontaneous capital liquid—turning it into culture recognizable as such in an
international marketplace—affirmed that the ineradicable differences among
peoples were not the outgrowth of the natural world but generated within
human societies. As such, their mutually respectful exchange symbolized the
capacity of humans to transcend the merely material, to overcome the limits
imposed by nature—the move that Vasconcelos urged in his 1926 lecture and
that the tourist promotions of the Southland constantly encouraged.

Keeping an Eye on the Invisible Export

But this small example can also be read as a sign of the difficulties governments faced in managing the nation's spontaneous culture for domestic benefit. If visitors from the United States could learn to perform traditional dances
as well as the natives, how long would such practices remain distinctively
national and therefore attractive to tourists? It turned out that even spontaneous capital, like so many of Mexico's natural resources, could be exploited or
even controlled by foreigners. Officials were concerned about this possibility
from the beginning of federal tourism promotion planning, not least because
of the plight of Cuba in the 1920s and 1930s. Indeed, Mexico's consul in Havana, Manuel Álvarez, offered the only strongly negative opinion of tourism
to be found in the reports requested in 1926. Criticizing tourism in terms
that remain sadly accurate for the twenty-first-century Caribbean, he noted
that most visitors to Havana bought their passage from U.S. and European
companies and stayed in U.S.-owned hotels, "with the result that the tourist
moves through Cuba by means of foreign properties, paying them the money
before leaving the United States. It is very sad that the citizens who spend
their money, sacrificing their wealth to prepare for the business, should have
to resign themselves to the scraps from the feast, such as employment in the
lowest jobs, in which they almost always suffer humiliations."[28] The consul
did not deny that tourism might bring considerable benefits to Mexico, but
he insisted it would only do so if the business remained in Mexican hands.

Although the head of the Bank of Mexico dismissed Álvarez's scathing
evaluation as misguided, the national government nevertheless tried to follow his advice by preventing foreign ownership of hotels, transportation, and
tourist services. Unfortunately, the economic devastation of the revolution

and chronic warfare in the 1920s, followed by the onset of the Great Depression in the 1930s, left Mexico desperately short of financial capital with which to develop its spontaneous capital. As a result, the effort was slow to get off the ground. Perhaps the most important contribution the national government made to tourism in the 1920s and 1930s was the construction of a national network of paved highways. When possible, federal officials also provided and guaranteed loans, especially for hotels, to ensure that national entrepreneurs and companies could compete in this field.[29]

But in a context in which big U.S. and European transportation firms already dominated regional tourism, economic nationalism could seriously hinder Mexican entrepreneurs, and not only for lack of money. That was the experience of Fernando Barbachano, the director of Mayaland Tours, based in Mérida, Yucatán, with branch offices at the Maya ruins of Chichén-Itzá, Uxmal, and Izamal. Neither a road nor a railroad linked the Yucatán Peninsula with the rest of Mexico, so Barbachano approached the state-owned Compañía de Transportes Marítimos y Fluviales (Maritime and River Transport Company) with a proposal typical of the industry: if the shipping company would guarantee high-quality, on-time service, Mayaland Tours would guarantee a certain number of passengers at a fixed price. Advised privately that the shipping company could not deliver good service, Barbachano sought to make the same arrangement with a foreign company, but the law permitted only Mexican ships to carry passengers between Mexican ports. This requirement discouraged the burgeoning Caribbean cruise industry from including Mexican ports on its itineraries and also retarded the development of beach resorts along the eastern coast, because most of the ships traveling the Caribbean were not of Mexican registry. By comparison, business leaders in Puerto Rico were stymied in their effort to get a U.S. government subsidy to improve passenger transport to the island because it was classified as within the United States for purposes of a law that banned federal subsidies for ships serving domestic ports. However, the same law defined the nearby Virgin Islands as outside the United States, and so with federal support they attracted more traffic than Puerto Rico in the 1930s.[30]

As these examples suggest, a critical part of making the invisible export of spontaneous culture pay both monetary and political dividends was reforming and elaborating border controls to ease the entrance of foreign visitors, whether individual or corporate. This was one of the recurrent motifs in the 1926 Mexican consular reports, which again identified European models for legal mechanisms designed to ease tourism without risking national security or economic controls. A 1928 cable from the Mexican consul in Spain noted that its National Tourism Board had won the right for those traveling in automobiles to enter the country by showing membership in another nation's automobile club, providing that nation gave the same privilege to Spanish citizens. The consul in Prague similarly credited the Czechoslovakian government with suppressing the requirements for passports and visas for some travelers and noted that automobile club membership cards were accepted throughout central Europe in place of passports. The consuls urged Mexico to follow suit in easing passage across the border for those who indicated a certain level of wealth, for example by owning a car, and the Mexican Automobile Association was prominent in tourism promotion efforts in the 1930s.[31]

But lowering the requirements for automobile owners addressed only a small part of the larger question. States inviting foreign tourists in also had to make sure that those entering the country were coming only to buy national culture and not to make other kinds of claims on the nation's resources. Doing so required codifying into law a previously unimportant distinction between tourists and other kinds of visitors, such as investors or immigrants, and making sure those who entered the country behaved in keeping with their initial categorization. Indeed, for many nations at the turn of the twentieth century, promoting orderly foreign tourism was an important element in larger efforts to manage immigration and foreign investment in order to ensure that the national economy operated primarily for the benefit of citizens. Thus plans to encourage and regulate tourism contributed to the universalization of the passport as proof of both individual identity and nationality.

Originally, a passport had been a document that requested freedom of passage for a ship belonging to one authority into a port controlled by another. By the early nineteenth century, it was a letter of reference in the process of becoming an identification card (just as letters of credit gradually became travelers' checks). Over the course of the nineteenth century a patchwork of local restrictions on people's movements gave way to national-level regulations. As national states aggregated powers once held by local governments and private entities to control the movement of individuals, they began to distinguish sharply between intranational movement by citizens, which was deregulated, and the movement of foreigners across national borders, which was increasingly regulated. States also now claimed the sole right to issue passports to their citizens and formalized the process for getting one. By the twentieth century, the document had become the primary way to prove one's nationality.[32]

According to scholarship on the subject, states had two chief motives for instituting or strengthening passport requirements in the mid- to late nineteenth century: immigration restriction and war. As western European and North American governments increasingly sought to limit or ban the entrance of some people, primarily those from China, Japan, and India, the absence of a widely accepted uniform document to establish a traveler's identity and nationality led to a profusion of paperwork, plentiful opportunities to manipulate the system, and considerable headaches for government agents trying to enforce the laws. The political problems caused by the invidious distinctions central to the original immigration restriction laws also pushed governments to find ostensibly equitable ways of excluding some people but not others. World War I then spurred European and North American governments to begin requiring passports to control both their own nationals (such as young men eligible for military service) and foreigners (especially nationals of enemy states). Then, in the 1920s the United States enacted comprehensive immigration restriction laws that set the standard for national control over the international flow of travelers and impelled many other nations to adopt paperwork that would be acceptable to U.S. consuls and immigration agents.[33] Ever since the interwar period, with notable exceptions in times of relative peace or among politically allied nations, international travelers typically have had to carry passports.

Mexico came to border regulation from a somewhat different position than the major immigrant-receiving nations did. Although interested in regulating immigration (usually in encouraging white, preferably Latin immigrants while discouraging African American, Afro-Caribbean, Asian, and Middle Eastern ones), it was also increasingly invested in attracting the wealthy pleasure travelers who usually went to Europe. In this enterprise Mexico was in good company. After 1900, the stars of the global tourist firmament—France, Switzerland, and Italy—faced stiff competition, as governments around the world spent more on tourism promotion and established national boards to manage it. These efforts were institutionalized internationally after World War I through organizations and events such as the Alliance Internationale de Tourisme (1919), Conseil Central du Tourisme International (1925), Federación Sudamericana de Turismo (ca. mid-1920s), World Travel Club (1929), Oriental Tourist Conference (1935), and the Inter-American Travel Conference (1939).[34]

Underwriting this institutional growth was money. "Putting completely aside the many advantages of tourism in drawing peoples together and awakening international understanding and better comprehension of the aspirations and ideals of nations," asserted a booklet for delegates to the Fourth Pan American Commercial Conference in 1931, "the revenues to be derived from the spending of foreign tourists have come to constitute a substantial factor in the national economies of many countries and a category of great importance in the balance of international payments." In 1929, tourism industry analyst A. J. Norval reported that France earned some $3.9 billion from the trade to lead his global list, with Canada, Italy, and Switzerland rounding out the top four. The director of the American Automobile Association's Office of Tourism noted that the tourist industry earned some $7.5 billion per year worldwide in the 1920s, with U.S. travelers dropping $25 million in Cuba and $50 million in Mexico's northern border cities (in a contrast that Mexican leaders were painfully aware of, they spent $400 million in Canada). The Department of Commerce considered the estimated $5.4 billion that U.S. tourists spent abroad between 1919 and 1938 a substantial factor in the international balance of payments.[35] Tourism was a major international enterprise by the 1930s.

It is not surprising, then, that nations increasingly took tourism, as well as war and immigration, into account when they wrote or revised border control laws. Even as states asserted their ability to bar entry to some individuals, they issued an invitation to others—and in the process, they defined tourists as people seeking culture. Many of the governments that rewrote their immigration codes in the late nineteenth century and early twentieth century specifically included pleasure travelers, usually as one category of travelers exempt from limits and fees imposed on immigrants. For example, as is well known, Chinese people faced steadily rising barriers to their movements from the 1870s. However, the U.S. law (first enacted in 1882 and renewed and revised thereafter until it was repealed piecemeal in 1952 and 1965) banned only Chinese *laborers*, not all Chinese travelers, and exempted some relatives of those already living in the United States. Most Chinese people seeking entrance therefore aimed to prove themselves either business people or family members of those who had arrived before the restrictions were enacted. But in at least one case, the would-be border crossers declared themselves to be tourists. The Lees, a Chinese Canadian family living in Victoria, British Columbia, and two of their friends sought permission to enter the United States as tourists in September 1908. In addition to filling out a form provided by the Canadian government that attested to their eligibility to enter the United States and getting a visa from the U.S. consul, the five applicants also had to show letters of reference from non-Chinese businessmen in Victoria con-firming their identities and class status, the partnership agreement for the business that Mr. Lee managed, and birth certificates for the three members of the party born in Canada.[36] Whether the Lees and their friends were tour-ists in the sense then beginning to emerge—temporary visitors seeking only to experience the local culture—or immigrants and investors cannot now be determined, but their case illustrates that the mechanisms for regulating im-migration also, initially by default, established categories of welcome travel-ers, including tourists.

Although the United States was slower than most of its neighbors to so-licit foreign tourism, it codified tourists as desirable travelers as early as 1924. In that year, the government enacted the notorious 1924 National Origins Act, which imposed draconian, racially based immigration restrictions. In this law, "immigrant" was defined entirely in terms of the kind of traveler an immigrant was not: "Definition of 'Immigrant.' Sec. 3. When used in this Act the term 'immigrant' means any alien departing from any place outside the United States destined for the United States, except" for six other types of aliens, including government officials and their families; foreigners in transit through the United States to another country; foreign sailors; foreign busi-ness people; and foreigners "visiting the United States temporarily as a tour-ist or temporarily for business or pleasure."[37] The National Origins Act thus extended the distinctions first applied only to Chinese travelers to all people seeking to enter the United States; "immigrant" and "tourist" were from this time on legally defined and distinct categories.

Mexican lawmakers first distinguished between tourists and immigrants in a new law on migration promulgated in 1926. This law defined four types of border crossers: immigrant workers, emigrants, colonists, and tourists; the last were exempt from some of the restrictions placed on the other three cate-gories. Four years later, the growing number of foreigners in the border cities and the increasing flow of tourists motivated amendments to this law. Among other things, the 1930 version created a registry for foreigners and added a new type of traveler, the local visitor to border towns and ports. The 1930 law defined the tourist as "the transient who comes to the country on a journey of recreation" and stays no more than six months. Such persons could not establish themselves in any business in the country and earn income from it without first changing their status to immigrants and paying a tax.[38]

The government also took other, regulatory steps to ease the passage of real tourists across the border. By 1930 it had instituted what it called the "forma 11," also known as the *tarjeta de turista* or tourist card. This card was all a white U.S. tourist needed to enter Mexico in the 1930s: no passport; no visa; no photographs; just the card, available at all Mexican consulates in return for a minimum of personal information, a signature, and a fee of about $1 U.S. (about $13 in 2010). (Black U.S. tourists faced much greater, often insuperable difficulties.) The size of a small index card, the document required the applicant to state his or her name, age, marital status, occupation, current nationality, residence address, destination, reason for traveling, and any other relevant facts (this *otros datos* field was quite small, suggesting the undesirability of having any such facts). The official who issued the form had to write in date of entry and expected date of departure and sign it. One copy remained with the tourist, the other on file in an office at the port of entry, until they were reunited upon the tourist's departure within the statutory six months. In contrast, travelers entering Mexico with the intention of staying longer than six months or working there had to obtain an identification card from a Mexican consulate by providing three front and three profile photographs of themselves; showing the officials their passports, birth certificates, or notarized affidavits proving their citizenship; and supplying a smallpox vaccination certificate. In addition, upon entry the migrant had to pay a $20 (about $260 in 2010) head tax.[39]

To put the Mexican requirements in context, consider that in 1936, Brazil required tourists to provide a valid passport, a smallpox vaccination certificate, a letter from a transportation or tour company attesting that he or she was a "bona-fide tourist," three identification forms filled out by the bearer and signed by a Brazilian consul, three photographs, and a visa fee of $4 (about $60 in 2010). Such persons were limited to a ninety-day stay in the country. Needless to say, the requirements for nontourists were even more onerous. Colombia required all of that, plus a health certificate, two letters of introduction to a Colombian consul attesting to the applicant's financial status and good character, and a return trip ticket. Increasingly, however, nations made exceptions for a certain kind of tourist—the kind traveling in an organized group on a defined circuit and possessing a round-trip ticket. In these cases, tour or transportation companies assumed the responsibility for ensuring that such people were financially sound, of good character, free of contagious disease, and transient.[40]

As the special provisions for tourists show, Mexico was far from alone in easing the rules for those seeking culture in the first half of the twentieth century. Countries closer to the United States and more enmeshed in its economy tended to impose fewer regulations on tourists, especially those from the United States. By 1936, Cuba required no documents at all from U.S. tourists, whereas pleasure travelers from other countries had to present valid passports. Panama not only required no documents from any tourist but also allowed them to stay in the country indefinitely—most countries imposed a three- or six-month limit. Many nations with Caribbean ports made an exception for cruise ship passengers; those travelers with round-trip tickets whose carrier would ensure their departure within a few hours of their arrival were allowed to enter without full documentation, although they often had to carry landing cards much like the Mexican tourist card. If they jumped ship, the carrier had to pay a fine and the immigrant head tax in many cases.[41]

Creating a special category of border crossers entailed an additional level of bureaucratic management. Letters from Mexico's Interior Department to the Department of Foreign Relations record ongoing efforts to make sure that consuls provided the tourist card only to bona fide tourists and a few other transients, such as students and travel agents—"that is to say, those who do not have . . . the character of immigrants." Making the determination could be difficult in some cases, as when consuls were called on to distinguish between "real" tourists and residents of the Mexico-U.S. border zone. Earlier, border consuls had been able to issue visas that had limited foreigners to a 24-hour visit, which effectively meant they could only visit the towns along the border with the United States. Discarding the limits on time and distance traveled encouraged travelers to come further into Mexico and reflected the government's desire for tourists to experience the national culture, not just the universal vices and Americanized Mexicanness available in Ciudad Juárez and Tijuana.[42]

The implementation of the tourist card forced consuls to decide who was a "real" tourist and who was just a local crossing the border to do business, shop, and visit family. The latter were supposed to get another document, the *tarjeta local* or local card, which relieved them of having to get the more expensive, time-limited passport (the United States offered a similar document to its citizens). But the Mexican government did not consider their travels, even if they included fiestas and visits to beach resorts, to be tourism properly understood. Tourists confirm the difference between nations, while "internationally local travelers," as one organization called them in complaining about the problem they posed for an accurate count of tourists, often blur it.[43] Only those whose trip had a precise temporal span, was designed only for leisure, began and ended outside Mexico, and had no other claim on the nation qualified for the tourist card.

In short, by the 1930s many governments had legally defined tourists as those whose relationship to a nation is transactional as much as geographic. Tourists buy culture and leave money, whereas immigrants bring their culture with them and seek money. The point of government involvement in tourism promotion, as one Mexican official wrote in 1929, should be to provide services for "the tourist, who leaves his country to spend his money and not in search of it, as does the emigrant." The tourist was a person explicitly not interested in labor or business investment but only in the cultural experience of the nation, so that pleasure travel would bolster just those claims of nationality, belonging, and sovereignty that immigration imperiled. In the words of Mexican travel promoter J. Rodolfo Lozada, the tourist was the person who came "to distract himself, to please his spirit, to satisfy a spiritual desire," whereas "all of those who move from one place to another out of necessity or for professional reasons are not tourists." Panama's Guillermo Andreve was more laconic: "Tourism is a love of travel for the pleasure of getting to know the usages and customs of peoples."[44] The tourist is the one who appreciates national culture without seeking to change it; the tourist's presence enriches the nation and removes no resources from it; the tourist is the one who goes home again.

As more American states began to encourage and regulate tourism, they brought their interests to the Pan American Union, a U.S.-sponsored organization intended to improve relations among the nations in the Western Hemisphere. Originating in the 1880s, it was the predecessor of today's Organization of American States. Among other things, the Pan American Union sponsored regular commercial conferences at which the participants discussed how to increase hemispheric trade. One of the subjects perennially mentioned as something that governments could do immediately and at little cost to promote tourism was to simplify or abolish passport and visa requirements. In 1931, tourism was one of the major themes of the conference. During the discussions, the Cuban delegation proposed creating a hemispheric tourist passport enabling all residents of signatory nations to travel to other signatory nations with a minimum of documentation. Four years later, at the 1935 conference in Buenos Aires, delegates signed the Pan American Tourist Passport Convention, which called on the member states to implement the Cuban proposal of 1931. This convention defined a tourist as "a resident of one of the countries [that are] members of the Pan American Union, not having the intention to move from it [whose] activities within the country must not have the direct object of providing his support [and whose] sojourn shall always be of limited character." The proposal came up again in 1939 at the First Inter-American Travel Conference. Nothing seems to have come of it, no doubt in large part because such mutual openness required a harmony of political and economic interests that did not exist.[45] Nevertheless, such high-level discussions helped to build a consensus about what tourism was, its legal construction and management, and its diplomatic and economic benefits.

Returning the Invitation

Tellingly, all the politicians and businesspeople involved in promoting the Southland focused on encouraging U.S. citizens to travel south, though the representatives of Latin American nations often paid lip service to tourism among Central and South American and Caribbean nations. U.S. economic power and the relatively greater wealth of its citizens had a great deal to do with the direction of travel, but equally important was the widely shared belief that culture at its most vibrant lived in the Southland or in Europe, but not in the industrial heartland of the United States. Compounding (or perhaps reflecting) that fact, the U.S. federal government was slow to get involved in the international tourism business. Several factors contributed to its foot dragging, not least the millions of immigrants and sojourners who entered the country between the 1880s and the immigration restrictions of the 1920s. Colonization overshadowed tourism as a border control issue until the legal dam reduced immigration from outside the Americas to a trickle. Moreover, the United States had a robust domestic tourist industry dominated by local and state governments, private companies, and trade groups—there was no obvious role for the federal government until the economic and diplomatic importance of the idea of culture became increasingly apparent amid the crisis of the 1930s. In this decade, the U.S. government officially took notice of the country's low standing in the international tourism rankings and began to heed promoters who promised extravagant profits from even a minuscule investment in advertising: "money spent to lure tourists, like the proverbial bread cast upon waters, often returns a hundredfold."[46]

Industry supporters often pointed out that the United States was losing considerable business by failing to compete on the same level as nations with national tourism promotion boards. As the U.S. Travel Bureau (USTB)—a division of the National Park Service (NPS) from February 1937 and established as a separate agency in July 1940—put it, "European nations have long appreciated the economic value of the tourist. They have realized that he is a commercial treasure chest. Here in America we have paid little attention to what is now our third largest industry." The memo then quoted leading newspapers and politicians arguing for the economic benefits of tourism and the importance of keeping U.S. residents at home while encouraging foreigners to visit—and spend money. In arguing for the creation of the travel bureau, the head of the NPS pointed out that such an agency "will place the United States on a par with other nations in the field of travel promotion." At the invitation of the park service, James W. Gerard, the former U.S. ambassador to Germany, pointed out in a radio broadcast that "for every dollar spent in America by foreign visitors eight dollars are spent abroad by American travelers. This is very likely attributable to the fact that 57 Foreign [*sic*] governments maintain offices in New York City and give active assistance in the promotion of travel."[47]

And it wasn't all about profits. Like its neighbors, the United States also turned to tourism to improve its international reputation. The USTB had as one of its aims to "develop international good will and understanding by encouraging foreign tourist and student groups to travel in the United States." In 1938, the bureau's radio program *America the Beautiful* began broadcasting on WNYC in New York, as well as by shortwave to Europe and South America in French, Spanish, German, and Portuguese. Episodes conducted virtual tours of the states of Maine, New Hampshire, Vermont, Massachusetts, Rhode Island, Connecticut, and Montana, as well as the territory of Hawai`i, with additional shows planned on Idaho, Oregon, Washington, Utah, Colorado, Wyoming, and the territory of Alaska.[48] (One can guess that major tourist destinations like Southern California and Florida were low on the program's list of priorities.)

A major focus of U.S. tourism promotion efforts in the 1930s was combating anti-Americanism and German and Japanese sympathies in Latin America. To this end, at some point in 1940 or 1941 the Office of Inter-American Affairs had its Inter-American Travel Committee take the unprecedented step of placing advertisements in the newspapers of several major Latin American countries inviting the locals to visit the United States. Reporting on the effectiveness of the campaign, researchers passed on comments from people who had seen the ads: "We already know the United States is the most wonderful country in the world," one remarked. "What I would like to see advertised is excursion rates to visit the United States or a special exchange rate for tourists, the way Germany, France and Italy did before the war to make it possible for us Chileans to go there." Echoing this complaint, others singled out the Grace Line—the U.S.-based steamship company that dominated passenger travel on the west coast of South America—for its prohibitive prices. A Venezuelan responded, "Congratulations on your United States travel advertisements! For the first time, South Americans are effectively invited to the United States, through their own newspapers. No longer are they simply expected to pose for the too-typical North American tourist." This writer considered the advertising campaign psychologically important for inter-American relations, even if it did not result in much actual travel.[49]

As this comment hints, just as Latin American governments believed that invisibly exporting their spontaneous capital to the United States would level the international playing field ideologically, U.S. officials believed they had to do the same to win the trust and friendship of the other peoples of the Western Hemisphere. As the United States entered the tourism lists, its advocates realized that they would have to confront U.S. racism and parochialism. Nazi propaganda, argued a statement of objectives for the Office of Inter-American Affairs, would harp on the negative stereotypes—deeply rooted in climatic determinism—that each side had of the other, such as "Latinos are niggers. Yanquis lynch niggers," "Latinos are dirty. Yanquis understand only a 'bathtub' culture," and "Latinos are hopeless [sic] inefficient. Yanquis are too damned efficient."[50] In combating such stereotypes, U.S. officials would have to elaborate a more welcoming vision of U.S. culture—something richer and warmer than homicidal bigotry and an obsession with hygiene and punctuality.

Such diplomatic campaigns were not the only way in which the circulation of the idea of culture challenged U.S. racial practices. Increasingly, the interest of promoters in multiplying circuits of travel and the number of people paying to move along them made white supremacy a political embarrassment and a hindrance to business. When U.S. officials in the Department of Territories and Insular Possessions (DTIP) and the Anglo-American Commission set about trying to promote the region in the late 1930s and early 1940s, they continually stumbled over the fact of U.S. whites' racism. In 1941, Virgin Islands acting governor Robert M. Lovett responded positively but cautiously to a proposal from the Alcoa Steamship Company to bring more pleasure travelers to the islands. Doing so would require expanded recreational facilities, which would in turn raise the question of whether the locals—mostly of Afro-Danish descent—would be able to use them. Any expansion of tourism "raises the awkward question of race discrimination," Lovett wrote. "I doubt whether the present Municipal Council will favor the extension of advantages which will be restricted, necessarily, to whites." Like Lovett, Coert DuBois trod delicately around the tendency of businesses serving foreign tourists to exclude nonwhite, nonelite locals from ostensibly public recreational facilities in his report to the Anglo-American Commission on the possibilities of developing the industry in the Caribbean. "Obviously," he wrote, "provision must be made for recreation and vacations of the local populations and this presents some problems." The solution was segregation: "Visitors from outside the area should not interfere with these established usages."[51]

The same problem hindered efforts to attract Latin Americans and Caribbeans to visit the United States. In a 1939 report to the Miami Chamber of Commerce on the benefits of setting up an "inter-American Trade Mart" in that city, general manager John L. Morris wrote that if Miami was to take advantage of the growing trade between the United States and its southern neighbors, its business leaders had to do something about racial segregation. This policy "has caused the defeat of the Trade Mart idea on other occasions," he pointed out. "Miami cannot hope to take her place in the favor of her South and Central American neighbors until such time as Miami makes provision for receiving properly and housing those neighbors. There can be very little cordiality, very little pretense of a Trade Mart and very little commerce in Miami from South and Central America until such time as the method of dealing with the foreign color line is changed." This was not a prediction but a reality: "That the President of Haiti and his official party could not remain in Miami overnight recently is to be deplored."[52] His solution was, like DuBois's, the provision of segregated facilities, in this case a luxurious "Western Hemisphere Club" where insufficiently pale officials and business people could stay during their visits.

Not surprisingly, U.S.-style segregation did not appeal to many in the Caribbean and Latin America. The political tensions and violence surrounding the construction of U.S. military bases on the islands during the war made that abundantly clear. In a 1940 discussion with the three members of the U.S. Commission to Study Social and Economic Conditions in the British West Indies, Jamaica's white governor warned his visitors that the islanders did not draw the color line. Black attorney and political activist Norman Manley—who would become the island's chief minister in the 1950s, after Jamaicans gained universal adult suffrage in 1944—begged to differ. He gave the officials "as an example his experience in the tourist hotels at Montego Bay. He said that no matter how empty they were he could not get reservations, the excuse always being that they were filled to capacity. This feeling on the part of Manley probably prompted a statement he made to the Chairman that the tourist trade was detrimental to the best interests of Jamaica."[53]

Manley's judgment reigns today among many scholars of tourism, especially tourism in the Caribbean and other tropical resorts, and for good reason.[54] But the fact that the Southland never realized the more progressive political and economic possibilities inherent in the romantic racialism of its promotional literature does not mean it merely sustained the existing web of inequalities. The transformation of the American tropics from the world's slave plantation to its luxury vacation resort reflected and contributed to considerable changes in mental and physical infrastructure, changes that made the tropics central to the way that Americans, at least, imagined modern bodies and societies. That modernity entailed the self-conscious revision of racial and sexual hierarchies into desirable cultural traits to be sold in an international marketplace. In the process of promoting this transformation, national governments and business leaders throughout the hemisphere rewrote laws and regulations to ensure that the tourist industry in the Southland severed the long-standing link between pleasure travel and colonization in the Americas.

CHAPTER 7

The Most Ideal Winter Resorts

By the 1930s, tourism, along with commercial horticulture, had come to seem the best, most civilized use of the tropics. The Southland, a transnational playground formed by an imputed tropicality, a sense of leisure and gaiety, Latin architecture and indigenous and African-flavored festivals, intense and constant sunshine, and amazingly plentiful fruits and flowers, had become a reality. Thanks to improvements in transportation and accommodations, the transformation of the landscape by plantations and resorts, and new ideas about health and the relationship between bodies and nature, the tropics no longer threatened the health and integrity of whites. Instead, they offered an essential vacation from the burdensome demands of civilization. Come and enjoy that "drowsy let-it-go-til tomorrow breeze," Jean Lane urged on behalf of the Panama Mail steamship line, for "it brings relaxation that contributes good capital in later eight hour working days."[1] Just as leisure had come to seem necessary for productive work, the tropics had become necessary for maintaining temperate civilization, a little darkness necessary for the success of whiteness. Natural differences had become cultural resources.

The rise of the Southland weakened the centuries-old link between colonization and pleasure travel in the Americas and correspondingly strengthened the idea that people would not be modified by moving to new places. Nature had lost its power to remake them. People could exchange places and the products of their differences freely because when properly managed such exchanges could only underscore, not blur, the critical cultural distinctions, and thus would produce mutually enriching relationships. The change in perspective is evident in the files of the Division of Territories and Insular Possessions, an office in the U.S. Department of the Interior, concerning the development of the Virgin Islands in the 1930s.

Purchased by the United States from Denmark for $25 million in 1917, the islands had hosted an important coaling station at the time and owning them bolstered U.S. naval power and commercial advantage in the region. At the port of Charlotte Amalie on St. Thomas, the lines of black women toiling up the ramps of steamships with baskets of coal on their heads were one of the characteristic tourist sights. But the shift to oil-fueled ships was already under way in 1917, and the people of St. Thomas, along with those on St. John and St. Croix, soon lost even this grueling source of income. Noting in 1937 that "it is difficult to comprehend on what the people of St. John live," the U.S.-appointed governor suggested to the secretary of the interior that the island be turned into a national park in the hope of stimulating more tourist travel.[2] In agreeing that tourism was the most feasible strategy for alleviating poverty and making the islands pay their own way, DTIP officials confirmed the transformation of temperate attitudes toward the tropics during the preceding fifty years.

The many proposals for developing the Virgin Islands that unemployed or underemployed travel industry managers and workers offered to the DTIP similarly underscored both the growing importance of the tourist industry and the sense that tourism was the chief purpose of tropical places. In one typical appeal, Ward M. Canaday, chairman of the board of Willy's Overland Motors, Inc., and Willy's American (a tour company), wrote to Secretary of the Interior Harold Ickes, "I am again impelled to call to your attention the fact that the Virgin Islands would make, with proper adjustment of transportation, one of the most ideal winter resorts in this hemisphere. The climate is perfect and the scenery, as you know, ideal." Moreover, in a point many made ·in this era of economic nationalism, "If Great Britain owned these islands, they would be rich with American tourist trade and transportation." Louise Redding, an experienced tour manager apparently laid off by the American Express Company, had both family in the Virgin Islands and extensive contacts in the industry: "I could use my knowledge to assist in a promotion that would spell returns on our $25,000000.00 [sic] a Mecca for tourists ALL OUR OWN, and a livelihood for myself." One self-described veteran hotel man wrote, "I can see the possibilities of making it [the Virgin Islands] a Resort place for Americans by Americans, that would put Bermuda in the shade, and I know personally lots and lots, who would be glad to go to a good United States Resort *if* we had one"—and he would like a job managing a hotel there to serve them.[3]

Although the DTIP responded to all these letters by informing the writers that the agency had no funds to support the proposed initiatives, in fact it had taken an active role in trying to develop tourism to the Virgin Islands and other federal dependencies, including Puerto Rico, Hawai`i, and Alaska. In 1931, the Virgin Islands governor had appealed to the DTIP for money to advertise the islands as a good home for summer and winter residents of moderate means, receiving $930 for publicity materials and postage, and a few people from the United States built vacation homes in the islands, while others rented cottages there for the winter in the late 1930s. Also in 1931, the federal government loaned money to the islands' business council to establish the Handicraft Cooperative to train the islands' palm-frond weavers to make items of interest to tourists and then sell them. In the mid-1930s, at the height of the New Deal, the DTIP funded the construction of the Bluebeard Hotel in Charlotte Amalie, promoted the erection of rental cottages on all three islands, and helped establish a local business development board. In a 1938 memo to his boss, the secretary of the interior, DTIP director Ernest Gruening was quite optimistic: "the Islands have finally arrived as a winter tourist resort, which certainly justifies the Federal Government's investment in the Bluebeard Castle Hotel, the adjoining cottages and apartment building," all of which had been leased to private companies and were sold out for the 1938–1939 winter season.[4]

But those who hoped that the Virgin Islands could rival the luxurious resorts of Nassau and Bermuda were disappointed, and not only because the federal government was redirecting its funds to war preparations by 1940. It became increasingly clear in the late 1930s that the islands would not be a winter home for the very wealthy but an afternoon's entertainment for well-to-do cruise passengers. By the 1930s, dozens of ships carried cruise passengers through the Caribbean each winter season, typically between November and April. The British line Cunard claimed to run eighteen West Indies cruises each winter in 1936, four of which were charters by the U.S. tour company Raymond-Whitcomb. Holland America offered six such tours in 1933, some twelve and some eighteen days long. Grace Line ran at least twelve sixteen-day cruises through the summer of 1938, with additional trips in the fall and winter seasons. United Fruit offered weekly sailings from New York and New Orleans by 1936–1937, taking tourists to Kingston and Havana along the way.[5]

The growing number of ships carried a growing number of passengers, particularly during the 1930s as the tourist class accommodations became more common and lines dropped prices to stay afloat during the Depression.

August Maffrey, a U.S. Department of Commerce analyst, counted 67,268 U.S. residents returning from cruises to Bermuda, the West Indies, and Central America (excluding Mexico) in 1932, a number that fluctuated for several years before reaching a prewar high of 85,835 in 1938. The Pan American Union's Travel Division found 71,359 U.S. residents cruising the West Indies (excluding Central America) in 1939, while more than 4,000 cruised to South America and another 4,200 to Central America.[6]

These numbers are small, whether compared to the total U.S. population in 1930—123 million—or the total of Caribbean cruise passengers in the early twenty-first century—5 million in 2008. But they represented a considerable increase in the number of tourists visiting Caribbean cities, and they became increasingly important to local economies, especially those that, like the Virgin Islands, had few other profitable enterprises. Tourism analyst A. J. Norval estimated that U.S. travelers spent between $10 and $16 million each year from 1929 to 1933 in the British West Indies alone. A 1939 Interior Department press release trumpeted the fact that "in 1934, the island [of St. Thomas, Virgin Islands] was visited by only eight cruise ships and the passengers purchased only $2,758 worth of native-made products," but by 1938, fifteen ships "carrying a total of 7,260 passengers, and spending a total of only about 90 hours in the island, left in their wake $11,179.93 at the Handicraft Cooperative alone." A table in the release listed each ship, the number of passengers, the total amount spent in port, and the average amount per passenger, from a low of 83¢ by the 646 passengers of Holland America's S.S. *Statendam* on February 8 to a high of $2.88 by the 674 traveling on Cunard's S.S. *Aquitania* on December 31.[7]

Although this report boasted that the cruise industry, in combination with the government-subsidized Handicraft Cooperative, would relieve the poverty of the Virgin Islanders, others were less sanguine. Travelers who came to stay, after all, would spend much more than a few dollars on hats and handkerchiefs; they would have to pay for hotel rooms, transportation, and meals, at a minimum, and at most they might become homeowners and investors. Thus a 1938 report on the convention trade in Cuba dismissed concerns over a decrease in the number of excursionists, meaning cruise passengers who lived aboard their ships and visited Cuba for only a day or two, by pointing to a rise in "tourists properly understood, that is, those who disembark and remain for several days, using our hotels and restaurants, visiting the interior of the republic and participating, during this time, in the life of the community."[8]

But as they made clear in the 1950s, many Cubans would have preferred a little less U.S. participation in the life of their community. Partially as a result of growing nationalism there and elsewhere, by the 1920s the old alliance between tourism and colonization ceased to represent the future of pleasure travel in the Southland. Contributing to this trend was the gradual extension of paid vacations to a growing number of U.S. workers. This new privilege enabled more to become tourists, but in a fashion quite unlike the leisurely, seasonal sojourns of late nineteenth-century travelers and without as much potential for residential construction and business investment. By 1938, the U.S. Bureau of Labor Statistics reported, nearly 40 percent of waged workers and 95 percent of salaried ones were employed by companies offering paid vacations. Typically these plans offered a week or two to long-term employees, raising the demand for short, relatively cheap tours. In the 1930s the steamship companies offered itineraries "to comply with current tourist trends," as Hamburg American put it, including cruises of seven, eight, nine, and thirteen, as well as the more usual nineteen days for prices ranging from $95 (the equivalent of about $1,400 in 2010) to $225 ($3,400). Given the speed of steamer travel, shorter cruises meant a focus on those places within a few days' sail of New York City. In thirteen days, one could go from New York to Kingston, Jamaica; Cartagena, Colombia; Colón, Panama; and Havana, Cuba, and return; in seven days, Nassau and Havana were the only ports of call.[9]

The cruise lines were not the only ones adjusting to the new reality in pleasure travel. The spread of automobile ownership and the construction of paved highways throughout the United States (Southern California and Florida were notable leaders in both) from the 1910s and Mexico from the 1920s similarly encouraged relatively short forays by people who might not have been able to afford steamship or rail fares, and auto camping by those who could not pay hotel charges. Compounding these new developments, the onset of the Great Depression encouraged tourist promoters throughout the Southland to offer short "bargain" vacations. For example, in 1933 Southern California's All Year Club advertised "a new 2 weeks vacation trip to CALIFORNIA," which if launched from the railroad hub of Chicago would give the visitor eleven days in the state. Assuming that all travelers would insist on hotel rooms with attached baths, the club outlined trips for "moderate," "average," and "better than average" budgets and promised "you'll come back with energy and enthusiasm renewed, your whole life enriched." In combination with the increasing availability of paid vacations, such developments help to explain why expenditures for travel fell less than spending on other recreational activities during the Depression. U.S. residents spent an estimated $495 million on vacations in 1909, rising to nearly $2.8 billion twenty years later. Although this sum fell to $1.8 billion in 1933, the nadir of the Depression, it rebounded to $2.3 billion just two years later, exceeding the figure for 1925.[10]

In responding to such trends and new border-crossing regimes, by the 1930s the industry was built around a form of tourism in which the host lands would be playgrounds for visitors, not places in which most would come to live, work, or invest. Whereas as late as 1919 at least one California businessman had called for the United States to invade Mexico and establish a government friendlier to U.S. investment, by 1930 the influential Automobile Club of Southern California was imploring Mexico's leaders to build more highways to encourage tourist travel: "The American people are spending $875,000,000 a year in Europe and $275,000,000 in Canada, and many of them are tiring of seeing the same sights year after year. They would welcome new sights and new customs if you will provide the roads."[11] The Southern Californians were particularly eager to see a highway extend down the Pacific Coast, erasing the material distinction between the two nations—a growing number of paved roads in California, few in northwestern Mexico—in order to enhance tourists' ability to experience the region's spiritual differences without hindrance and, presumably, to leave more money in local coffers while doing so.

Summing up a generation of change in the meaning of tourism in the region is a report prepared for the Anglo-American Caribbean Commission, formed by the U.S. and British governments in 1940 to plan for transferring control over the British West Indies to the United States in the event that Germany conquered Great Britain. One of the key issues was economic development, and in this context tourism merited an extensive study in 1943–1944. To begin with, participants rehearsed the truisms of the field: "It was brought out that this industry required little plant or supplies, that it could be quickly organised and that it would bring a market to the source of supply for many native arts, crafts, skills and products. That the area offered many exceptional recreational advantages was obvious but these had never been systematically surveyed." Stating that "people go vacationing in search of a better climate than their own, new and exotic scenery, interesting foreign peoples, arts and cultures, sports, points of historical and scientific interest, social gaiety, health and rest and peace," author Coert DuBois considered it obvious that all of these features could be found in the Caribbean—a notable transformation of attitude since the 1880s. The climate, in particular, was perfect: "It is considerably cooler than many parts of North America in the summer and delightfully warm in the winter." The 1944 report that followed proposed "a comprehensive recreational development plan for the British and American island possessions in the Caribbean Sea" with the hope of enlisting other nations and colonies in the region as the project showed its worth.[12]

An expression of Depression-era populism and the growing interest of states in managing their citizens' leisure, DuBois's report also demonstrates the extent to which sixty years of publicity had made the tropics everyone's fantasy and thus something that governments should actively seek to realize. Thus DuBois wrote, "Measures should be adopted by the local governments to insure that recreational areas which are essential to any area-wide scheme of development are made available for such use as will best serve the public interest." He proposed creating a Caribbean Vacation Travel Authority that would have the power to buy, sell, and lease property, initiate or approve development plans, and directly manage specific projects through private concessionaires or public agencies. An essential element in successfully transforming the region into a single, unified playground was lowering the barriers to international travel: "All Governments concerned should modify their existing laws, rules and regulations and enact whatever enabling legislation is necessary in order to facilitate in every possible way the entry and free passage from one jurisdiction to another with the minimum of documentation, customs and other charges and official routine of all visiting travellers and their personal effects"—the unrealized aim of several Pan American commercial conferences since 1931.[13]

Needless to say, nothing came of this ambitious plan after World War II. The difficulties of creating an agency that would treat the Caribbean islands solely in terms of where tourists might want to go, regardless of international borders, imperial affiliations, and other business interests, probably would have been insuperable under most circumstances. After the war, however, the United States retreated rapidly from its New Deal progressive activism, the European powers lay in ruins, and long-simmering independence movements came to a full boil on many islands. Still, the report's ambitions underscore the extent to which tourism seemed to many to be the region's best use, for the good of both residents and visitors. By summing up the transformation in attitudes toward the tropics, this document, along with the files of the DTIP and the plans—realized and unrealized—of U.S. tourism providers, demonstrates that the foundations of postwar efforts to jumpstart the development of the "third world" through tourism were laid well before that war.[14] The incorporation of the tropics by temperate peoples in the multiple ways described in this study was the mortar holding these foundations together because it became the idea of culture—the idea that the tropics offered a lifestyle through which sensual joy might be recovered without challenging the order of civilization.

The development of the Southland might have amounted to nothing more than the usual story of imperial incorporation and capitalist commodification, of course; that it did amount to more is because of the political events of the times. However conventional and profit oriented, the tourist businesses and writers who celebrated the Southland deployed elements of a romantic critique of civilization generated to a considerable degree by anti-imperial and antiracist movements around the world. To argue that U.S. whites needed the youthful gaiety of tropical peoples was not a declaration of solidarity with nationalists in Jamaica or Mexico, much less Cuba; it was not necessarily an endorsement of even the most conservative versions of mestizaje or racial democracy; but it was a concession that the white supremacist civilization born of the temperate zones of Europe and North America was not adequate to human happiness. That in itself marked a redrafting of the meaning of humanity, producing one more prone to admit the value, if not the equality, of nonwhite peoples. Responding to this romantic racialism, many U.S. tourists—most of them white, wealthy, and convinced of their own and their nation's superiority—accepted the invitation to go south and became in some measure tropical whites.

Today's global tourist South was constructed on these early twentieth-century foundations. To make this argument means acknowledging the extent to which modern notions of selfhood, encompassing romantic racialism, heterosexual liberalism, and the relationship with nature that undergirds both, were shaped by the conversion of the tropics from necessary peril to desirable resort for North American and European whites. It also means recognizing the significant role of the tourist industry in remaking the ways that people conceived of and encountered human and environmental variation in the early decades of the twentieth century. Although people and places have differed from each other in systematic as well as idiosyncratic ways forever, since the 1880s the culture concept and the tourist industry have been integral elements in organizing and teaching such differences. In the early twenty-first century, we are very much creatures of the ecosystem they established.

NOTES

The following abbreviations appear in the notes.

AACC	Anglo-American Caribbean Commission
AFA	Allen Family Archive, Palo Alto, California
AGE	Archivo Genaro Estrada (Mexico)
ANC	Autry National Center
Bennett	Eleanor F. Bennett Diaries
BL	Braun Library, Autry National Center
CDC	Carrie Dunlap Collection
CEHM	Centro de Estudios de la Historia Mexicana (Mexico)
CL	Columbus Library, Organization of American States
CSWR	Center for Southwest Research, University of New Mexico
Dexter	Samuel Frank Dexter Papers
DL	Degolyer Library, Southern Methodist University
DTIP	Division of Territories and Insular Possessions (United States)
EFP	Ed Fletcher Papers
GFP	Gilpin Family Papers
HL	Huntington Library
HM	HistoryMiami (formerly the Historical Museum of South Florida)
Ingram	Selena Gray Galt Ingram Diaries
JJK	Joseph John Kirkbride Papers
KMEC	Kemble Maritime Ephemera Collection
LMDO	Luis Montes de Oca Collection
LST	Lottie S. Tillotson Collection
MDLC	Manuscript Division, Library of Congress (United States)
MSC	Mandeville Special Collections
Munroe	Kirk Munroe Papers
NARA I	National Archives and Records Administration, Washington, D.C. (United States)
NARA II	National Archives and Records Administration, College Park, Md. (United States)
NPSCCF	National Park Service Central Classified Files (United States)

OCPC   Ocean Cruise Pamphlet Collection
OFIAA   Office of Inter-American Affairs (United States)
OTCF   Office of the Territories Classified Files (United States)
PAAC   Pan American Airways Collection
Remondino   Peter C. Remondino Papers
RG   Record group
SC   Seaver Center for Western History, Los Angeles County Museum of Nat-
              ural History
SCRL   Special Collections, Richter Library, University of Miami
SDHS   San Diego Historical Society
SRE   Secretaria de Relaciones Exteriores (Mexico)
UCSD   University of California, San Diego

Introduction

1. Ida M. H. Starr, *Garden of the Caribbees: Sketches of a Cruise to the West Indies and the Spanish Main*, vol. 1 (Boston: L. C. Page, 1903): 11; *Go East by Sea* (Panama Mail, ca. 1920s): back cover, Panama Mail folder 1, KMEC, HL; illustration captioned "A Market in Barbados," *Travel* 40:1 (November 1922): 24; Stacy May and Galo Plaza, *The United Fruit Company in Latin America*, 7th Case Study in an NPA Series on United States Business Performance Abroad (n.p.: National Planning Association, 1958): 18.

2. Anne McClintock, *Imperial Leather: Race, Gender and Sexuality in the Colonial Contest* (New York: Routledge, 1995): 31, 61, 163, 214, 230–231.

3. Starr, *Garden of the Caribbees*, vol. 1, 11, 37.

4. Stephen Graham, *In Quest of El Dorado* (New York: D. Appleton, 1923): 167; Ward M. Canaday, chairman, Willy's Overland Motors, Inc., Willy's Americar, to Harold L. Ickes, secretary of the interior, February 25, 1941, file DTIP—Virgin Islands—Tourist and Winter Residence Development—General, box 1313, Virgin Islands Tourist Development, 9-11-42, OTCF, 1907–1951, RG 126, NARA II.

5. Untitled, *Travel* 1:4 (October 1901): 9; untitled, *Travel* 1:6 (December 1901): 24; John R. Gilpin to his sister, Mrs. W. P. (Sue) Hazard, January 18, 1880, 1, folder 1, box 1, GFP, HM.

6. Adolph Sutro, journal of a trip to Mexico, Cuba, and Florida, February–April, 1889: A19, B9, HL; Charles Warner, *Our Italy* (New York: Harper and Bros., 1891); *Plan of Two Excursions to Florida, by the Florida Excursion Co.* (Boston: Florida Excursion Co., 1884): 1; *Florida and Cuba, Winter 1913–14* (Thomas Cook and Son, Programme No. 42, 1913): 3; *Raymond-Whitcomb Cruises: West Indies, 1926* (Raymond-Whitcomb, 1925): 7, in Norddeutscher Lloyd folder 42, KMEC, HL; Matthew Pratt Guterl, "An American Mediterranean: Haiti, Cuba, and the American South," in Caroline F. Levander and Robert S. Levine, eds., *Hemispheric American Studies* (New Brunswick,

N.J.: Rutgers University Press, 2008): 96–115. Conevery Bolton Valenčius, *The Health of the Country: How American Settlers Understood Themselves and Their Land* (New York: Basic Books, 2002): 231, notes that some antebellum U.S. residents regarded the middle Mississippi valley (the states of Missouri and Arkansas) as tropical.

7. Philip Sanford Marden, *Sailing South* (Boston: Houghton Mifflin, 1921): 19–21, describing the "vague notions" U.S. residents had of the Caribbean islands; Philip J. Pauly, *Fruits and Plains: The Horticultural Transformation of America* (Cambridge, Mass.: Harvard University Press, 2007): 203–207; Jill Casid, *Sowing Empire: Landscape and Colonization* (Minneapolis: University of Minnesota Press, 2005); Krista A. Thompson, *An Eye for the Tropics: Tourism, Photography, and Framing the Caribbean Picturesque* (Durham, N.C.: Duke University Press, 2006).

8. David Arnold, *The Problem of Nature: Environment, Culture and European Expansion* (Oxford: Blackwell, 1996): 141–168; Felix Driver and Luciana Martins, eds., *Tropical Visions in an Age of Empire* (Chicago: University of Chicago Press, 2005); Edmundo Desnoes, "El caribe: paraiso/infierno," in Rose S. Minc, ed., *Literatures in Transition: The Many Voices of the Caribbean Area* (Montclair, N.J.: Montclair State College, Ediciones Hispamérica, 1982): 9–16; on environmental determinism, see, among many others, Gary Y. Okihiro, *Pineapple Culture: A History of the Tropical and Temperate Zones* (Berkeley: University of California Press, 2009); David N. Livingstone, "The Moral Discourse of Climate: Historical Considerations on Race, Place and Virtue," *Journal of Historical Geography* 17:4 (1991): 413–434, and "Climate's Moral Economy: Science, Race and Place in Post-Darwinian British and American Geography," in Anne Godlewska and Neil Smith, eds., *Geography and Empire* (Oxford: Blackwell, 1994): 132–154; Warwick Anderson, "Climates of Opinion: Acclimatization in Nineteenth-Century France and England," *Victorian Studies* 32:2 (1992): 135–157.

9. Arnold, *Problem of Nature*, 141–168; Driver and Martins, *Tropical Visions*; and the sources cited for environmental determinism in the previous note. On tropicality in the twentieth century, see Nancy Leys Stepan, *Picturing Tropical Nature* (London: Reaktion Books, 2001); David Arnold, "'Illusory Riches': Representations of the Tropical World, 1840–1950," *Singapore Journal of Tropical Geography* 21:1 (March 2000): 6–18. For the literature on beach resorts, see John K. Walton, "Introduction," in John K. Walton, ed., *Histories of Tourism: Representation, Identity and Conflict* (Clevedon, U.K.: Channel View Publications, 2005): 12.

10. George W. Stocking, Jr., *Race, Culture, and Evolution: Essays in the History of Anthropology* (Chicago: University of Chicago Press, 1982); Adam Kuper, *Culture: The Anthropologists' Account* (Cambridge, Mass.: Harvard University Press, 2000); Elazar Barkan, *The Retreat of Scientific Racism: Changing Concepts of Race in Britain and the United States Between the World Wars* (Cambridge: Cambridge University Press, 1992). These are complex, sophisticated intellectual histories; it is their reduction to simplistic teleology that I criticize in the next paragraph of the text.

11. Scholars have long recognized the inadequacy of the usual story of race and culture, as an abundant literature on the two topics shows; see, among many others,

Michael A. Eliot, *The Culture Concept: Writing and Difference in the Age of Realism* (Minneapolis: University of Minnesota Press, 2002); Brad Evans, *Before Cultures: The Ethnographic Imagination in American Literature, 1865–1920* (Chicago: University of Chicago Press, 2005); Matthew Pratt Guterl, *The Color of Race in America, 1900–1940* (Cambridge, Mass.: Harvard University Press, 2001); Susan Hegeman, *Patterns for America: Modernism and the Concept of Culture* (Princeton, N.J.: Princeton University Press, 1999); Christopher Herbert, *Culture and Anomie: Ethnographic Imagination in the Nineteenth Century* (Chicago: University of Chicago Press, 1991); Kuper, *Culture*; Walter Benn Michaels, "Race into Culture: a Critical Genealogy of Cultural Identity," *Critical Inquiry* 18:4 (Summer 1992): 655–685; Ann Laura Stoler, "Racial Histories and Their Regimes of Truth," *Political Power and Social Theory* 11 (1997): 183–206; Donald S. Moore, Anand Pandian, and Jake Kosek, "The Cultural Politics of Race and Nature: Terrains of Power and Practice," in Donald S. Moore, Jake Kosek, and Anand Pandian, eds., *Race, Nature, and the Politics of Difference* (Durham, N.C.: Duke University Press, 2003): 1–70.

12. Hegeman, *Patterns for America*, 1–14, 64; Walter Benn Michaels, *Our America: Nativism, Modernism, and Pluralism* (Durham, N.C.: Duke University Press, 1995); Akhil Gupta and James Ferguson, eds., *Culture, Power, Place: Explorations in Critical Anthropology* (Durham, N.C.: Duke University Press, 1997); Carrie Tirado Bramen, *The Uses of Variety: Modern Americanism and the Quest for National Distinctiveness* (Cambridge, Mass.: Harvard University Press, 2000).

13. Michaels, "Race into Culture," 655–685; Stoler, "Racial Histories and Their Regimes of Truth," 183–206; Diana Selig, *Americans All: The Cultural Gifts Movement* (Cambridge, Mass.: Harvard University Press, 2008).

14. On romantic racialism, see Partha Chatterjee, *Nationalist Thought and the Colonial World: A Derivative Discourse?* (London: Zed, 1986); George Frederickson, *The Black Image in the White Mind: The Debate on Afro-American Character and Destiny, 1817–1914* (Middletown, Conn.: Wesleyan University Press, 1987); Wilson J. Moses, *The Golden Age of Black Nationalism, 1850–1925* (New York: Oxford University Press, 1978); Marianna Torgovnick, *Gone Primitive: Savage Intellects, Modern Lives* (Chicago: University of Chicago, 1990); Kuper, *Culture*, 23–46. On desire and the idea of culture, see Herbert, *Culture and Anomie*. I use "heterosexual liberalism" to describe what is usually (but misleadingly) termed the sexual revolution; see my essay "Rethinking Sexuality in the Progressive Era," *Journal of the Gilded Age and Progressive Era* 5:2 (April 2006): 94–118. The term "sexual liberalism" originates with John D'Emilio and Estelle Freedman, *Intimate Matters: A History of Sexuality in America* (New York: Harper and Row, 1988): xviii, 241, who intend "liberal" to be understood in the classic sense of the assumption that individuals' pursuit of their own happiness will produce a good society. I added the "hetero" because liberalization initially involved the stigmatization of same-sex affections and relationships; see Jonathan Ned Katz, *The Invention of Heterosexuality* (New York: Dutton, 1995); Christina Simmons, *Making Marriage Modern: Women's Sexuality from the Progressive Era to World War II* (Oxford: Oxford University Press, 2009).

15. W. E. B. Du Bois, *The Gift of Black Folk: The Negroes in the Making of America*, with an introduction by Carl A. Anderson (Garden City, N.Y.: Square One, 2009 [1924]): 151, and *The Souls of Black Folk*, with an introduction by Donald B. Gibson (New York: Penguin, 1989 [1903]): 5. Du Bois wrote *The Gift* at the invitation of the Knights of Columbus, which sponsored a series on the Jewish, African American, and German gifts to U.S. society in response to the rise of the Ku Klux Klan and anti-immigrant sentiment after World War I. On Du Bois's romantic writings, see Susan Gillman and Alys Eve Weinbaum, eds., *Next to the Color Line: Gender, Sexuality, and W. E. B. Du Bois* (Minneapolis: University of Minnesota Press, 2007).

16. I critique this portrayal at greater length in "Rethinking Sexuality in the Progressive Era"; see also D'Emilio and Freedman, *Intimate Matters*, 171–235; Simmons, *Making Marriage Modern*; and Christine Stansell, *American Moderns: Bohemian New York and the Creation of a New Century* (New York: Henry Holt, 2000).

17. On race and sexuality, see Ann Laura Stoler, *Carnal Knowledge and Imperial Power: Race and the Intimate in Colonial Rule* (Berkeley: University of California Press, 2002); McClintock, *Imperial Leather*; Laura Briggs, *Reproducing Empire: Race, Sex, Science, and U.S. Imperialism in Puerto Rico* (Berkeley: University of California Press, 2002); Eileen J. Suárez Findlay, *Imposing Decency: The Politics of Sexuality and Race in Puerto Rico, 1870–1920* (Durham, N.C.: Duke University Press, 1999); Glenda Gilmore, *Gender and Jim Crow: Women and the Politics of White Supremacy in North Carolina, 1896–1920* (Chapel Hill: University of North Carolina Press, 1996); Julian B. Carter, *The Heart of Whiteness: Normal Sexuality and Race in America, 1880–1940* (Durham, N.C.: Duke University Press, 2007), among many others.

18. Rebecca Steinitz, "The Illusion of Exchange: Gift, Trade, and Theft in the Nineteenth-Century British Voyage Narrative," *LIT* 7:2–3 (1996): 153–165; Mary Louise Pratt, *Imperial Eyes: Travel Writing and Transculturation* (New York: Routledge, 1992): 78–85.

19. Herbert, *Culture and Anomie*; compare the transformation in the meaning of wilderness in William Cronon, "The Trouble with Wilderness or, Getting Back to the Wrong Nature," *Environmental History* 1:1 (January 1996): 7–28.

20. Leonard Keene Hirshberg, "Doctors of Preventive Medicine Finding New Sanitary Weapons," *Chicago Daily Tribune* (April 20, 1913): E4; Michael Berkowitz, "A 'New Deal' for Leisure: Making Mass Tourism During the Great Depression," in Shelley Baranowski and Ellen Furlough, eds., *Being Elsewhere: Tourism, Consumer Culture, and Identity in Modern Europe and North America* (Ann Arbor: University of Michigan Press, 2001): 185–212; Kristin L. Hoganson, *Consumers' Imperium: The Global Production of American Domesticity, 1865–1920* (Chapel Hill: University of North Carolina Press, 2007): 153–208; for the examples, in the order they are given in the text, see Arthur W. Page, "Our Nearest Latin Neighbor," *Travel* 16:3 (January 1911): 112–115; "Harding Leaves Marion for South," *Boston Globe* (January 21, 1921): 11; "Hoover, Sun-Tanned, Starts for Capital," *New York Times* (February 16, 1930): 1; Mme. X, "News of Chicago Society/Jamaica a Land of Enchantment for Northern Tourists," *Chicago*

Daily Tribune (March 7, 1920): E4; F. P. Dunne, "Mr. Dooley on Vacations," *Boston Globe* (August 15, 1909): 45; Ring Lardner, "'Unique and Extraordinary,'" *Boston Globe* (March 4, 1923): A5; "That Piratical Film," *New York Times* (September 29, 1929): X8; "Movie Facts and Fancies," *Boston Globe* (May 11, 1924): A10; Patricia King Hanson and Alan Gevinson, eds., *The American Film Institute Catalog of Motion Pictures Produced in the United States, Feature Films, 1911–1920, Credit and Subject Indexes* (Berkeley: University of California Press, 1988), and *The American Film Institute Catalog of Motion Pictures Produced in the United States, Feature Films, 1931–1940, Credit and Subject Indexes* (Berkeley: University of California Press, 1993), and Kenneth W. Minden, ed., *The American Film Institute Catalog of Motion Pictures Produced in the United States, Feature Films, 1921–1930, Credit and Subject Indexes* (New York: R. R. Bowker, 1971), works that list about four hundred films on Mexico, Mexicans, and the U.S.-Mexico border, with hundreds more featuring California, Florida, and the Caribbean; "Golfers Going South," *New York Times* (December 13, 1908): S3; "Western Golfers in Lead in Palm Beach Tournament," *Chicago Daily Tribune* (February 15, 1910): 12; "Robins on Holiday in Florida Camp," *New York Times* (March 17, 1924): 11; Kenneth L. Roberts, *Sun Hunting: Adventures and Observations Among the Native and Migratory Tribes of Florida, Including the Stoical Time-Killers of Palm Beach, the Gentle and Gregarious Tin-Canners of the Remote Interior, and the Vivacious and Semi-Violent Peoples of Miami and Its Purlieus* (Indianapolis: Bobbs-Merrill, 1922): 85–102.

21. Stuart Hall, "Conclusion: The Multi-cultural Question," in Barnor Hesse, ed., *Un/Settled Multiculturalisms: Diasporas, Entanglements, "Transruptions"* (London: Zed Books, 2000): 210; William Deverell, *Whitewashed Adobe: The Rise of Los Angeles and the Remaking of Its Mexican Past* (Berkeley: University of California Press, 2004); Andrew Sackett, "Fun in Acapulco? The Politics of Development on the Mexican Riviera," in Dina Berger and Andrew Wood, eds., *Holiday in Mexico: Critical Reflections on Tourism and Tourist Encounters* (Durham, N.C.: Duke University Press, 2010): 161–182; Frank Fonda Taylor, *To Hell with Paradise: A History of the Jamaican Tourist Industry* (Pittsburgh: University of Pittsburgh Press, 1993); Richard Rosa, "Business as Pleasure: Culture, Tourism, and Nation in Puerto Rico in the 1930s," *Nepantla: Views from the South* 2:3 (2001): 449–488; Thompson, *An Eye for the Tropics*; Lawrence Culver, *The Frontier of Leisure: Southern California and the Shaping of Modern America* (Oxford: Oxford University Press, 2010); Rick A. López, *Crafting Mexico: Intellectuals, Artisans, and the State After the Revolution* (Durham, N.C.: Duke University Press, 2010); Christine Skwiot, *The Purposes of Paradise: U.S. Tourism and Empire in Cuba and Hawai'i* (Philadelphia: University of Pennsylvania Press, 2010); Polly Pattullo, *Last Resorts: The Costs of Tourism in the Caribbean* (London: Cassell, 1996); Mimi Sheller, *Consuming the Caribbean: From Arawaks to Zombies* (London: Routledge, 2003).

Chapter 1. A Regulated Arcadia

1. "Potts, the Troubadour," *Overland Monthly* (August 1870): 170–171, 175.
2. "Potts, the Troubador," 175.

3. Michael Dawson, *Selling British Columbia: Tourism and Consumer Culture, 1890–1970* (Vancouver: University of British Columbia Press, 2004); Catherine Cocks, *Doing the Town: The Rise of Urban Tourism in the United States, 1850–1915* (Berkeley: University of California Press, 2001): 106–142; Marguerite S. Shaffer, *See America First: Tourism and National Identity, 1880–1940* (Washington, D.C.: Smithsonian Institution Press, 2001); Robert Campbell, *In Darkest Alaska: Travel and Empire Along the Inside Passage* (Philadelphia: University of Pennsylvania Press, 2007); Christine Skwiot, *The Purposes of Paradise: U.S. Tourism and Empire in Cuba and Hawai'i* (Philadelphia: University of Pennsylvania Press, 2010).

4. Jefferson qtd. in A. Cash Koeniger, "Climate and Southern Distinctiveness," *Journal of Southern History* 54:1 (1988): 21; Charles de Secondat, Baron de Montesquieu, *The Spirit of the Laws*, trans. and ed. Anne M. Collier, Basia Carolyn Miller, and Harold Samuel Stone (Cambridge: Cambridge University Press, 1989 [1748]): 232–233 (quotation), 236, 246–252, 269, 271. The literature on climate and race is quite large; among many others, see Gary Y. Okihiro, *Pineapple Culture: A History of the Tropical and Temperate Zones* (Berkeley: University of California Press, 2009); David N. Livingstone, "The Moral Discourse of Climate: Historical Considerations on Race, Place and Virtue," *Journal of Historical Geography* 17:4 (1991): 413–434, and Livingstone, "Climate's Moral Economy: Science, Race and Place in Post-Darwinian British and American Geography," in Anne Godlewska and Neil Smith, eds., *Geography and Empire* (Oxford: Blackwell, 1994): 132–154; on European attitudes toward the tropics, David Arnold, *The Problem of Nature: Environment, Culture and European Expansion* (Oxford: Blackwell, 1996): 22–23.

5. Hadley Cantril, "Representative Opinion and Information Concerning Latin America: Confidential Report for James Young," folder American Social Surveys Export Information Bureau #9, box 137, OFIAA, general records, central files, RG 229, NARA II. The records do not offer any information on respondents' demographics. The three terms mentioned in the text were the second, third, and sixth most often selected; first was "dark-skinned," the choice of 76.9 percent; fourth was "religious" (42.6) and fifth "backward" (41.7).

6. David N. Livingstone, "Human Acclimatization: Perspectives on a Contested Field of Inquiry in Science, Medicine and Geography," *History of Science* 25 (1987): 359–394; Mark Harrison, "'The Tender Frame of Man': Disease, Climate, and Racial Difference in India and the West Indies, 1760–1860," *Bulletin of the History of Medicine* 70 (1996): 68–93; Karen Ordahl Kupperman, "Fear of Hot Climates in the Anglo-American Colonial Experience," *William and Mary Quarterly*, 3rd series, 41:2 (April 1984): 213–240; Philip Curtin, *Death by Migration: Europe's Encounter with the Tropical World in the Nineteenth Century* (Cambridge: Cambridge University Press, 1989); Nancy Leys Stepan, *"The Hour of Eugenics": Race, Gender, and Nation in Latin America* (Ithaca, N.Y.: Cornell University Press, 1991).

7. Arnold, *Problem of Nature*, 26–30; Livingstone, "Climate's Moral Economy" and "Human Acclimatization"; Harrison, "'The Tender Frame of Man.'"

8. Ellsworth Huntington, *The Character of Races as Influenced by Physical Environment, Natural Selection and Historical Development* (New York: Charles Scribner's Sons, 1924): 33; Ellen Churchill Semple, *Influences of Geographic Environment on the Basis of Ratzel's System of Anthropo-Geography* (New York: Henry Holt, 1911): 629, 635. For context, see Arnold, *Problem of Nature*, 158–160, and his " 'Illusory Riches': Representations of the Tropical World, 1840–1950," *Singapore Journal of Tropical Geography* 21:1 (March 2000): 6–18.

9. Arnold, *Problem of Nature*, 48, 144–147; Richard H. Grove, *Green Imperialism: Colonial Expansion, Tropical Island Edens and the Origins of Environmentalism, 1600–1800* (Cambridge: Cambridge University Press, 1995): 153, 476–478.

10. James Anthony Froude, *The English in the West Indies; Or, The Bow of Ulysses* (New York: Negro Universities Press, 1969 [1888]): 49–50; Semple, *Influences*, 620.

11. Harriet Beecher Stowe, *Palmetto Leaves*, with introductions by Mary B. Graff and Edith Cowles (Gainesville: University Press of Florida, 1999 [1873]): 155 (similarly, Froude, *English in the West Indies*, 23, wrote that upon entering the tropics "we had passed suddenly from winter into perpetual summer, as Jean Paul says it will be with us in death"); Semple, *Influences*, 621. On the cycle of seasons and Christian theology, see Michael Kammen, *A Time to Every Purpose: The Four Seasons in American Culture* (Chapel Hill: University of North Carolina Press, 2004).

12. Harrison, " 'Tender Frame of Man' "; Arnold, " 'Illusory Riches.' "

13. Robert De C. Ward, "The Acclimatization of the White Race in the Tropics," *Annual Report of the Board of Regents of the Smithsonian Institution, 1930* (Washington, D.C.: Government Printing Office, 1931; reprinted from the *New England Journal of Medicine* 201:13 [September 26, 1929]: 617–627): 561; Semple, *Influences*, 37; on English colonists' fears, see Kupperman, "Fear of Hot Climates," 214–215.

14. Joseph Kirkbride, Monday, February 15, and Friday, February 26, 1897, 1896 journal, JJK, MDLC; Ward, "Acclimatization," 566; on the epidemics and government reactions, see Mariola Espinosa, *Epidemic Invasions: Yellow Fever and the Limits of Cuban Independence, 1878–1930* (Chicago: University of Chicago Press, 2009); *Documents Required and Visa Fees for Tourists Entering Latin American Republics; Also, Requirements for Leaving These Countries* (Washington, D.C.: Pan American Union, 1931): 3, 12.

15. Ward, "Acclimatization," 564; T. Philip Terry, *Terry's Mexico: Handbook for Travellers*, 2nd ed. (London: Gay and Hancock; Boston: Houghton Mifflin; Mexico City: Sonora News, 1911): xxx (this warning, along with other health concerns, had vanished by the 1940 edition); on physicians' concerns, see Dane Kennedy, "The Perils of the Midday Sun: Climatic Anxieties in the Colonial Tropics," in John M. McKenzie, ed., *Imperialism and the Natural World* (Manchester: Manchester University Press, 1990): 118–140; Simon Carter, *Rise and Shine: Sunlight, Technology, and Health* (Oxford: Berg, 2007).

16. Charles Woodruff, *The Effects of Tropical Light on White Men* (New York: Rebman, 1905): 4, 323 (quotation, italics in the original), 326, 328, 334–335, 340, 345–346; see also Ward, "Acclimatization," 564, 565; Warwick Anderson, "The Trespass Speaks:

White Masculinity and Colonial Breakdown," *American Historical Review* 102:5 (December 1997): 1343–1370.

17. Semple, *Influences*, 626; Huntington, *Civilization and Climate* (New Haven, Conn.: Yale University Press, 1915): 41.

18. Charles Dudley Warner, *Our Italy* (New York: Harper & Brothers, 1891): 88; Emma Gilpin to Mrs. W. P. (Sue) Hazard, May 8, 1890, 1, folder 5, box 1, GFP, HM; Stephen Graham, *In Quest of El Dorado* (New York: D. Appleton, 1923): 165; C. W. Johnston, *Along the Pacific by Land and Sea: Through the Golden Gate* (Chicago: Rand McNally, 1916): 252, 248.

19. A. Grenfell Price, with additional notes by Robert G. Stone, *White Settlers in the Tropics*, American Geographical Society Special Publication No. 23 (New York: American Geographical Society, 1939): 31, 69; Ruth Bryan Owen to Carrie Dunlap, August 9, 1911, 2, folder 29, CDC, SCRL. Kitty's relationship to Owen is unclear; she might have been a sister, niece, or cousin. The daughter of prominent U.S. politician William Jennings Bryan, Owen was married to an officer in the British army who was stationed in Jamaica. In the 1930s, after divorce, remarriage, and a career in public service, she advocated the creation of the U.S. Travel Bureau (see Chapter 6).

20. Addison Awes, Jr., *"Son of a Revolutionary Sire," Why a Rich Yankee Did Not Settle in California* (Boston: Cubery, 1900): 5, 37, 38, 56 (quotations), 61.

21. Julius Muller, "The Caribbean Tropics: A Rich Man's Heaven and a Poor Man's Hell," *Century* 87 (January 1914): 369; Charles Dudley Warner, "Race and Climate," *Land of Sunshine* 4:3 (February 1896): 103.

22. Muller, "Caribbean Tropics," 373; Montesquieu, *Spirit of the Laws*, 251; Henry Fairfield Osborn, foreword to Madison Grant, *Passing of the Great Race: Or, The Racial Basis of European History*, 4th rev. ed. (New York: Charles Scribner's Sons, 1923): 10–11; Ronald G. Walters, "The Erotic South: Civilization and Sexuality in American Abolitionism," *American Quarterly* 25:2 (May 1973): 177–201; Eric T. Love, *Race over Imperialism: Racism and U.S. Imperialism, 1865–1900* (Chapel Hill: University of North Carolina Press, 2004). A counterdiscourse emerged in Australia: Price, *White Settlers in the Tropics*, 52–76; Warwick Anderson, *The Cultivation of Whiteness: Science, Health, and Racial Destiny in Australia* (Durham, N.C.: Duke University Press, 2006).

23. Muller, "Caribbean Tropics," 374; Lothrop Stoddard, *The Rising Tide of Color Against White World-Supremacy* (New York: Charles Scribner's Sons, 1920): 107–108, 113.

24. Price, *White Settlers in the Tropics*, 47; Warner, "Race and Climate," 105; Fredrik B. Pike, *The United States and Latin America: Myths and Stereotypes of Civilization and Nature* (Austin: University of Texas Press, 1992); Mark C. Anderson, "What's to Be Done with 'Em? Images of Mexican Cultural Backwardness, Racial Limitations, and Moral Decrepitude in the United States Press, 1913–1915," *Mexican Studies/Estudios Mexicanos* 14:1 (Winter 1998): 23–70; David J. Weber, "Here Rests Juan Espinosa: Toward a Clearer Look at the Image of the 'Indolent' Californios," *Western Historical Quarterly* 10:1 (January 1979): 61–69, and *New Spain's Far Northern Frontier: Essays on Spain in the American*

West, 1540–1821 (Dallas: Southern Methodist University Press, 1979): 295–307; James William Park, *Latin American Underdevelopment: A History of Perspectives in the United States, 1870–1965* (Baton Rouge: Louisiana State University Press, 1995).

25. Skwiot, *Purposes of Paradise*; Louis A. Pérez, Jr., *Cuba and the United States: Ties of Singular Intimacy*, 2d ed. (Athens: University of Georgia Press, 1997); William Schell, Jr., *Integral Outsiders: The American Colony in Mexico City, 1876–1911* (Wilmington, Del.: Scholarly Resources, 2001); John Mason Hart, *Empire and Revolution: The Americans in Mexico Since the Civil War* (Berkeley: University of California Press, 2002).

26. Charles J. Kenworthy, M.D., *Climatology of Florida* (Savannah, Ga.: Morning News Steam Printing House, 1881): 17; for context, see Conevery Bolton Valenčius, *The Health of the Country: How American Settlers Understood Themselves and Their Land* (New York: Basic Books, 2002).

27. Peter C. Remondino, first typescript, p. 5, folder 10, box 4, Remondino, SDHS; for context, see Valenčius, *Health of the Country*; John E. Baur, *The Health Seekers of Southern California, 1870–1900* (San Marino, Calif.: Huntington Library, 1959); Billy M. Jones, *Health-Seekers in the Southwest, 1817–1900* (Norman: University of Oklahoma Press, 1967); Linda Nash, *Inescapable Ecologies: A History of Environment, Disease, and Knowledge* (Berkeley: University of California Press, 2006).

28. William F. Hutchinson, *Under the Southern Cross: A Guide to the Sanitariums and Other Charming Places in the West Indies and Spanish Main* (Providence, R.I.: Ryder & Dearth, 1891): 17; Kenworthy, *Climatology of Florida*, 7 (he is quoting Tanner, *Practice of Medicine*, 782, but gives no publication information); see also James Johnson, *Jamaica: The New Riviera: a Pictorial Description of the Island and Its Attractions* (London: Cassell, 1903): 7, 24.

29. *Tropical Trips and Tourist Hotel Directory, Season 1910–11* (Wilmington, Del.: Atlantic Coast Line, 1910): 1–2; Hutchinson, *Southern Cross*, 9; for context, see W. M. L. Jay, *My Winter in Cuba* (New York: E. P. Dutton, 1871); Julia Ward Howe, *A Trip to Cuba* (New York: Negro Universities Press, 1969 [1870]); Froude, *English in the West Indies*, 297, 309; Johnson, *Jamaica*; Mary Blume, *Côte d'Azur: Inventing the French Riviera* (London: Thames and Hudson, 1992); Jim Ring, *Riviera: The Rise and Rise of the Côte d'Azur* (London: John Murray, 2004); Susan C. Anderson and Bruce H. Tabb, *Water, Leisure and Culture: European Historical Perspectives* (Oxford: Berg, 2002); Theodore Corbett, *The Making of American Resorts: Saratoga Springs, Ballston Spa, Lake George* (New Brunswick, N.J.: Rutgers University Press, 2001); Thomas A. Chambers, *Drinking the Waters: Creating an American Leisure Class at Nineteenth-Century Mineral Springs* (Washington, D.C.: Smithsonian Institution Press, 2002); John K. Walton, *The English Seaside Resort: A Social History, 1750–1914* (New York: St. Martin's Press, 1983), and "The Seaside Resorts of Western Europe, 1750–1939," in Stephen Fisher, ed., *Recreation and the Sea* (Exeter, U.K.: University of Exeter Press, 1997): 36–56; Alain Corbin, *The Lure of the Sea: The Discovery of the Seaside in the Western World, 1750–1840*, trans. Jocelyn Phelps (Berkeley: University of California Press, 1994; orig. *Le territoire du vide*, 1988).

30. F. C. S. Sanders, *California as a Health Resort* (San Francisco: Bolte & Braden, 1916): 37; Kenworthy, *Climatology of Florida*, 46; P. C. Remondino, *The Mediterranean Shores of America: Southern California: Climatic, Physical, and Meteorological Conditions* (Philadelphia: F. A. David, 1892): 127; Anna Dexter, February 5, 1901, Dexter, HL. Hutchinson, *Southern Cross*, 21, called sightseeing "that hardest of work" and advised the sick to avoid it.

31. Hutchinson, *Southern Cross*, 13; Kenworthy, *Climatology of Florida*, 14–16, 34; Remondino, *Mediterranean Shores*, iv.

32. W. A. Evans, "How to Keep Well," *Chicago Daily Tribune* (June 4, 1912): 6; Remondino, first typescript, 3; for context, see Margaret A. Cleaves, *Light Energy: Its Physics, Physiological Action and Therapeutic Applications* (New York: Rebman, 1904); Kennedy, "Perils"; Carter, *Rise and Shine*; Baur, *Health Seekers*, 6.

33. Michael and Virginia Scully, *The Motorists' Guide to Mexico (Pan-American Highway)*, junior ed. (Dallas: Turner, 1935): 5; on germ theory and medical geography, see Gregg Mitman and Ronald L. Numbers, "From Miasma to Asthma: The Changing Fortunes of Medical Geography in America," *History and Philosophy of the Life Sciences* 25 (2003): 391–412; Rod Edmond, "Returning Fears: Tropical Disease and the Metropolis," in Felix Driver and Luciana Martins, eds., *Tropical Visions in an Age of Empire* (Chicago: University of Chicago Press, 2005): 175–194; Nash, *Inescapable Ecologies*; Earl B. McKinley, "Climate and Health," *Scientific Monthly* 39:2 (August 1934): 117–128.

34. Nash, *Inescapable Ecologies*; Espinosa, *Epidemic Invasions*.

35. Graham, *In Quest of El Dorado*, 167 (quotation); for context, see Curtin, *Death by Migration*, 136; Nancy Leys Stepan, *Picturing Tropical Nature* (London: Reaktion, 2001): 149–179; Livingstone, "Human Acclimatization," 379–388; Kennedy, "Perils," 120–121; for contemporary self-congratulation, Huntington, *Civilization and Climate*, 40; A. Hyatt Verrill, *Cuba Past and Present* (New York: Dodd, Mead, 1924): i, ii, 11; "Healthy Havana," *Four-Track News* [later *Travel*] 1:5 (November 1901): 8; "Outwitting Climate," *Science News-Letter* 20:553 (November 14, 1931): 311.

36. Jean Lane, "Panama Mail Cruise Between New York and California Ports," *San Francisco, Los Angeles, Mexico, Central America, Panama, Cuba, New York, the De Luxe Tour* (Panama Mail, ca. 1920s): 4, Panama Mail folder 1, KMEC, HL.

37. Clarence E. Edwards, "The Wonderland of the Pacific Slope," *Travel* 15:1 (Oct. 1909): 25; Irvin S. Cobb, *Roughing It De Luxe*, illustrated by John T. McCutcheon (New York: George H. Doran, 1914): 110; Gloria Goddard, "The Flowery Crescent of the Caribbean," *Travel* 50:2 (December 1927): 9; John T. Faris, "Florida's Seaboard Magnificent," *Travel* 38:3 (January 1922): 30; George Allan England, "America's Island of Felicity," *Travel* 50:3 (January 1928): 14; on naturalists and painters, see Driver and Martins, *Tropical Visions*; Katherine Emma Manthorne, *Tropical Renaissance: North American Artists Exploring Latin America, 1839–1879* (Washington, D.C.: Smithsonian Institution Press, 1989).

38. Thanks to Reiko Hillyer for first articulating for me the oddity of the "palm courts" common in nineteenth-century U.S. hotels. Douglas Cazaux Sackman, *Orange*

Empire: California and the Fruits of Eden (Berkeley: University of California Press, 2005); John McPhee, *Oranges* (New York: Farrar, Strauss and Giroux, 2000); Steve Striffler and Mark Moberg, *Banana Wars: Power, Production, and History in the Americas* (Durham, N.C.: Duke University Press, 2003); B. R. Mitchell, *International Historical Statistics: The Americas, 1750–2005*, 6th ed. (New York: Palgrave Macmillan, 2007): 238, table C8; Virginia Scott Jenkins, *Bananas: An American History* (Washington, D.C.: Smithsonian Institution Press, 2000): 110 (citing a *Good Housekeeping* article). U.S.-owned companies also produced or bought many other tropical products, including coffee, rubber, and livestock, causing enormous environmental degradation; see Richard P. Tucker, *Insatiable Appetite: The United States and the Ecological Degradation of the Tropical World* (Berkeley: University of California Press, 2000). These items were not as potently symbolic as oranges and bananas.

39. Sackman, *Orange Empire*, 84–116; Jenkins, *Bananas*, 45–49, 56–125; Gordon T. McClelland and Jay T. Last, *Fruit Box Labels: An Illustrated Price Guide to Citrus Labels* (Santa Ana, Calif.: Hillcrest Press, 1995).

40. Sackman, *Orange Empire*, 119–253; Matt Garcia, *A World of Its Own: Race, Labor, and Citrus in the Making of Greater Los Angeles, 1900–1970* (Chapel Hill: University of North Carolina Press, 2001); Philip J. Pauly, *Fruits and Plains: The Horticultural Transformation of America* (Cambridge, Mass.: Harvard University Press, 2007): 195–229; David Vaught, *Cultivating California: Growers, Specialty Crops, and Labor, 1875–1920* (Baltimore: Johns Hopkins University Press, 1999).

41. *Souvenir Views of Pomona, Cal., and Vicinity* (n.p.: Bailey Bros., 1893): 5, LST, ANC; Arthur Paine, "In Southern California," *Travel* 16:2 (December 1910): 64; Samuel Dexter to his children, January 25 and 27, 1901, Dexter, HL; Augustus Franklin Tripp, "Notes of an Excursion to California" (1893): 22–23, 38, HL; see also J. R. Gilpin to Mrs. W. P. (Sue) Hazard, April 3, 1888: 1–2, folder 4, box 1, GFP, HM.

42. Winthrop Packard, *Florida Trails, as Seen from Jacksonville to Key West and from November to April, Inclusive* (Englewood, Fla.: Pineapple Press, 1983 [1910]): 104; Cobb, *Roughing It De Luxe*, 98.

43. Mrs. Neal Wyatt Chapline, *Florida the Fascinating, Profusely Illustrated from Original Photos* (New York: Broadway, 1914): 20; Kenworthy, *Climatology of Florida*, 43 (the impulse to overeat has not vanished; see David Foster Wallace, "A Supposedly Fun Thing I'll Never Do Again," in his *A Supposedly Fun Thing I'll Never Do Again: Essays and Arguments* [Boston: Little, Brown, 1997]); McPhee, *Oranges*; Sackman, *Orange Empire*.

44. B. Kroupa, *An Artist's Tour: Gleanings and Impressions of Travels in North and Central America and the Sandwich Islands* (London: Ward and Downey, 1890): 251; Emma Gilpin to Mrs. W. P. (Sue) Hazard, April 18, 1890, 7–8, folder 5, box 1, GFP, HM; Robert E. Bloomfield Diaries, December 24, 1907, MDLC; Selena Ingram, May 10, 1909, 1909 volume, box 1, Ingram, HL. I could add hundreds more examples in support of this point.

45. Kroupa, *An Artist's Tour*, 251; Adolph Christian Fera, *Post Cards of a Tourist (Mr. "Skinny" East): Cartoons of Southern California* (Los Angeles: Henry J. Pauly, 1910): 6.

46. J. R. Gilpin to Mrs. W. P. (Sue) Hazard, April 3, 1888: 1–2, folder 4, box 1, GFP, HM; Les Standiford, *Last Train to Paradise: Henry Flagler and the Spectacular Rise and Fall of the Railroad That Crossed an Ocean* (New York: Three Rivers Press, 2002): 65; David Leon Chandler, *Henry Flagler: The Astonishing Life and Times of the Visionary Robber Baron who Founded Florida* (New York: Macmillan, 1986): 167; *Cool Vacation Cruises to Foreign Lands Nearby from New Orleans: Havana, Nicaragua, Panama, Old Mexico* (1938), miscellaneous, OCPC, SC; material on United Fruit in OCPC, SC, and also KMEC, HL; Gates' Third Tour Through Mexico, "The Egypt of the New World" January 14, 1896): 30, DL (quotation).

47. *Wayside Notes Along the Sunset Route* (Southern Pacific, 1916): 16; John Sebastian, *California* (Rock Island Lines, 1906): 10; Samuel Dexter to his children, January 25, 1901, Dexter, HL (this passage describes Redlands, California; a passage in the letter of January 24 describes a similar scene in San Bernardino); see also Eleanor F. Bennett, January 1, 1907, 1906–1908 diary, HL; *Side Trips Along Sunset Route: New Orleans to Los Angeles and San Francisco* (Southern Pacific Lines, 1916): 50; Cobb, *Roughing It De Luxe*, 111; Los Angeles Chamber of Commerce, *Climate and Health in Los Angeles and Southern California* (January 1899): 2; and practically every publication of the All Year Club.

48. E. H. Blichfeldt, *A Mexican Journey*, 2d ed. (Chautauqua, N.Y.: Chautauqua Press, 1919): 6 (the first edition was published in 1911); *Mexico: Itineraries of a Motor Trip* (Mexico City: Pemex Travel Club, ca. 1930s): cover; see also Terry, *Terry's Mexico* (1911): xxiii.

49. Ward, "Acclimatization," 571; Anderson, *Cultivation of Whiteness*.

50. "Outwitting Climate," 311.

Chapter 2. More and More Attractive Each Year

1. Kirk Munroe, November 28, 30, 1881; on mosquitoes and fleas, see January 18 and 20, 1882; on alligators, ducks, turkeys, and fish, see December 13, 1881, and January 17, 22, and 27, 1882; closing quotations, February 3 and 5, 1882, diary for 1881–1882, box 1, Munroe, MDLC.

2. Mary Barr, 1884 diary (Barr enjoyed neither camping nor being separated from the camping enthusiast she had married), Munroe, December 10, 1881, both in box 1, Munroe, MDLC; *The New Overland and Short Sea Route: Florida and Cuba from the North and West, Through Florida to the Gulf of Mexico, and on to Cuba via the Plant System* (n.p.: Geo. E. Matthews, 1892): 3.

3. Charles W. Paget to Harold L. Ickes, secretary of the interior, January 15, 1937, File DTIP—Virgin Islands—Tourist and Winter Residence Development—General, February 5, 1935–December 26, 1937; box 1313, 9-11-42, Virgin Islands, Tourist Development, RG 126, OTCF, 1907–1951, NARA II; on the Munroes' house in South Florida, 1903 diary, box 1, Munroe, MDLC.

4. *Plan of Two Excursions to Florida, by the Florida Excursion Co.* (Boston: Florida Excursion Co., 1884): 13; J. R. Gilpin to Mrs. W. P. (Sue) Hazard, January 18, 1880: 4, folder 1, box 1, GFP, HM; see also Reiko Hillyer, "The New South in the Ancient City:

Flagler's St. Augustine Hotels and Sectional Reconciliation," *Journal of Decorative and Propaganda Arts* 25 (2005): 104–134; Harriet Beecher Stowe, *Palmetto Leaves*, with introductions by Mary B. Graff and Edith Cowles (Gainesville: University Press of Florida, 1999 [1873]); *Plan of Two Excursions to Florida*, 7; Philip J. Pauly, *Fruits and Plains: The Horticultural Transformation of America* (Cambridge, Mass.: Harvard University Press, 2007): 203–207. Like the Gilpins, Kirk Munroe stayed with the Jones family, remarking on December 19, 1881, "Mrs. J. sets best table in Florida," 1881 diary, box 1, Munroe, MDLC. I have no evidence that the Gilpins met Kirk here, but they later became frequent visitors to Ralph Munroe's camp in Coconut Grove and good friends with the Munroe clan.

5. See, for example, *The New Overland and Short Sea Route; Tropical Trips and Tourist Hotel Directory, Season 1910–11* (Wilmington, Del.: Atlantic Coast Line, 1910); *Florida: Winter Pleasure Tours Under Personally-Conducted System of the Pennsylvania Railroad* (Philadelphia: Pennsylvania Railroad Company, 1890); Gregg M. Turner, *A Journey into Florida Railroad History* (Gainesville: University Press of Florida, 2008).

6. J. R. Gilpin to Mrs. W. P. (Sue) Hazard, January 12, 1880: 4, March 24, 1880: 1, and April 2, 1880: 2–3, all in folder 1, box 1, GFP, HM.

7. Gregory W. Bush, " 'Playground of the USA': Miami and the Promotion of Spectacle," *Pacific Historical Review* (1999): 153–172; David Leon Chandler, *Henry Flagler: The Astonishing Life and Times of the Visionary Robber Baron Who Founded Florida* (New York: Macmillan, 1986); Susan R. Braden, *The Architecture of Leisure: The Florida Resort Hotels of Henry Flagler and Henry Plant* (Gainesville: University Press of Florida, 2002); Les Standiford, *Last Train to Paradise: Henry Flagler and the Spectacular Rise and Fall of the Railroad That Crossed an Ocean* (New York: Three Rivers Press, 2002); "Florida Theme Issue," *Journal of Decorative and Propaganda Arts* 23 (1998); Pauly, *Fruits and Plains*, 195–229.

8. Emma Gilpin, 1905 diary, entries for February 22, 23, and 24, 2–6, folder 1, box 2, GFP, HM; *Golden Days on the East Coast of Florida* (St. Augustine, Fla.: Passenger Traffic Department, Florida East Coast Railway, 1927): 7, 36.

9. Glenn S. Dumke, *The Boom of the Eighties in Southern California* (San Marino, Calif.: Huntington Library, 1991 [1944]); Carey McWilliams, *Southern California: An Island on the Land* (Layton, Utah: Gibbs Smith, 1999 [1946]): 96–164.

10. Samuel Dexter to his children, January 19 through January 24, Dexter, HL; Emma Gilpin to Kate, February 28, 1903: 4–5, folder 9, box 1, GFP, HM; McWilliams, *Southern California*, 130; Frederick E. Emmons, *American Passenger Ships: The Ocean Lines and Liners, 1873–1983* (Newark: University of Delaware Press; London: Associated University Presses, 1985): 46–49. Steamship passengers could cross the Isthmus of Panama by rail rather than rounding South America, but this journey still took longer than the transcontinental trip within the United States.

11. *Redondo Beach and the Pleasures You May Have There* (Los Angeles and Redondo Beach Railway, ca. 1909): 14, 17; Coronado Beach Company, *Coronado Beach, San Diego, California* (Chicago: Rand, McNally & Co., 1886): 3, 4; on the development

of tourism in Southern California, see Lawrence Culver, *The Frontier of Leisure: Southern California and the Shaping of Modern America* (Oxford: Oxford University Press, 2010); Clark Davis, "From Oasis to Metropolis: Southern California and the Changing Context of American Leisure," *Pacific Historical Review* 61:3 (August 1992): 357–385; Tom Zimmerman, "Paradise Promoted: Boosterism and the Los Angeles Chamber of Commerce," *California History* 64:1 (Winter 1985): 22–33, 73–75. Southern California had no shortage of ruthless or charismatic developers and Florida had institutional promoters (notably the state Department of Agriculture), so the different emphases reflect historiographical rather than historical distinctions. In general, Florida has received less attention from academic historians than has California, with the result that the eastern state's historical importance is undervalued.

12. Samuel Dexter to his children, January 17 and February 1, 1901; Anna Dexter to her children, February 21, 1901, both in Dexter, HL.

13. Selena Ingram, 1908 and 1909 volumes, box 1, Ingram, HL; her trip to Mexico City occurred in May 1909; see also Grace Owen Bowen, *The Tour of the 400 to Mexico* (privately printed, 1908), in which the tourists visit mines in which they have invested; William Schell, Jr., *Integral Outsiders: The American Colony in Mexico City, 1876–1911* (Wilmington, Del.: Scholarly Resources, 2001).

14. John Mason Hart, *Empire and Revolution: The Americans in Mexico Since the Civil War* (Berkeley: University of California Press, 2002): 106–130; Daniel Lewis, *Iron Horse Imperialism: The Southern Pacific of Mexico, 1880–1951* (Tucson: University of Arizona Press, 2007): 15–40.

15. O. F. Fassett, *Diary on a Journey to Mexico and California* (St. Albans, Vt.: Wallace Printing, 1888): 31; *Mexico: Tropical Tours to Toltec Towns* (Chicago: Knight, Leonard, 1892); *Gates' Third Tour Through Mexico* (1895); *Gates' Tenth Annual Tours* (1904); *15th Season Gates' Tours* (1907); *Gates' 19th Annual Tours* (1911) (the Gates brochures are all at the DL); untitled editorial, *Modern Mexico* 7:3 (September 1899): 4 (quotation), CSWR; Wabash Railroad, "A Thirty Day Tour of Old Mexico by Special Train from $291.25," *Modern Mexico* 7:3 (September 1899): 17, CSWR; Andrea Boardman, "The U.S.-Mexican War and the Beginnings of American Tourism in Mexico," in Dina Berger and Andrew Grant Wood, eds., *Holiday in Mexico: Critical Reflections on Tourism and the Tourist Encounter* (Durham, N.C.: Duke University Press, 2010): 21–53; for numbers of U.S. tourists in Mexico, see Dina Berger, *The Development of Mexico's Tourism Industry: Pyramids by Day, Martinis by Night* (New York: Palgrave Macmillan, 2006), appendix; Dennis Merrill, *Negotiating Paradise: U.S. Tourism and Empire in Twentieth-Century Latin America* (Chapel Hill: University of North Carolina Press, 2009). The U.S. federal government did not generate statistics on foreign tourism until the 1930s.

16. *Monterey [sic], Mexico* (Chicago: Poole Bros., 1882); Culver, *Frontier of Leisure*, 132; Paul J. Vanderwood, *Satan's Playground: Mobsters and Movie Stars at America's Greatest Gaming Resort* (Durham, N.C.: Duke University Press, 2010); Charles Dudley Warner, *On Horseback: A Tour in Virginia, North Carolina, and Tennessee; with Notes of Travel in Mexico and California* (Boston: Houghton Mifflin, 1889): 297; C. M. St.

Hill, *Pocket Guide to Mexico* (n.p.): 4–5, in Alice D. Perkins Scrapbook, 1882–1920, HL.

17. Emmons, *American Passenger Ships*, on the Alexandre Line, which began service from the United States to Mexico and the Caribbean in 1867, and the Ward Line, which began in 1878; Michael Craton and Gail Saunders, *Islanders in the Stream: A History of the Bahamian People*, vol. 2: *From the Ending of Slavery to the Twenty-first Century* (Athens: University of Georgia Press, 1998): 80–82. The U.S. merchant marine was small, weak, and lacking in governmental support compared with European companies, which dominated Caribbean shipping until the 1930s.

18. *The New Overland and Short Sea Route*, 33–34; *Trade and Travel: An Illustrated Volume Descriptive of the Commercial, Financial Transportation and Hotel Interests of the United States, 1895* (New York: Commercial Travelers Club of New York, 1895): 129; Frederick A. Ober, *Our West Indian Neighbors; The Islands of the Caribbean Sea, 'America's Mediterranean': Their Picturesque Features, Fascinating History, and Attractions for the Traveler, Nature-Lover, Settler and Pleasure-Seeker* (New York: James Pott, 1904): 16–17; Susan De Forest Day, *The Cruise of the Scythian in the West Indies* (New York: F. Tennyson Neely, 1899); *A Delightful Cruise Around the Islands of the West Indies* (Hamburg American, n.d.), brochure enclosed in a letter from Ruth Bryan Owen to Carrie Dunlap, March 27, 1911, folder 26, CDC, SCRL.

19. Franklin W. Knight, *The Caribbean: The Genesis of a Fragmented Nationalism*, 2nd ed. (New York: Oxford University Press, 1990), 182–188; Frank Fonda Taylor, *To Hell with Paradise: A History of the Jamaican Tourist Industry* (Pittsburgh: University of Pittsburgh Press, 1993); Duncan McDowell, *Another World: Bermuda and the Rise of Modern Tourism* (London: Macmillan Education, 1999); Krista A. Thompson, *An Eye for the Tropics: Tourism, Photography, and Framing the Caribbean Picturesque* (Durham, N.C.: Duke University Press, 2006).

20. Walter LaFeber, *Inevitable Revolutions: The United States in Central America*, 2nd ed. (New York: W. W. Norton, 1993); Knight, *The Caribbean*; see the flyers preserved in the OCPC (SC) and the KMEC (HL) for evidence for the entrance of the Grace, Panama Mail, and Panama Pacific Lines into the Caribbean.

21. *Cruising the Spanish Main: United Fruit Company Steamship Service* (United Fruit Co. Steamship Service, 1913): 23, United Fruit Company folder 1, KMEC, HL (quotation); on the fruit companies and Caribbean tourism, see Marcelo Bucheli, "United Fruit Company in Latin America," in Steve Striffler and Mark Moberg, eds., *Banana Wars: Power, Production, and History in the Americas* (Durham, N.C.: Duke University Press, 2003): 80–100; Stacy May and Galo Plaza, *The United Fruit Company in Latin America*, 7th Case Study in an NPA Series on United States Business Performance Abroad (n.p.: National Planning Association, 1958): 18; Taylor, *To Hell with Paradise*, 45–49, 59–60; 68–93; *Cool Vacation Cruises* (Illinois Central Railroad and the Standard Fruit Company, 1938), miscellaneous, not in folder, OCPC, SC; Culver, *Frontier of Leisure*; Christine Skwiot, *The Purposes of Paradise: U.S. Tourism and Empire in Cuba and Hawai'i* (Philadelphia: University of Pennsylvania Press, 2010).

22. Emma Gilpin to Mrs. W. P. (Sue) Hazard, March 9, 1899, 3, folder 6, box 1, GFP, HM; Amy Bridges, December 21, 1886, and February 27, 1887, 1886–1887 diary, HL; on hotels, see A. K. Sandoval-Strausz, *Hotel: An American History* (New Haven, Conn.: Yale University Press, 2007); Catherine Cocks, *Doing the Town: The Rise of Urban Tourism in the United States, 1850–1915* (Berkeley: University of California Press, 2001): 70–105; Chandler, *Henry Flagler*, 87–88. The Gilpins preferred Lake Worth before Flagler built the high society resort of Palm Beach there. After it opened, they began to spend their Florida winters on a houseboat, often using Ralph Munroe's camp in Coconut Grove as a home base.

23. *Tropical Tours to Toltec Lands*, 6, 8, 13, 14, 18, 23, 33; *Gates' Third Tour Through Mexico*, 8; *Gates' Tenth Annual Tours*, 20; *Gates' 19th Annual Tours*, 33.

24. Ella Wheeler Wilcox, *Sailing Sunny Seas: A Story of Travel in Jamaica, Honolulu, Haiti, Santo Domingo, Porto Rico, St. Thomas, Dominica, Martinique, Trinidad and the West Indies* (Chicago: W. B. Conkey, 1909): 14, 17, 38, 139, 189, 196 (Wilcox weaves reminiscences of several voyages together, so it is not possible to know just when she was in Havana, but it seems likely that she visited during the 1890s, when the city was in poor condition because of Cuba's final war against Spain); L. Vernon Briggs, *Arizona and New Mexico, 1882, California 1886, Mexico 1891* (New York: Argonaut Press, 1966 [1932]): 201; Ingram, May 11, 1909, 1909 volume, Ingram, HL.

25. Briggs, *Arizona and New Mexico*, 201; Warner, *On Horseback*, 231; Josephine Tozier, *The Traveler's Handbook: A Manual for Transatlantic Travelers* (New York: Funk & Wagnalls, 1907): 23; *Ocean Records: A Pocket Handbook for Travelers*, 8th ed. (New York: World Traveler, 1925): 22.

26. Anne McClintock, *Imperial Leather: Race, Gender and Sexuality in the Colonial Contest* (New York: Routledge, 1995): 207–231; Nancy Tomes, *The Gospel of Germs: Men, Women, and the Microbe in American Life* (Cambridge, Mass.: Harvard University Press, 1998); Warwick Anderson, "Excremental Colonialism: Public Health and the Poetics of Pollution," *Critical Inquiry* 21 (Spring 1995): 640–669; Mark Harrison, *Climates and Constitutions: Health, Race, Environment and British Imperialism in India* (Oxford: Oxford University Press, 1999): 22–23.

27. "Consideraciones para Llevar a Cabo el Proyecto de Financiar la construcción, adaptación y equipo de hoteles y paradores en distintas poblaciones del país y lugares adecuados en las carreteras," 1, doc. 28684, folder 311/493, files 1/132, June 1937, documents 28683–28815, LMDO, CEHM. On Cuba, see Skwiot, *Purposes of Paradise*; Rosalie Schwartz, *Pleasure Island: Tourism and Temptation in Cuba* (Lincoln: University of Nebraska Press, 1997): 42–47; on Mexico, see Merrill, *Negotiating Paradise*; on Puerto Rico, see Enrique Ortega, "Annual Report of the Institute of Tourism, Fiscal Year Ending June 30, 1938," 43, folder Institute of Tourism 1938, box 986, 9-8-88, Puerto Rico, Reports, Annual, Institute of Tourism; F. Benitez Rexach, "Memorandum for Mr. Corcoran on the Tourist Problem" (ca. 1935), 6–8, folder Tourist Development—General, box 1012, 9-8-92, Puerto Rico, Tourist Development; William Cattron Rigby of Rigby, Malone and Hutchinson, attorneys at law, to Major General Blanton Winship, governor of Puerto

Rico, January 26, 1935, file 2, folder Tourist Development—Hotels—Condado, box 1012, 9-8-92, Puerto Rico, Tourist Development; all Puerto Rico documents in OTCF, 1907–1951, RG 126, NARA II; Taylor, *To Hell with Paradise*; McDowell, *Another World*; on the Canadian National Steamship Line establishing a tourist hotel in Trinidad, see Louis E. Tuffin to secretary of the interior Harold Ickes, undated, stamped received by Interior Department May 18, 1938, file DTIP—Virgin Islands—Tourist and Winter Residence Development—General, box 1313, 9-11-42, Virgin Islands, Tourist Development, OTCF, 1907–1951, RG 126, NARA II.

28. Roger Cartwright and Carolyn Baird, *The Development and Growth of the Cruise Industry* (Boston: Butterworth Heinemann, 1999): 1–26; Kristoffer A. Garin, *Devils on the Deep Blue Sea: The Dreams, Schemes and Showdowns That Built America's Cruise Empires* (New York: Viking, 2005).

29. Philip Dawson, *Cruise Ships: An Evolution in Design* (London: Conway Maritime Press, 2000): 7–22, and *The Liner: Retrospective and Renaissance* (New York: W. W. Norton, 2006): 42; John Maxtone-Graham, *Liners to the Sun* (New York: Macmillan, 1985).

30. *West Indies, South America, Panama Canal . . . "S.S. New York"* (American Line, 1911): 15, American Line folder 4, KMEC, HL; R. A. Fletcher, *Travelling Palaces: Luxury in Passenger Steamships* (London: Sir Isaac Pitman & Sons, 1913): 1.

31. Dawson, *Cruise Ships*, 10–13, and *The Liner*, 25; Maxtone-Graham, *Liners to the Sun*; Tozier, *The Traveler's Handbook*, 21. Cartwright and Baird, *Development and Growth*, 23, cite the Oceanic Yachting Company's 1881 effort as the first cruise. Another inspiration for sea cruises must have been river and lake steamer tours, the most famous of which was the journey up the Nile to see the pyramids.

32. *Winter Tours to the Tropics* (Quebec & Gulf Ports Steamship Company, 1879), KMEC, HL; *Guide to Winter Resorts in Southern Seas* (Quebec Steamship Co., ca. 1885).

33. Wilcox, *Sailing Sunny Seas*, 140; Joseph Kirkbride, February 6, 1897, JJK, MDLC; Ida M. H. Starr, *Gardens of the Caribbees: Sketches of a Cruise to the West Indies and the Spanish Main*, vol. 1 (Boston: L. C. Page, 1903): 22. Ship's biscuit, also known as hardtack, was a cracker made of flour, water, and salt. Kirkbride's steward offered champagne and oranges instead; see the February 7 entry in his 1897 diary.

34. Harry A. Franck, *Roaming Through the West Indies* (New York: Blue Ribbon Books, 1920): 21; William Thomas Corlett, *The American Tropics: Notes from the Log of a Midwinter Cruise* (Cleveland: Burrows Brothers, 1908): 17; Carlos Patiño Jaramillo, *Por México y California: Recuerdos de Viaje* (Bogota: Librería Nueva, 1899), 37. Patiño was traveling from Ecuador to San Francisco, so he obviously was not on the Caribbean but the Pacific Ocean.

35. Kirkbride, entries for February 14, 16, 17, and 23, 1897, JJK, MDLC; Wilcox, *Sailing Sunny Seas*, 199, 206; Corlett, *American Tropics*, 58–59; Patiño Jaramillo, *Por México y California*, 47.

36. *The New Overland and Short Sea Route*, 35; *Winter Cruises to the West Indies* (New York: Hamburg American, 1912): 5, Hamburg American folder 8, KMEC, HL;

Dawson, *Cruise Ships*, 14; *Raymond-Whitcomb Cruises West Indies, 1926* (Raymond-Whitcomb, ca. 1925): back cover, Norddeutscher Lloyd folder 42, KMEC, HL.

37. Lorraine Coons and Alexander Varias, *Tourist Third Cabin: Steamship Travel in the Interwar Years* (New York: Palgrave Macmillan, 2003): xxi; Maxtone-Graham, *Liners to the Sun*, 55; Dawson, *Cruise Ships*, 22, 38–39.

38. Maxtone-Graham, *Liners to the Sun*, 109, 111; Dawson, *Cruise Ships*, 21–27; *Winter Cruises to the West Indies*, 6–7; *"Today's Programme of Events" . . . R.M.S. "Franconia": Canada-St. Pierre-Bermuda-Cruise* (Cunard, 1933), Cunard folder 137, KMEC, HL.

39. *Cruising the Spanish Main: United Fruit Company Steamship Service* (United Fruit Company Steamship Service, 1913): 5, 8, 9, United Fruit folder 1, KMEC, HL; *Grace Line/Route of Romance* (San Francisco: March, 1936), OCPC, SC; *Cool Vacation Cruises*; see also *Cruising the Spanish Main*, 9; *Coast to Coast: New York–California Via the Isthmus* (Panama Pacific Line, 1924): 1–5, Panama Pacific folder 1, KMEC, HL. For "large and airy," see *Caribbean Cruises, Great White Fleet* (United Fruit Company Steamship Service, 1924): 11, United Fruit folder 2, KMEC, HL; Dawson, *Cruise Ships*, 28; Maxtone-Graham, *Liners to the Sun*, 111, 190–208.

40. Dawson, *The Liner*, 9; *Cuba via New Orleans . . . Southern Pacific Co.* (Southern Pacific: ca. 1907): 7–8, Southern Pacific folder 2, KMEC, HL; Fletcher, *Travelling Palaces*, 115.

41. Dawson, *Cruise Ships*, 22–23.

42. Maxtone-Graham, *Liners to the Sun*, 54–55, 58–60; Coons and Varian, *Tourist Third Cabin*; Dawson, *The Liner*, 13.

43. Patiño Jaramillo, *Por México y California*, 34–35; F. Frankfort Moore, *Shipmates in Sunshine: The Romance of a Caribbean Cruise* (New York: D. Appleton, 1903): 75; *Ocean Records*, 26 (inflation calculated using the website http://www.westegg.com/inflation/, accessed November 2, 2010); Tozier, *The Traveler's Handbook*, 67. Madeline Allen, sailing on a small Italian liner from San Francisco to Europe in 1931, reported that the passengers played bridge, shuffleboard, jacks, and chess, jumped rope, swam and sunbathed, and listened or danced to phonograph records; see her letter to "Dearest Family," March 18, 1931, AFA.

44. Corlett, *American Tropics*, 144; *List of Passengers on the Yachting Cruise in the West Indies by the American Line, S.S. New York . . . Leaving New York March 4th, 1911* (American Line, 1911): 4, American Line folder 4, KMEC, HL; *Winter Cruises to the West Indies*, 5.

45. For the cruise staff, see *The Cunard Cruise News* (S.S. *Franconia*, 1933), bulletin no. 1, Cunard folder 138; for the social programs on this cruise, see Cunard folder 137, which contains several daily program cards; the golf pro appears on p. 1 of *Cunard Cruise News* (R.M.S. *Mauretania*, 1933), bulletin no. 6, Cunard folder 160; *1937 West Indies Cruises, Hamburg-American Line/North German Lloyd* (October 1936): 16, Hamburg American folder 8; *A Manual of Instructions for Pursers—Cruise Conductors: How to Conduct Cruise Programs Aboard Passenger Ships of the Great White Fleet* (United Fruit, ca. 1932–1934), United Fruit folder 36; all materials in this note from KMEC, HL.

There were no actual horses on board. On some ships, the "horses" were wooden figures manipulated by passengers. On others, female passengers were asked to represent the horses, but it's not clear whether they in fact ran races. I assume the turtles were real and probably intended for dinner.

46. *Ships and Ports of the Great White Fleet* (United Fruit, ca. 1930s): 3, United Fruit folder 3, KMEC, HL; *Caribbean Cruises*, 8; George W. Seaton, *Let's Go to the West Indies (How to Get the Most out of Your Trip)* (New York: Prentice-Hall, 1938): 17–18.

47. *Winter Cruises to the West Indies*, 10 (inflation here and below calculated using the website http://www.westegg.com/inflation/, accessed January 15, 2012); *Florida and Cuba, Winter 1913–14* (Thos. Cook & Son, Programme No. 42, 1913): 2, SCRL. The pricing got quite complicated as the brochure elaborated on the travelers' options; see 14–19, 29, and 32. The prices in the text represent the range of fares available.

48. For the 1920s, see *Go East by Sea, Reduced Summer Excursion Fares* (Panama Pacific, ca. 1920s), Panama Pacific folder 1, KMEC, HL; for the 1930s, see *Panama Vacations, Panama Pacific Line* (Panama Pacific, ca. 1930s), Panama Pacific folder 2, KMEC, HL; *A New Ocean Route to Mexico from Miami in the Canadian National T.S.S.* Prince Henry (Canadian National Steamship Co., 1937), Canadian National folder 14, KMEC, HL; Seaton, *Let's Go to the West Indies*, 16–17.

49. *United Fruit Company Great White Fleet* (United Fruit, ca. 1920): 14, United Fruit Company folder 1, KMEC, HL (see also *United Fruit Company Great White Fleet* [New York: 1922, 1924, and 1926 editions], United Fruit Company folder 2, KMEC, HL, for the same instruction); *Grace Line 16 Day Cruises to the Caribbean* (Grace Line, April 1938): under the header "General Information," Grace Line folder 8, KMEC, HL; *1938 April, May, June, Sailing List, Standard Fruit & Steamship Co.* (Standard Fruit, 1938), Standard Fruit folder 2, KMEC, HL.

50. Daniel Rochford, "Flying the West Indies—Concluding Portions of Articles in the Series," *Boston Evening Transcript* (November 29, 1929): 2 (a reprint of this series appears in folder 8, Magazine Articles, 1918–1936, box 8, accession 1, PAAC, SCRL); people with Spanish names and Mexican, Central American, or Caribbean cities of residence are common in *Passenger Traffic Statistics from Dec. 18th 1929 to Dec. 5th, 1934*, a handwritten record of Pan American's earliest passengers, in folder 2, Passenger Travel Statistics, box 49, accession 1, PAAC, SCRL. The few women who traveled by air in these years were almost all Latin Americans.

51. *Tropical Chatter* (Panama Mail: S.S. *Ecuador*, 1930): 7, 59–75, Panama Mail folder 7, KMEC, HL; M. Touissant to Luis Montes de Oca, June 11, 1937, doc. 28761, file 311, LMDO, CEHM. On the *Tropical Chatter* list, there are several people with non-Hispanic surnames who listed Central American cities as their residence. I have assumed that they were North Americans or Europeans doing business in Latin America. See also Patiño Jaramillo, *Por México y California*, 34, on a fellow passenger who was a "Guatemalan with very brown skin and a vulgar appearance who had come from Paris, although he didn't look it."

52. *Passenger List for a voyage from New York to Los Angeles and San Francisco . . .*

(Grace Line, 1936), Grace Line folder 42, KMEC, HL; passenger list for the Holland America cruise in the West Indies Cruise Photo Album, 1928, SC; *List of Passengers, New York & Cuba Mail Steamship Company, S.S.* Siboney, *April 1938*, New York & Cuba Mail folder 6, KMEC, HL; Mrs. Eloisa M. de Won Yiu is listed in the *Souvenir Passenger List, San Francisco New York Service, Panama Mail S.S. Co S.S. Ecuador, Voy. 74* (Panama Mail, 1931), Panama Mail folder 7, KMEC, HL; Mr. Mitsuji Sawaura and Mr. Yutaka Tsukatani appear on the passenger list for a Cunard cruise on the S.S. *Mauretania* in November 1933, Cunard folder 161, KMEC, HL. I address gender, age, and marital status in Chapter 5.

53. Richard Bond, *The Ship's Steward's Handbook: The Complete Guide to the Victualling and Catering Departments on Board Ship* (Glasgow: James Munro, 1918). Bond had worked his way up from mess boy to chief steward before becoming chief instructor at the Nautical Training School for Stewards and Cooks in Liverpool. He seems to have been a man of indestructible good temper and extraordinary energy.

54. Moore, *Shipmates in Sunshine*, 3; Isabel Anderson, *Odd Corners* (New York: Dodd, Mead, 1917): 63; Philip Sanford Marden, *Sailing South* (Boston: Houghton Mifflin, 1921): 132; for officers, see the *Passenger List for a Voyage from New York*, 3, including one Julian A. Palacios, assistant purser, the only Hispanic name I saw on such lists.

55. *United Fruit Company Great White Fleet*, 2; *Caribbean Cruises*, 11, 12; *West Indies Winter 1910 Program* (issue no. 4, December 3): 2, Hamburg American folder 43, KMEC, HL.

56. *Ocean Records*, 22; Kirkbride, 1897 diary, JJK, MDLC. Moore, *Shipmates in Sunshine*, 128, 164, 259, similarly had his gossip-mongering protagonist go for a walk or a carriage ride in most ports of call.

57. Kirkbride, February 28, 1897, 1897 diary, JJK, MDLC; Day, *The Cruise of the Scythian*, 279; Joseph Mattingly, comp. and ed., *Souvenir and Log of My Voyage via Panama Mail S. S. Co.* (Panama Mail S. S. Co, 1920): 8, 11, 12; Allen, March 27, 1931, AFA.

58. *Cruise News* (January 22, 1912): 2, White Star folder 1, KMEC, HL; *Winter Cruises to the West Indies*, 33; *Raymond-Whitcomb Cruises*, back cover; Allen, March 27, 1931, AFA (many tropical towns relied on vultures to dispose of street garbage, much as North Americans had long relied on pigs); Corlett, *American Tropics*, 62; see also the Mexican American toddlers who had learned to demand a penny before allowing tourists to take their pictures, in Bowen, *The Tour of the 400*, 25.

59. *Raymond-Whitcomb Cruises*, inside second fold, 1; Clare Sheridan, *My American Diary* (New York: Boni & Liveright, 1922): 141, 142.

60. Seaton, *Let's Go to the West Indies*, 46, 47, 79; *Comisión Nacional para el Fomento del Turismo, Memoria Annual*, 1928–1929 (Havana, 1929): 19, 20; Merrill, *Negotiating Paradise*, 103–140; L. A. Miranda and R. González, eds., *Tourist's Guide of Puerto Rico* (San Juan, P.R., 1937): 74. This guide was probably published by Puerto Rico's Institute of Tourism, a government agency; this copy is in folder Publicity—Publications—Institute of Tourism—Booklets/Folders, box 957, entry 1, 9-8-84, Puerto Rico, Publicity, Publications, OTCF, 1907–1951, RG 126, NARA II.

61. Allen, March 27, 1931, AFA; Seaton, *Let's Go to the West Indies*, 22, 23 (quotation), 24; *Raymond-Whitcomb Cruises*, 40–41; for a tour of Panama City, see Mattingly, *Souvenir and Log*, 28; the West Indies Cruise Photo Album contains several booklets describing shore excursions in Havana, Kingston, Colón (Panama), Curaçao, La Guayra, Trinidad, Barbados, Martinique, St. Thomas, San Juan, and Bermuda during a Holland America cruise; see also *Cunard Cruise News* (R.M.S. *Mauretania*, 1933), bulletin no. 6, 2.

62. Seaton, *Let's Go to the West Indies*, 95, 111, 118; *Facts About Puerto Rico U.S.A. Where the Americas Meet* (Institute of Tourism, Government of Puerto Rico, n.d., ca. 1939): 47, folder Publicity—Publications—Institute of Tourism—Facts About Puerto Rico, box 958, 8-8-84, Puerto Rico, Publicity, Publications, OTCF, 1907–1951, RG 126, NARA II.

63. Similar cultural enterprises arose elsewhere in the context of increased development and travel; see, for example, Erika Marie Bsumek, *Indian-Made: Navajo Culture in the Marketplace, 1868–1940* (Lawrence: University Press of Kansas, 2008); David E. Whisnant, *All That Is Native and Fine: The Politics of Culture in an American Region* (Chapel Hill: University of North Carolina Press, 1983); Rick A. López, *Crafting Mexico: Intellectuals, Artisans, and the State After the Revolution* (Durham, N.C.: Duke University Press, 2010).

64. United States Department of the Interior memorandum for the press, February 19, 1939: 3, file: DTIP—Virgin Islands—Tourist and Winter Residence Development—General, box 1313, 9-11-42, Virgin Islands, Tourist Development, OTCF, 1907–1951, RG 126, NARA II. Greater dependence on the seasonal, changeable tourist trade was usually at best a mixed blessing.

65. On Curaçao, see *Six Superb Cruises to the West Indies* (Holland America Line, 1933), OCPC, SC; on Martinique, see *West Indies* (American Line), 6, American Line folder 4, KMEC, HL; on Jamaica, see *Sailing from New Orleans . . . Winter Season 1939* (American Express, 1938), American Express folder, OCPC, SC; on Barbados, see *1937 West Indies Cruises*, 7.

66. Starr, *Gardens of the Caribbees*, vol. 2, 232; Marden, *Sailing South*, 232, 233 (quotation). Although some travelers remarked on black medical and customs officials, black police officers earned the most ink; see, for example, "The dignified coal black native policemen in their trim blue uniforms . . . and their beaming smiles, are a sight worth seeing" in Bermuda, in *Cunard Cruise News* (S.S. *Franconia*, 1933): bulletin no. 4, 2, Cunard Line folder 138, KMEC, HL.

67. Starr, *Gardens of the Caribbees*, vol. 2, 231.

Chapter 3. Fountain of Youth

1. Charles Dudley Warner, "Race and Climate," *Land of Sunshine* 4:3 (February 1896): 104–105, 106.

2. Frank Parker Stockbridge and John Holliday Perry, *So This Is Florida* (New York: Robert M. McBridge, 1938): vii, 1, 8, 27.

3. Amy L. Bridges, February 27, 1887, Bridges diary, 1886–1887, HL.

4. Charles J. Kenworthy, M.D., *Climatology of Florida* (Savannah, Ga.: Morning News Steam Printing House, 1881).

5. Kenworthy, *Climatology of Florida*, 15 (quotation), 10 (quotation), 3, 4, 21, 24. The mortality figures are deceptive because the author focused on phthisis (tuberculosis), a disease associated with cold weather, and ignored or denied the prevalence of the diseases associated with warm weather, particularly malaria.

6. Kenworthy, *Climatology of Florida*, 21; see also Grace Ellery Channing, "Italy and 'Our Italy,'" *Land of Sunshine* 11:1 (June 1899): 24–29.

7. "Where to Go This Winter for Rest, Recreation, or Sport," *New York Times* (January 4, 1903): WR1; T. Philip Terry, *Terry's Guide to Mexico: A Handbook for Travellers* (Boston: Houghton Mifflin, 1911): xxv (the same language appears in the 1923 edition); *Plan of Two Excursions to Florida, by the Florida Excursion Co.* (Boston: Florida Excursion Co., 1884); *Four Tours to Florida and Nassau* (Raymond-Whitcomb Company, 1907): title page, SCRL; *Winter Cruises to the West Indies* (New York–Hamburg American Line, 1912): 3, Hamburg American folder 8, KMEC, HL; J. R. Gilpin to Mrs. W. P. (Sue) Hazard, March 22, 1899: 1; Emma Gilpin to Mrs. W. P. (Sue) Hazard, March 30, 1899: 1–2; both in folder 6, box 1, GFP, HM.

8. Southern Pacific Railroad advertisement, *Travel* 8:2 (February 1905): 54 (of the separately numbered advertising section); Los Angeles Chamber of Commerce, *Climate and Health in Los Angeles and Southern California* (January 1899): 1, HL; Harry Ellington Brook, comp., *Land of Sunshine: Southern California* (Los Angeles: World's Fair Association and Bureau of Information, 1893): 9; *Plan of Two Excursions to Florida*, 1, 20; Bradford Torrey, *A Florida Sketch-Book* (Boston: Houghton Mifflin; Cambridge: Riverside Press, 1924 [1894]): 67; L. A. Miranda and R. González, eds., *Tourist's Guide of Puerto Rico* (San Juan, P.R., 1937): 37, folder Publicity—Publications—Institute of Tourism—Booklets/Folders, box 957, 9-8-84, Puerto Rico, Publicity, Publications, OTCF, 1907–1951, RG 126, NARA II; T. Philip Terry, *Terry's Guide to Mexico: The New Standard Guidebook to the Mexican Republic, with Chapters on the Railways, Automobile Roads, and the Ocean Routes to Mexico* (Hingham, Mass.: n.p., 1940): xii; J. J. Aubertin, *A Fight with Distances: The States, the Hawaiian Islands, Canada, British Columbia, Cuba, the Bahamas* (London: Kegan Paul, Trench, 1888): 336.

9. Silvia Sunshine [Abbie M. Brooks], *Petals Plucked from Sunny Climes* (Nashville: Southern Methodist Publishing House, 1880): 171; Emma H. Adams, *To and Fro in Southern California, with Sketches in Arizona and New Mexico* (Cincinnati: W. M. B. C. Press, 1887): 60, 68, 73, 76 (quotation); Irvin S. Cobb, *Roughing It De Luxe*, illustrated by John T. McCutcheon (New York: George H. Doran, 1914): 97.

10. Clarence E. Edwards, "The Wonderland of the Pacific Slope," *Travel* 15:1 (October 1909): 23, 24; *Mexico: Tropical Tours to Toltec Towns* (Chicago: Knight, Leonard, 1892): 4, 7, 8, 11, 25 (quotation), 26; *Gates' Third Tour Through Mexico* (1896): cover, 4, DL; see also John Sebastian, *California* (Rock Island Lines, 1906): 8, 10, BL; Cora Hayward Crawford, *The Land of the Montezumas* (Troy, N.Y.: Nims and Knight, 1890):

55; R. C. Noble, *Our Trip to California* (Shelbyville, Ill.: Our Best Words, 1890): 25; "Bermuda—Playground of Eternal Springtime," Furness, Withy Company advertisement, *Travel* 44:5 (March 1925): inside front cover.

11. George Wharton James, *The Influence of the Climate of California upon Its Literature* (n.p.: printed brochure, ca. 1910): 7, HL; Maude Littlefield Baillard, "Creating the New Florida," *Travel* 38:3 (January 1922): 9; *Trade and Travel: An Illustrated Volume Descriptive of the Commercial, Financial Transportation and Hotel Interests of the United States, 1895* (New York: Commercial Travelers Club of New York, 1895): 129; United Fruit Company advertisement, *Travel* 8:3 (March 1905): 59 (of separately paginated advertising section); see also Los Angeles Chamber of Commerce, *Climate and Health*, 1; Federal Writers' Project, comp., *Florida: A Guide to the Southernmost State* (New York: Oxford University Press, 1939): 7–8; *Guide to Southern Georgia and Florida, Containing a Brief Description of Points of Interest to the Tourist, Invalid or Emigrant, and How to Reach Them* (Savannah, Ga.: General Passenger Department, Atlantic and Gulf Railroad, 1879): 66.

12. Los Angeles Chamber of Commerce, *Climate and Health*, 4; "United States Department of the Interior, Harold L. Ickes, Secretary, Division of Territories and Island Possessions, General Information, Puerto Rico," 1, in folder Publicity—Publications—General Information—Puerto Rico, box 957, 9-8-84, Puerto Rico, Publicity, Publications, OTCF, 1907–1951, RG 126, NARA II (although the flyer appears in records from the 1930s, it looks like an old, oft-reproduced document dating from the 1910s); Charles B. Reynolds, *Standard Guide to Cuba: A New and Complete Guide to the Island of Cuba, with Maps, Illustrations, Routes of Travel, History, and an English-Spanish Phrase Book* (Havana: Foster & Reynolds, 1913): 119; see also Los Angeles Chamber of Commerce, *Climate and Health*, 4; Miranda and González, *Tourist's Guide of Puerto Rico*, 28; William A. Edwards, M.D., and Beatrice Harraden, *Two Health-Seekers in Southern California* (Philadelphia: J. B. Lippincott, 1896): 45–47, 52–54, 56–57, 60; Kenworthy, *Climatology of Florida*, 5, 21, 30. I rounded off the Celsius equivalents.

13. Coronado Beach Company, *Coronado Beach, San Diego, California* (Chicago: R. R. Donnelly, 1889): 30; Ratcliffe Hicks, *Southern California, or the Land of the Afternoon* (Springfield, Mass.: Springfield Printing and Binding, 1898), 7; James Johnson, *Jamaica: The New Riviera, a Pictorial Description of the Island and Its Attractions* (London: Cassell, 1903): 7, 8; Kenworthy, *Climatology of Florida*, 21.

14. Ralph Henry Barbour, *Let's Go to Florida! Information for Those Who Haven't Been but Are Going, Those Who Have Been and Are Going Back, and Those Who Don't Expect to Go but Will* (New York: Dodd, Mead, 1926): 81; Mrs. Neal Wyatt Chapline, *Florida the Fascinating* (New York: Broadway, 1914): 27; Miranda and González, *Tourist's Guide of Puerto Rico*, 39; Reynolds, *Standard Guide to Cuba*, 119; "Climate and Clothes," *Real Mexico* 1:1 (April 1932): 34; Edwards and Harraden, *Two Health-Seekers*, 66; Selena Ingram, June 26, 1907, 1907 volume, Ingram, HL; see also Johnson, *Jamaica*, 23; Eleanor Early, *Ports of the Sun: A Guide to the Caribbean, Bermuda, Nassau, Havana and Panama* (Boston: Houghton Mifflin, 1937): 45–46. Kenneth Roberts, in *Florida*

(New York: Harper & Brothers, 1926), 288, notes that on hearing northerners complain about the heat, "the Floridian promptly proceeds to show—to his own satisfaction if not to that of any one else—that the cities of Blagoviestchensk, Siberia; Oslo, Norway; and Boston, Massachusetts, are sweltering furnaces in the summer months by comparison with almost any Florida city."

15. Barbour, *Let's Go to Florida*, 81; Chapline, *Florida the Fascinating*, 71; see also Rex Beach, *The Miracle of Coral Gables* (Coral Gables, Fla: 1926): 41, 43.

16. Samuel Dexter to his children, January 29, 1901, and similar statements in the letters of February 14, 18, 21, and February 28–March 1, Dexter, HL; Marie Robinson Wright, *Picturesque Mexico* (Philadelphia: J. B. Lippincott, 1897): 192.

17. Adams, *To and Fro in Southern California*, 82–83; Terry, *Terry's Mexico*, xxvii, xxx (the language on clothing does not change substantially in the 1923 and 1940 editions, but there is far more material on warmer sites in 1940, reflecting the development of coastal resorts); Ingram, November 7, 1908, 1908 diary, Ingram, HL; on air conditioning, see Gail Cooper, *Air-conditioning America: Engineers and the Controlled Environment, 1900–1960* (Baltimore: Johns Hopkins University Press, 1998).

18. *Mexico? Si Señor* (Mexico City: Tourist Department of Wells Fargo & Co., S.A., 1938): 7; Stockbridge and Perry, *So This Is Florida*, 25; William Corlett, *The American Tropics: Notes from the Log of a Midwinter Cruise* (Cleveland: Burrows Brothers, 1908): 19; Nancy Johnstone, *Sombreros Are Becoming* (New York: Longmans, Green, 1941): 61.

19. Jim Ring, *Riviera: The Rise and Rise of the Côte d'Azur* (London: John Murray, 2004): 104–116; Mary Blume, *Côte d'Azur: Inventing the French Riviera* (London: Thames and Hudson, 1992): 74–76; Miranda and González, *Tourist's Guide of Puerto Rico*, 38; *1937 West Indies Cruises*, Hamburg-American Line/North German Lloyd (October 1936): 3, Hamburg American folder 8, KMEC, HL; Cooper, *Air-conditioning America*; John Maxtone-Graham, *Liners to the Sun* (New York: Macmillan, 1985): 149, 192.

20. *Mexico: The Faraway Land Nearby* (n.p.: Asociación Mexicana de Turismo, ca. 1930s): 4; Susan Barton, *Healthy Living in the Alps: The Origins of Winter Tourism in Switzerland, 1860–1914* (Manchester: Manchester University Press, 2008); Hal K. Rothman, *Devil's Bargains: Tourism in the Twentieth-Century American West* (Lawrence: University Press of Kansas, 1998): 168–201.

21. *California: Tourist Sleeper Excursions* (Santa Fe Railroad, ca. 1905–1910): 3; "Bermuda," Furness, Withy advertisement; *Trade and Travel*, 85; Florida East Coast Railway, *Golden Days on the East Coast of Florida* (St. Augustine, Fla.: Passenger Traffic Department, Florida East Coast Railway, 1927), 7, SCRL; "The Land of Mid-Winter Roses," *Four-Track News* [later *Travel*] 1:6 (December 1901): 5.

22. Gloria Goddard, "The Flowery Crescent of the Caribbean," *Travel* 50:2 (December 1927): 8.

23. Florida East Coast Railway, *Golden Days*, 3; [Richard J. Levis], *Diary of a Spring Holiday in Cuba* (Philadelphia: Porter & Coates, 1872): 11 (Levis finished this phrase with references to sugarcane fields and toiling slaves, images probably common to many U.S. fantasies of the tropics, since African slavery was the foundation of the plantation

economy in the Americas); *Cool Vacation Cruises* (Illinois Central and Standard Fruit and Steamship Co.), miscellaneous not in folder, OCPC, SC; "Bermuda and the West Indies," *Travel* 15:3 (December 1909): 132.

24. *Guide to Southern Georgia and Florida*, 67; James, *The Influence of the Climate of California*, 7; *Guide to Southern Georgia and Florida*, 68 (the guide did acknowledge that Floridians suffered from the usual intermittent fevers—probably malaria—but regarded this as an unavoidable minor problem); George W. Seaton, *Cue's Guide to What to See and Do in Florida: How to Get the Most out of Your Trip* (New York: Prentice-Hall, 1940): 82; Peter C. Remondino, *The Mediterranean Shores of America. Southern California: Climatic, Physical, and Meteorological Conditions* (Philadelphia: F. A. David, 1892): 118; Cobb, *Roughing It De Luxe*, 109; see also Chapline, *Florida the Fascinating*, 50, 71; *The Standard Guide to Florida* (New York: Foster & Reynolds, 1925): 105.

25. A. W. and Julian Dimock, *Florida Enchantments* (New York: Outing, 1908): 6; "Why Not Visit Puerto Rico?" *Home Pictorial: A Rotogravure Monthly for the Home* 7:5 (May 1936): n.p., clipping in second file, folder Tourist Development—Hotels—Condado, box 1012, Puerto Rico, Tourist Development 9-8-92, OTCF, 1907–1951, RG 126, NARA II; see also John E. Jennings, *Our American Tropics* (n.p.: Thomas Y. Crowell, 1938): 17. The dyspeptic A. Hyatt Verrill noted on the very first page of *Romantic and Historic Florida* (New York: Dodd, Mead, 1935) that the Spanish explorer believed the fountain of youth to be in the Bahamas and only poor navigation brought him to Florida.

26. Peter MacFarlane, "California the Land of Promise," *Sunset* 33:1 (July 1914): 44; *1937 West Indies Cruises*, 20.

27. Channing, "Italy and 'Our Italy,'" 24; George Wharton James, *California Romantic and Beautiful* (Boston: Page, 1914): 165, 373, and *The Influence of the Climate of California*, 7.

28. *Spanish Americas* (Panama Mail, n.d.): 5–6, Panama Mail folder 1, KMEC, HL; Elizabeth Gray Potter and Mabel Thayer Gray, *The Lure of San Francisco: A Romance amid Old Landmarks* (San Francisco: Paul Elder, 1915): 14; see also Carey McWilliams, *Southern California: An Island on the Land* (Layton, Utah: Gibbs Smith, 1999 [1946]): 96–164; William Deverell, *Whitewashed Adobe: The Rise of Los Angeles and the Remaking of Its Mexican Past* (Berkeley: University of California Press, 2004).

29. Advertisement for the Hotel Cecil, *The Standard Guide to Florida*, 6 (of a separately paginated advertising section); *Sailing from New Orleans: 3 West Indies Cruises . . . Winter Season 1939* (American Express, 1938), American Express folder, OCPC, SC; *Six Superb Cruises* (Holland America Line, 1933), Holland America folder, OCPC, SC; Elise S. Haas, *Letters from Mexico* (San Francisco: privately printed, 1937): 6; *Mexico? Si Señor!* 32.

30. Lisa Pinley Covert, "Colonial Outpost to Artists' Mecca: Conflict and Collaboration in the Development of San Miguel de Allende's Tourist Industry," in Dina Berger and Andrew Grant Wood, eds., *Holiday in Mexico: Critical Reflections on Tourism and Tourist Encounters* (Durham, N.C.: Duke University Press, 2010): 183–220; Heath Bowman

and Stirling Dickinson, *Mexican Odyssey* (Chicago: Willett, Clark, 1936); Helen Delpar, *The Enormous Vogue of Things Mexican: Cultural Relations Between the United States and Mexico, 1920–1935* (Tuscaloosa: University of Alabama Press, 1992); Faith Berry, *Langston Hughes: A Biography: Before and Beyond Harlem* (New York: Citadel Press, 1983); Rebecca M. Schreiber, "Dislocations of Cold War Culture: Exile, Transnationalism, and the Politics of Form," in Sandhya Shukla and Heidi Tinsman, eds., *Imagining Our Americas: Toward a Transnational Frame* (Durham, N.C.: Duke University Press, 2007): 282–312.

31. Chapline, *Florida the Fascinating*, 25; Verrill, *Romantic and Historic Florida*, 239; *Souvenir and Log of My Voyage* (Panama Mail Steamship Co., n.d., ca. 1930): 1, KMEC, HL (this sentence also appears in Joseph Mattingly, *Souvenir and Log of My Voyage via Panama Mail S. S. Co.* [Panama Mail S. S. Co, 1920]: 1); *Mexico: Tropical Tours*, 13; *"Mexico" guía de turismo* (July 1929): 47, file 6, Asunto: Folletos relativos a la organización del Turismo, 1929, Consular Dept., IV-300-1:VI, SRE, AGE (the author of this piece was particularly badly served by the translator); Miranda and González, *Tourist's Guide of Puerto Rico*, 52.

32. Charles M. Pepper, "The Spanish Population of Cuba and Porto Rico," *Annals of the American Academy of Political and Social Science* (July 1901): 170; "Discurso del Señor Elmer Jenkins: Gerente de la Oficina de Turismo Nacional de la Asociación Americana de Automovilistas" (October 7, 1931, 4th Pan American Commercial Conference), 2, III-192-9, SRE, AGE; see also Fredrick B. Pike, *The United States and Latin America: Myths and Stereotypes of Civilization and Nature* (Austin: University of Texas Press, 1992); John T. Reid, *The Spanish American Image of the United States, 1790–1960* (Gainesville: University Press of Florida, 1977). Special thanks to the Mexico City police officer who refused to answer my plea for directions until I uttered a polite "Buenos días, señor."

33. I. A. Wright, *Havana Ways and By-Ways* (New York: Ward Line, New York & Cuba Mail Steamship Co., 1924): 4; *Spanish Americas*, 11–12; [Levis], *Diary of a Spring Holiday in Cuba*, 9; *West Indies* (American Lines, 1911): 2, American Lines folder 4, KMEC, HL; "Bermuda," Furness, Withy advertisement; *Six Superb Cruises*; Clayton Sedgwick Cooper, "Uncle Sam's Great Winter Playground," *Travel* 46:1 (November 1925): 35; Sidney A. Clark, *Cuban Tapestry* (New York: National Travel Club, 1936): 190.

34. Clark, *Cuban Tapestry*, ix, 98; Derek Walcott, *The Antilles: Fragments of Epic Memory, The Nobel Lecture* (New York: Farrar, Straus and Giroux, 1992): n.p.; Harry L. Foster, *A Gringo in Mañana-Land* (New York: Dodd, Mead, 1924): 49, 65, 9.

35. Arthur W. Page, "Our Nearest Latin Neighbor," *Travel* 16:3 (January 1911): 113; Goddard, "The Flowery Crescent of the Caribbean," 47; Jean Lane, "Panama Mail Cruise Between New York and California Ports," *San Francisco, Los Angeles, Mexico, Central America, Panama, Cuba, New York: The De Luxe Tour* (Panama Mail, n.d.): 1, Panama Mail folder 1, KMEC, HL.

36. Reynolds, *Standard Guide to Cuba*, 113; *West Indies 1927 Raymond-Whitcomb Cruises* (Raymond-Whitcomb, 1926): 34, Norddeutscher Lloyd folder 42, KMEC, HL. This comment was specifically about the people of Curaçao.

37. Philip Sanford Marden, *Sailing South* (Boston: Houghton Mifflin, 1921): 225 (Marden was referring to Kingston, Jamaica, but he acknowledged that begging and extortionate prices were common "in any land where tourist travel is common" [224]); *West Indies 1927*, 39; Pepper, "The Spanish Population of Cuba and Porto Rico," 176; Hadley Cantril, American Social Surveys, "Opinion in the United States Concerning Latin America: Third Report" (February 12, 1942): 1, folder American Social Surveys, Export Information Bureau #3, box 137, Reports and Surveys, Regional, Commercial and Financial, OFIAA, general records, central files, RG 229, NARA II. This report was based on a poll taken December 10–20, 1940, and context makes clear that "South Americans" meant the people today called "Latin Americans."

38. Jennings, *Our American Tropics*, 20; see also Verrill, *Romantic and Historic Florida*, 63, 79.

39. James, *California Romantic and Beautiful*, xii; *California* (Automobile Club of Southern California, 1930): 9, BL; Clark, *Cuban Tapestry*, 255. McWilliams, *Southern California*, first identified this appropriation and mystification of the Spanish colonial era; Deverell, *Whitewashed Adobe*, 60, notes that in U.S. accounts of Spanish colonial and Mexican California, the residents are nearly always dancing.

40. *The Exclusive Grace Cruise Route* (Grace Line, ca. 1935), 7, Grace Line folder, OCPC, SC; *Spanish Americas*, 11; *Raymond-Whitcomb Cruises West Indies 1926* (Raymond-Whitcomb, 1925): 32, Norddeutscher Lloyd folder 42, KMEC, HL; Agnes Laut, "The Richest, Cruelest Land on Earth," *Travel* 35:3 (July 1920): 6.

41. Cleveland Amory, *The Last Resorts* (New York: Harper and Bros., 1952): 357; Susan Braden, *The Architecture of Leisure: The Florida Resort Hotels of Henry Flagler and Henry Plant* (Gainesville: University Press of Florida, 2002); "Florida Theme Issue," *Journal of Decorative and Propaganda Arts* 23 (1998); Beach, *The Miracle of Coral Gables*; Mark S. Foster, *Castles in the Sand: The Life and Times of Carl Graham Fisher* (Gainesville: University Press of Florida, 2000); Laura Cerwinske, *Tropical Deco: The Architecture and Design of Old Miami Beach* (New York: Rizzoli, 1981); *Florida: The Southernmost State*, 211–212.

42. Phoebe Kropp, *California Vieja: Culture and Memory in a Modern American Place* (Berkeley: University of California Press, 2006): 159–206; Lawrence Culver, *The Frontier of Leisure: Southern California and the Shaping of Modern America* (Oxford: Oxford University Press, 2010): 198–238; "Florida Theme Issue"; *Florida: The Southernmost State*, 210–211; Beach, *Miracle of Coral Gables*, 19, 58.

43. Eleanor F. Bennett, January 1, 1906, folder 1905–1906, Bennett, HL (the "steamer" was actually an automobile decorated to look like a miniature train engine); *Florida: The Southernmost State*, xxiii–xxvi.

44. Deverell, *Whitewashed Adobe*, 49–90; *Florida: The Southernmost State*, 210, 286; Catherine Cocks, "The Chamber of Commerce's Carnival: City Festivals and Urban Tourism in the United States, 1890–1915," in Shelley Baranowski and Ellen Furlough, eds., *Being Elsewhere: Tourism, Consumer Culture and Identity in Modern Europe and America* (Ann Arbor: University of Michigan Press): 89–107.

45. Julian Street, Jr., "Report on Carnavals [*sic*] in American Republics as a Stimulus to Tourist Travel" (February 5, 1941): 5, folder Carnivals—Tourist Travel, box 135, Reports and Surveys, Regional, Commercial and Financial, central file, general records, OFIAA, RG 229, NARA II; Guillermo Andreve, *Cómo atraer el turismo a Panamá*, Edición Oficial (Panama City, 1929): 26; Robin D. Moore, *Nationalizing Blackness: Afrocubanismo and Artistic Revolution in Havana, 1920–1940* (Pittsburgh: University of Pittsburgh Press, 1997): 62–86; on carnivals, see Andrew Grant Wood, "On the Selling of Rey Momo: Early Tourism and the Marketing of Carnival in Veracruz," in Berger and Wood, *Holiday in Mexico*, 77–106; Cocks, "The Chamber of Commerce's Carnival"; David Glassberg, *American Historical Pageantry: The Uses of Tradition in the Early Twentieth Century* (Chapel Hill: University of North Carolina Press, 1990).

Chapter 4. Dressing for the Tropics

1. Adam Singleton, "What Is a Gentleman?—A Lady?" *Cosmopolitan* (August 1900): 400; Selena Ingram, August 26, 1904, 1904 volume, Ingram, HL; on the dress code on Santa Catalina Island, see Lawrence Culver, *The Frontier of Leisure: Southern California and the Shaping of Modern America* (Oxford: Oxford University Press, 2010): 90.

2. "On Way to Fishnet Canyon," Elizabeth Chandler, photograph album, 1899–1904: 15, HL; see also Isabel Rintoul Shankland, photograph album, 1904: 11, HL.

3. William Thomas Corlett, *The American Tropics: Notes from the Log of a Midwinter Cruise* (Cleveland: Burrows Brothers, 1908), 58; Charles Dudley Warner, *On Horseback: A Tour in Virginia, North Carolina, and Tennessee; with Notes of Travel in Mexico and California* (Boston: Houghton Mifflin; Cambridge: Riverside Press 1889): 162; Charles M. Pepper, "The Spanish Population of Cuba and Porto Rico," *Annals of the American Academy of Political and Social Science* (July 1901): 176; Dane Kennedy, "The Perils of the Midday Sun: Climatic Anxieties in the Colonial Tropics," in John M. McKenzie, ed., *Imperialism and the Natural World* (Manchester: Manchester University Press, 1990): 118–140; Charles Woodruff, *The Effects of Tropical Light on White Men* (New York: Rebman, 1905): 323; T. Philip Terry, *Terry's Mexico: Handbook for Travellers*, 2nd ed. (London: Gay and Hancock, 1911): xxix (the same text appears in the 1923 edition on xxix; in the 1940 edition, the entire section was replaced with an affirmation that Mexico was as healthy as any civilized country [xxx]).

4. Kenneth L. Roberts, *Sun-Hunting: Adventures and Observations Among the Native and Migratory Tribes of Florida, Including the Stoical Time-Killers of Palm Beach, the Gentle and Gregarious Tin-Canners of the Remote Interior, and the Vivacious and Semi-Violent Peoples of Miami and Its Purlieus* (Indianapolis: Bobbs-Merrill, 1922): 26, 27, 167; Frank Parker Stockbridge and John Holliday Perry, *So This Is Florida* (New York: Robert M. McBridge, 1938): 9, 10.

5. Madeline Allen to her family, March 21, 1931, AFA; on this kind of clothing and lifestyle, see William R. Scott, "California Casual: Lifestyle Marketing and Men's Leisurewear, 1930–1960," in Regina Lee Blaszczyk, ed., *Producing Fashion: Commerce, Culture, and Consumers* (Philadelphia: University of Pennsylvania Press, 2008): 169–186;

Deirdre Clemente, "Made in Miami: The Development of the Sportswear Industry in South Florida, 1900–1960," *Journal of Social History* 41:1 (2007): 127–148; Patricia Campbell Warner, *When the Girls Came Out to Play: The Birth of American Sportswear* (Amherst: University of Massachusetts Press, 2006); Jane Farrell-Beck and Colleen Gau, *Uplift: The Bra in America* (Philadelphia: University of Pennsylvania Press, 2002); Jill Field, *An Intimate Affair: Women, Lingerie, and Sexuality* (Berkeley: University of California Press, 2007).

6. Allen, March 21; *Ships and Ports of the Great White Fleet* (United Fruit, ca. 1930s): 12, United Fruit folder 3, KMEC, HL; *Vagabond Cruises* (United Fruit, ca. 1930s): n.p., United Fruit folder 13, KMEC, HL; *Spanish Americas* (Panama Mail, ca. 1930s): 14, Panama Mail folder 1, KMEC, HL; Eleanor Early, *Lands of Delight: A Cruise Book to Northern South America and the Caribbean* (Boston: Houghton Mifflin, 1939): 4.

7. F. P. Garretson, *A Snap-Shot in the West Indies. A Thirty-Five Day Trip* (Newport, R.I.: Herald, 1902): 47.

8. John K. Walton, *The English Seaside Resort: A Social History, 1750–1914* (New York: St. Martin's Press, 1983); James Walvin, *Beside the Seaside: A Social History of the Popular Seaside Holiday* (London: Allen Lane, 1978); Cindy S. Aron, *Working at Play: A History of Vacations in the United States* (New York: Oxford University Press, 1999); John Kasson, *Amusing the Million: Coney Island at the Turn of the Century* (New York: Hill and Wang, 1978); Charles E. Funnell, *By the Beautiful Sea: The Rise and High Times of That Great American Resort Atlantic City* (New York: Knopf, 1975). Orvar Löfgren, *On Holiday: A History of Vacationing* (Berkeley: University of California Press, 1999): 224, says "the beach is very much the site of the making of the modern body."

9. F. H. Taylor, "A Trip to Bermuda," *Guide to Winter Resorts in Southern Seas* (Quebec Steamship Co., ca. 1880s): 14, 15, SCRL; *Jamaica, Hayti & the Spanish Main* (Hamburg American Line, 1906): 14, 16, 18, 20, 28 (the Bog Walk, reportedly a corruption of the Spanish "Boca del Agua," was a stroll along a river to a waterfall), SCRL; Ida M. H. Starr, *Gardens of the Caribees: Sketches of a Cruise to the West Indies and the Spanish Main*, vol. 2 (Boston: L. C. Page, 1903): 221; *Plan of Two Excursions to Florida, by the Florida Excursion Co.* (Boston: Florida Excursion Co., 1884): 9. See also James Johnson, *Jamaica: The New Riviera: A Pictorial Description of the Island and Its Attractions* (London: Cassell, 1903): 8–9, who wrote "one of the greatest diversions of the visitor who remains for any time in Jamaica is the sea-bathing." Notably, when Richard Henry Dana, Jr., visited Havana, Cuba, in the 1850s, the sea baths were literally baths, concrete boxes protecting bathers from the waves, sharks, and the gaze of passersby, intended to improve city dwellers' hygiene; see *To Cuba and Back: A Vacation Voyage* (Boston: Houghton, Mifflin, 1881): 55.

10. Samuel Dexter to his children, February 14, 1901, Dexter, HL; Eleanor F. Bennett, June 1, 1905, folder 1905–1906, Bennett, HL (even after acquiring a hand-me-down bathing suit shortly after the beach visit mentioned here, Bennett rarely entered the water, and although she loved to lie on the beach, getting a tan was never her goal); *Plan of Two Excursions to Florida*, 13; for context, see Walton, *The English Seaside Resort*,

and "The Transatlantic Seaside from the 1880s to the 1930s: Blackpool and Coney Island," in Neil Campbell, Jude Davies, and George McKay, eds., *Issues in Americanisation and Culture* (Edinburgh: Edinburgh University Press, 2004): 111–125.

11. J. R. Gilpin to Mrs. W. P. (Sue) Hazard, April 7, 1880:4, folder 1, box 1; and J. R. Gilpin to Mrs. W. P. (Sue) Hazard, April 20, 1888: 2, folder 4, box 1, both in GFP, HM.

12. On Daytona, see Clifton Johnson, *Highways and Byways of Florida: Human Interest Information for Travellers in Florida; and for Those Other Travellers Who Are Kept at Home by Chance or Necessity, but Who Journey Far and Wide on the Wings of Fancy* (New York: Macmillan, 1918): 73; Cecil Roberts, *Gone Sunwards* (New York: Macmillan, 1936): 101; [Carita Dogget Corse], *Florida* (Tallahassee, Fla.: Florida State Hotel Commission, 1930): 27, 38, 50; on Coronado, see Coronado Beach Company, *Coronado Beach, San Diego, California* (Chicago: Rand, McNally, 1886): 4, 7, and the nearly identical 1887 edition, both at the HL.

13. Ingram, February 20 and 21, 1909, 1909 volume, Ingram, HL.

14. Ingram, May 9, 1903, 1903 volume, Ingram, HL ("the boys" were her four sons; Selena Pope was her daughter and youngest child. The car was a train car at the family's disposal because Ingram's husband, Robert, was an official of the Southern Pacific Railroad. The family made regular visits to Long Beach and Santa Monica for a few years after coming to Los Angeles in 1902, but starting in 1904, they spent their summers on Santa Catalina Island and did all their swimming there); Samuel Dexter to his children, February 21, 1905, Dexter, HL; Stockbridge and Perry, *So This Is Florida*, 25; for context, see Jeff Wiltse, *Contested Waters: A Social History of Swimming Pools in America* (Chapel Hill: University of North Carolina Press, 2007).

15. C. W. Johnston, *Along the Pacific by Land and Sea: Through the Golden Gate* (Chicago: Rand McNally, 1916): 158–159; Ingram, diaries for 1904 through 1915; Stockbridge and Perry, *So This Is Florida*, 66; J. T. Boumphrey, *Down Where There's No Tomorrow* (Los Angeles: House of Ralston, 1928): 104; see also George W. Seaton, *Cue's Guide to What to See and Do in Florida: How to Get the Most out of Your Trip* (New York: Prentice-Hall, 1940): 24.

16. "Hawaiian Beauty in a Bathing Suit," *Los Angeles Times* (November 5, 1899): 6; Wiltse, *Contested Waters*, 121–153; Culver, *The Frontier of Leisure*; Marsha Dean Phelts, *An American Beach for African Americans* (Gainesville: University Press of Florida, 1997); Frank Fonda Taylor, *To Hell with Paradise: A History of the Jamaican Tourist Industry* (Pittsburgh: University of Pittsburgh Press, 1993); Christine Skwiot, *The Purposes of Paradise: U.S. Tourism and Empire in Cuba and Hawai'i* (Philadelphia: University of Pennsylvania Press, 2010); Langston Hughes, *I Wonder as I Wander: An Autobiographical Journey* (New York: Hill and Wang, 1993 [1956]): 11–15. I have come across no evidence of efforts to segregate beaches in Mexico but there, as elsewhere, the privatization of beaches for wealthy tourists tended to dispossess poor locals of all races.

17. William D'Egilbert, commissioner general, Virgin Islands Commission, to Ernest Gruening, director, DTIP, Department of the Interior, November 26, 1934: 3; F. Benítez Rexach, "Memorandum for Mr. Corcoran on the Tourist Problem" (ca. 1935);

F. Benítez Rexach to Ernest Gruening, November 16, 1934; all three items in folder Tourist Development—General, box 1012, Puerto Rico, Tourist Development, 9-8-92, OTCF, 1907–1951, RG 126, NARA II (Benítez was trying to raise money to complete the Escambron Beach Club and apparently had few friends in the Puerto Rican legislature, although U.S. officials backed him); Coert DuBois, "Travel Facilities and Vacation Opportunities in the Caribbean Area," 15–16, folder Vacation Travel Survey, 1943–July 1944, box 44, AACC, 1940–1946, and Caribbean Commission, 1946–1948, records of international commissions, RG 43, NARA II; Andrew Sackett, "Fun in Acapulco? The Politics of Development on the Mexican Riviera," in Dina Berger and Andrew Grant Wood, eds., *Holiday in Mexico: Critical Reflections on Tourism and Tourist Encounters* (Durham, N.C.: Duke University Press, 2010): 161–182; Dina Berger, *The Development of Mexico's Tourism Industry: Pyramids by Day, Martinis by Night* (New York: Palgrave Macmillan, 2006).

18. Claudia B. Kidwell, "Women's Bathing and Swimming Costume in the United States," *United States National Museum Bulletin* 250 (Washington, D.C.: Smithsonian Institution Press, 1968): 3–32; Angela J. Latham, *Posing a Threat: Flappers, Chorus Girls, and Other Brazen Performers of the American 1920s* (Hanover, N.H.: Wesleyan University Press, pub. by the University Press of New England, 2000): 65–97; Walton, *The English Seaside Resort*; Walvin, *Beside the Seaside*; Douglas Booth, "Nudes in the Sand and Perverts in the Dunes," *Journal of Australian Studies* 53 (1997): 170–182; Cameron White, "Picnicking, Surf-Bathing and Middle-Class Morality on the Beach in the Eastern Suburbs of Sydney, 1811–1912," *Journal of Australian Studies* 80 (2004): 101–110.

19. Kidwell, "Women's Bathing and Swimming Costume"; Latham, *Posing a Threat*, 65–97.

20. Cleveland Amory, *The Last Resorts* (New York: Harper and Bros., 1952): 339; Kidwell, "Women's Bathing and Swimming Costume," 26–27; Latham, *Posing a Threat*, 65–97; Roberts, *Sun-Hunting*, 34, 183–184 (quotations); see also "Gowns Cause It All; Park Commissioners Worry About Women's Bathing Costumes," *Chicago Daily Tribune* (August 4, 1895): 2; "Not Suited to Ocean Grove," *Chicago Daily Tribune* (August 29, 1891): 16; Bruce Henstell, *Sunshine and Wealth: Los Angeles in the Twenties and Thirties* (San Francisco: Chronicle Books, 1984): 52, offers a photograph of the Los Angeles chief of police posing with women in bathing suits identified as approved for use on city beaches; Kimberly Hamlin, "Bathing Suits and Backlash: The First Miss America Pageants, 1921–1927," in Elwood Watson and Darcy Martin, eds., *There She Is, Miss America: The Politics of Sex, Gender, and Race in America's Most Famous Pageant* (New York: Palgrave/St. Martin's, 2004): 27–51.

21. George W. Seaton, *Let's Go to the West Indies (How to Get the Most out of Your Trip)* (New York: Prentice-Hall, 1938): 22; Allen, March 21. This young man turned out to be an Argentine film star.

22. Johnston, *Along the Pacific*, 158, 160 (quotation); Kidwell, "Women's Bathing and Swimming Costume," 27, 30; Clemente, "Made in Miami," 135–136; Latham, *Posing a Threat*, 74; Adolph Christian Fera, *Post Cards of a Tourist (Mr. "Skinny" East): Cartoons*

of Southern California (Los Angeles: Henry J. Pauly, 1910): 43; Marcella Seiden Scrapbook, 1926–1929, HM.

23. Löfgren, *On Holiday*, 226, notes the same timing.

24. Roberts, *Sun-Hunting*, 136; Cecil Roberts, *Gone Sunwards* (New York: Macmillan, 1936): 182–183 (quotation), 204; Seaton, *Cue's Guide*, 81; see also Stockbridge and Perry, *So This Is Florida*, photograph of young women in bathing suits following p. 4; Hamlin, "Bathing Suits and Backlash."

25. *The Air Gateway Between the Americas* (Pan American, 1938), last page and inside back cover, folder 9, box 624, accession 1, PAAC, SCRL; *1937 West Indies Cruises, Hamburg-American Line/North German Lloyd* (October 1936): 2; *Six Superb Cruises* (Holland America Line, 1933); both in the OCPC, SC; Miguel Covarrubias, plate 1, "Peoples of the Pacific," *Pageant of the Pacific* (1940), HL; Heath Bowman and Stirling Dickinson, *Mexican Odyssey* (Chicago: Willett, Clark, 1936): 102. Löfgren, *On Holiday*, 237, notes that tourists' scanty clothing continued to dismay locals in the late twentieth century.

26. [Corse], *Florida*, 45, 60.

27. Laura Torbet, ed., *Helena Rubinstein's Book of the Sun* (New York: Times Books, 1979): 3–4; Kerry Segrave, *Suntanning in 20th Century America* (Jefferson, N.C.: MacFarland, 2005); James Walvin, "Selling the Sun: Tourism and Material Consumption," *Revista/Review Interamericana* 22 (Spring 1992): 208–225; Simon Carter, *Rise and Shine: Sunlight, Technology and Health* (Oxford: Berg, 2007); Marguerite S. Shaffer, "The Environmental Nude," *Environmental History* 13:1 (January 2008): 126–139; Leone Huntsman, *Sand in Our Souls: The Beach in Australian History* (Melbourne: Melbourne University Press, 2001); Booth, "Nudes in the Sand"; White, "Picnicking, Surf-Bathing and Middle-Class Morality"; Caroline Daley, *Leisure and Pleasure: Reshaping and Revealing the New Zealand Body, 1900–1960* (Auckland: Auckland University Press, 2003): 83–159; Löfgren, *On Holiday*, 168, 222–223.

28. Segrave, *Suntanning*, 5, acknowledges that the negative connotations attributed to dark skin had to be overcome for the practice to flourish in North America, but he does not attempt to explain how this happened or how it was compatible with the persistence of racism. Carter, *Rise and Shine*, places Britons' concern with staying pale in the context of British colonialism, but he drops the issue in explaining the vogue for tanning. See also Marilyn Lake and Henry Reynolds, *Drawing the Global Colour Line: White Men's Countries and the International Challenge of Racial Equality* (Cambridge: Cambridge University Press, 2008); Jonathan Peter Spiro, *Defending the Master Race: Conservation, Eugenics, and the Legacy of Madison Grant* (Hanover, N.H.: University Press of New England for the University of Vermont Press, 2009).

29. Eric Lott, *Love and Theft: Minstrelsy and the American Working Class* (New York: Oxford University Press, 1993); Baz Dreisinger, *Near Black: White-to-Black Passing in American Culture* (Amherst: University of Massachusetts Press, 2008); Shaffer, "The Environmental Nude"; Phil Deloria, *Playing Indian* (New Haven, Conn.: Yale University

Press, 1998); Shari M. Huhndorf, *Going Native: Indians in the American Cultural Imagi-nation* (Ithaca, N.Y.: Cornell University Press, 2001).

30. Mary Cathryn Cain, "The Art and Politics of Looking White: Beauty Practice Among White Women in Antebellum America," *Winterthur Portfolio* 42:1 (Spring 2008): 27–50; Gail Bederman, *Manliness and Civilization: A Cultural History of Gender and Race in the United States, 1880–1917* (Chicago: University of Chicago Press, 1995); Glenda Elizabeth Gilmore, *Gender and Jim Crow: Women and the Politics of White Supremacy in North Carolina, 1896–1920* (Chapel Hill: University of North Carolina Press, 1996); Kathy Peiss, *Hope in a Jar: The Making of America's Beauty Culture* (New York: Metro-politan Books, 1998); Franz Mraček, *Atlas of Diseases of the Skin, Including an Epitome of Pathology and Treatment*, trans. from the German by Henry W. Stelwagon (London: Rebman, 1900): 132; Henry W. Stelwagon, *Treatise on Diseases of the Skin, for the Use of Advanced Students and Practitioners*, 2nd ed. (Philadelphia: W. B. Saunders, 1903): 475–476; Christie MacDonald, "Good Complexions," *Delineator* 78:3 (September 1911): 204; "Care of the Arms," *Chicago Daily Tribune* (November 10, 1907): F8; "New Aid to Beauty; Pouring Rain Said to Wash Freckles Away," *Chicago Daily Tribune* (April 9, 1898): 16.

31. Emma Gilpin to Ellie, April 4, 1880, 2, folder 1, box 1, GFP, HM (in the late nine-teenth century, people used "burn" to describe both the reddening and the browning of the skin. The later restriction of "sunburn" to the former reflected the popularization of tanning and its construction as healthy); Samuel Dexter to his children, February 28–March 1, 1901, Dexter, HL; Laura Jean Libbey, "Laura Jean Libbey's Advice: Summer Brownies," *Chicago Daily Tribune* (July 12, 1912): 11; John Maxtone-Graham, *Liners to the Sun* (New York: Macmillan, 1985): 120.

32. "In the Boudoir," *Chicago Daily Tribune* (August 19, 1907): 7 (Segrave's earliest source is a 1905 *New York Times* article; see *Suntanning*, 185 n. 5); Christie MacDon-ald, "Good Complexions," *Delineator* 78:3 (September 1911): 204; W. A. Evans, "How to Keep Well," *Chicago Daily Tribune* (June 4, 1912): 6 (Evans continued this fight, with growing exasperation, into the 1930s; see "How to Keep Well," *Chicago Daily Tribune* [July 14, 1933]: 14). Readers attending to the footnotes will see that the *Chicago Daily Tribune* seems to have paid far more attention to tanning than any other newspaper except the smaller *Los Angeles Times*. I have no explanation for this. In addition to these two newspapers, I searched the *New York Times*, the *Washington Post*, the *Boston Globe*, the *San Diego Union*, and the *Atlanta Constitution* for articles on tanning and Florida and California vacations. Unfortunately, no Florida newspapers were available to me for the period of my study. The issue of tanning hardly appears at all in dermatology text-books between the 1880s and 1930s; recipes for freckle removers appear in the earlier editions, whereas later volumes summarize the state of knowledge about skin pigmenta-tion, but tanning as a practice earned little prose. By contrast, in the 1930s public health officials made regular pronouncements on tanning, sunburn, and vitamin D.

33. Margaret A. Cleaves, M.D., *Light Energy: Its Physics, Physiological Action and Therapeutic Applications* (New York: Rebman, 1904): xiii; Carter, *Rise and Shine*, 49–70; Segrave, *Suntanning*, 4–5, 12–26.

34. Bennett, February 25, 1907, 1906–1908 diary, Bennett, HL (her specific ailment was apparently gynecological, but far more damaging to her health was her resentment at having to work as a domestic or a seamstress to support herself. She eventually wrote her travels around Southern California into a career in local journalism); Peter C. Remondino, *The Mediterranean Shore of America: Southern California: Climatic, Physical, and Meteorological Conditions* (Philadelphia: F. A. David, 1893): 127; Remondino, first typescript, 3, folder 10, box 4, Remondino, SDHS; W. A. Evans, "How to Keep Well," *Chicago Daily Tribune* (July 8, 1920): 8; see also the same column in the *Chicago Daily Tribune* (July 20, 1912): 4.

35. Ratcliffe Hicks, *Southern California, or the Land of the Afternoon* (Springfield, Mass.: Springfield Printing and Binding, 1898): 9; Cleaves, *Light Energy*, 311; Los Angeles Chamber of Commerce, *Climate and Health in Los Angeles and Southern California* (January 1899): 2, 3, HL; *Florida: A Guide to the Southernmost State*, American Guide Series (New York: Oxford University Press, 1939): 260; Seaton, *Cue's Guide*, 82; John E. Jennings, *Our American Tropics* (n.p.: Thomas Y. Crowell, 1938): 45; Stockbridge and Perry, *So This Is Florida*, 1, 4; see also "Sunrays are Powerful Curative Agents Experts Say," *Florida Sunshine Greeter* 5:9 (February 3, 1934): 8.

36. Cleaves, *Light Energy*; Victor E. Levine, "Sunlight and Its Many Values," *Scientific Monthly* 29:6 (December 1929): 551–557; Edwin E. Slosson, "Sunshine for Brains," *Scientific Monthly* 21:5 (November 1925); 551–555; Guy Hinsdale, "The Sun, Health and Heliotherapy," *Scientific Monthly* 9:3 (September 1919): 253–262; J. H. Kellogg, *Light Therapeutics: A Practical Manual of Phototherapy for the Student and the Practitioner* (Battle Creek, Mich.: Good Health, 1910): 3; see Segrave, *Suntanning*, for a survey of sunlamps and related devices; John E. Baur, *The Health Seekers of Southern California, 1870-1900* (San Marino, Calif.: Huntington Library, 1959), 49, on Kellogg's sanitarium in Glendale, near Los Angeles; "Sunrays are Powerful Curative Agents," 8; [Corse], *Florida*, 8, 17, 79 (this work was also published as *Florida, Empire of the Sun*); *Comisión Nacional para el Fomento del Turismo, Memoria Annual, 1928–1929* (Havana: 1929): 32 (quotation).

37. Edgar Mayer, *The Curative Value of Light: Sunlight and Sun-Lamp in Health and Disease* (New York: D. Appleton, 1932): 7–15; Levine, "Sunlight and Its Many Values"; Frank Hammond Krusen, *Light Therapy*, 2nd ed. (New York: Paul B. Hoeber, Medical Book Department of Harper & Brothers, 1937); Herbert Bailey, *The Vitamin Pioneers* (Emmaus, Pa.: Rodale Books, 1968): 159–179; Rima D. Apple, *Vitamania: Vitamins in American Culture* (New Brunswick, N.J.: Rutgers University Press, 1996); "History of Vitamin D," University of California, Riverside, Vitamin D Workshop, http://vitamind.ucr.edu/history.html, accessed September 27, 2009; Michael F. Holick, "Sunlight, UV-Radiation, Vitamin D and Skin Cancer: How Much Sunlight Do We Need?" in Jörg Reichrath, ed., *Sunlight, Vitamin D and Skin Cancer,* Advances in Experimental Medicine and Biology, no. 624 (New York: Springer Science & Business, 2008): 1–15. Although this substance is still popularly known as vitamin D, scientists now consider it a steroid hormone.

38. Apple, *Vitamania*, 7–53; Ronald Millar, in collaboration with Dr. E. E. Free, *Sunrays and Health* (New York: Robert M. McBride, 1929): 82. Carter, *Rise and Shine*, explores the debate over providing access to sunlight versus improving children's diets in Britain (cod liver oil proved the cheaper option), and Apple notes that U.S. sales of cod liver oil soared in the mid-twentieth century. Daniel Freund, *American Sunshine: Diseases of Darkness and the Quest for Natural Light* (Chicago: University of Chicago Press, 2012) appeared too late to be incorporated in my study.

39. Mayer, *The Curative Value of Light*, 41; Millar, *Sunrays and Health*, 40, 29.

40. Juliet Dixon, "Saving Your Face from Sunburn," *Delineator* 99:2 (September 1921): 34; Celia Caroline Cole, "Romance and Red Lips," *Delineator* 105:20 (August 1924): 22; Alma Whitaker, "Sun Tans Win in Movieland," *Los Angeles Times* (July 27, 1930): B9. For context, see Peiss, *Hope in a Jar*; Sarah Berry, "Hollywood Exoticism: Cosmetics and Color in the 1930s," in David Desser and Garth Jowett, eds., *Hollywood Goes Shopping* (Minneapolis: University of Minnesota Press, 2000): 108–138; Shaffer, "The Environmental Nude"; Sigrid Schultz, "Claim Adam and Eve 'Were Happy'; So 6,000 Go Naked," *Chicago Daily Tribune* (March 16, 1931): 13.

41. "The Bronze Age," *Los Angeles Times* (July 11, 1929): A4.

42. Rhea Seeger, "Bathing Suits Get Praise of Wets and Drys," *Chicago Daily Tribune* (June 29, 1932): 15; Tom Pettey, "Getting a Tan, It Appears, Is Quite an Art," *Chicago Daily Tribune* (July 25, 1929): 29; "Laughing at the Sun," J. W. Robinson Co. ad, *Los Angeles Times* (June 20, 1934): 9; Ruth Seinfel, "The Burning Question," *Collier's* 92 (July 8, 1933): 24; see also Antoinette Donnelly, "Summer Complexion Ills: How to Reduce the Annual Crop of Freckles, Tan, and Sunburn," *Chicago Daily Tribune* (June 19, 1924): F2; the caption of the accompanying photograph of women sitting on the beach in one-piece bathing suits was, "They'll be sorry tomorrow for flirting with the sun."

43. Cleaves, *Light Energy*, 327; Walter H. Eddy, "Take It Easy," *Good Housekeeping* 104:6 (June 1937): 140; William J. Fielding, *How the Sun's Rays Will Give You Health and Beauty*, Little Blue Book No. 1556 (Girard, Kans.: Haldeman-Julius Publications, 1930): 13; Millar, *Sunrays and Health*, 88.

44. Fielding, *How the Sun's Rays*, 13; Millar, *Sunrays and Health*, 45 (quotation); and Stanley Hoffland, "Tan Is the Smart Shade This Summer," *Los Angeles Times* (July 18, 1926): B7 (quotation).

45. J. W. Sturmer, "The Modern Sun Cult," *Annual Report of the Board of Regents of the Smithsonian Institution, 1930* (Washington, D.C.: Government Printing Office, 1931): 191–206, originally a lecture given at Philadelphia College of Pharmacy and Science, 1929, and first published in the *American Journal of Pharmacy* 102:2 (February 1930); Edwin E. Slosson, "The Progress of Science: Health from Ultra-Violet Rays," *Scientific Monthly* 22:1 (January 1926): 81, 82.

46. Hoffland, "Tan Is the Smart Shade This Summer," B7; Jack London, "A Son of the Sun," in *A Son of the Sun* (Garden City, N.Y.: Doubleday, Page, 1912): 12, 27–28, 29; see also Anne-Marie Harvey, "Sons of the Sun: Making White, Middle-Class Manhood in

Jack London's David Grief Stories and the *Saturday Evening Post*," *American Studies* 39:3 (Fall 1998): 37–68.

47. "In the Boudoir," *Chicago Daily Tribune* (August 19, 1907): 7; Weare Holbrook, "Tarred and Weathered," *Los Angeles Times* (January 6, 1929): H10; the "rising tide" phrase refers to Lothrop Stoddard, *The Rising Tide of Color Against White World-Supremacy* (New York: Charles Scribner's Sons, 1920).

48. Stuart Chase, "Confessions of a Sun-Worshiper," *Nation* 128: 3338 (June 26, 1929): 763, 765. Chase mentions sunbathing nude with his family, making him part of the small U.S. nudist movement; see Shaffer, "The Environmental Nude."

49. [Corse], *Florida*, 17, 19, 29, 33 (part 1 of this guide opens with a fanciful depiction of an ancient Florida sun ceremony. The author lost track of her sunshine and health theme as she turned her attention to contemporary attractions, much to my disappointment); Millar, *Sunrays and Health*, 6; see also Cleaves, *Light Energy*, 311–312; Herman Goodman, *The Basis of Light in Therapy* (New York: Medical Lay Press, 1928): 39–40; Kellogg, *Light Therapeutics*, 9; Krusen, *Light Therapy*, 3; Mayer, *The Curative Value of Light*, 1–5.

50. Millar, *Sunrays and Health*, 43; Chase, "Confessions," 762; Pettey, "Getting a Tan," 29; see also Leonard Falkner, "The Burning Question," *American Magazine* 110 (August 1930): 50.

51. Walter H. Eddy, "Nature Gives Us Sunlight—Let's Use It!" *Good Housekeeping* 107:1 (July 1938): 51; Josephine Hemenway Kenyon, "The Sun Cure and Rickets," *Good Housekeeping* 86 (March 1928): 106. Scientists today regard skin pigmentation as an evolutionary adaptation enabling the skin to regulate the amount of ultraviolet light that penetrates the body; dark skins block more, pale skins less. See Nina G. Jablonski, *Skin: A Natural History* (Berkeley: University of California Press, 2006): 65–96.

52. Hazel Rawson Cades, "The Beautiful and Tanned," *Collier's* 79 (June 18, 1927): 14, 58; Dorothy Cocks (no relation to me), "From Berry Brown to Lily White," *Ladies' Home Journal* 50:10 (October 1933): 22; Seinfel, "The Burning Question," 24; see also Doris Lee Ashley, "Tempering Your Tan," *Pictorial Review* 31:12 (September 1930): 32.

Chapter 5. Lands of Romance

1. Sidney A. Clark, *Cuban Tapestry* (New York: National Travel Club, 1936): 28, 29, 30. Clark quoted the "star-eyed" phrase from the popular guidebook *Terry's Guide to Cuba*; in the 1926 edition (T. Philip Terry, *Terry's Guide to Cuba, Including the Isle of Pines* [Boston: Houghton Mifflin, 1926]), the quotation appears on 200. Havana employed a special, English-speaking police brigade to serve and protect U.S. tourists; rumor had it that good looks were a job requirement.

2. Ann Laura Stoler, *Carnal Knowledge and Imperial Power: Race and the Intimate in Colonial Rule* (Berkeley: University of California Press, 2002); Anne McClintock, *Imperial Leather: Race, Gender and Sexuality in the Colonial Contest* (New York: Routledge, 1995); Laura Briggs, *Reproducing Empire: Race, Sex, Science, and U.S. Imperialism in Puerto Rico* (Berkeley: University of California Press, 2002); Eileen J. Suárez Findlay,

Imposing Decency: The Politics of Sexuality and Race in Puerto Rico, 1870–1920 (Durham, N.C.: Duke University Press, 1999); Gail Bederman, *Manliness and Civilization: A Cultural History of Gender and Race in the United States, 1880–1917* (Chicago: University of Chicago Press, 1995); Kristin L. Hoganson, *Fighting for American Manhood: How Gender Politics Provoked the Spanish-American and Philippine-American Wars* (New Haven, Conn.: Yale University Press, 1998); Warwick Anderson, *Colonial Pathologies: American Tropical Medicine, Race, and Hygiene in the Philippines* (Durham, N.C.: Duke University Press, 2006); Vicente L. Rafael, *White Love and Other Events in Filipino History* (Durham, N.C.: Duke University Press, 2000); Marilyn Lake and Henry Reynolds, *Drawing the Global Colour Line: White Men's Countries and the International Challenge of Racial Equality* (Cambridge: Cambridge University Press, 2008): 95–113; Amy Kaplan, *The Anarchy of Empire in the Making of U.S. Culture* (Cambridge, Mass.: Harvard University Press, 2002): 92–120.

3. On race and heterosexual liberalization, see Kevin J. Mumford, *Interzones: Black/White Sex Districts in Chicago and New York in the Early Twentieth Century* (New York: Columbia University Press, 1997); Chad Heap, *Slumming: Sexual and Racial Encounters in American Nightlife, 1885–1940* (Chicago: University of Chicago Press, 2007); Alys Eve Weinbaum, "Interracial Romance and Black Internationalism," in Susan Gillman and Alys Eve Weinbaum, eds., *Next to the Color Line: Gender, Sexuality, and W. E. B. Du Bois* (Minneapolis: University of Minnesota Press, 2007): 96–123; Saloni Mathur, "Wanted Native Views: Collecting Colonial Postcards of India," in Antoinette Burton, ed., *Gender, Sexuality and Colonial Modernities* (New York: Routledge, 1999): 95–115.

4. Harriet Beecher Stowe, *Palmetto Leaves*, with introductions by Mary B. Graff and Edith Cowles (Gainesville: University Press of Florida, 1999 [1873]): 36 (quotation), 138, 140; José J. Nuñez y Dominguez, "The Legend of 'El Tajin,'" *Lands of Romance* 1:1 (August 1935): 9; Edward W. Barnard, "When Winter Widows All the North," *Land of Sunshine* 5:5 (October 1896): 191; Roy Pittard Stewart, "The Land of Some Other Time," *Lands of Romance* 1:6 (February 1936): 4; Amy Oakley, *Behold the West Indies* (New York: D. Appleton-Century, 1941): x, xii; *Year Round Vacation Trips* (Panama Pacific, ca. 1930s): inside fold, Panama Pacific folder 2, KMEC, HL.

5. Marie Robinson Wright, *Picturesque Mexico* (Philadelphia: J. B. Lippincott, 1897): 54; for examples, see *Cool Vacation Cruises* (Illinois Central and Standard Fruit and Steamship Co., 1938): cover, OCPC, SC; *Sailing from New Orleans: 3 West Indies Cruises, Winter Season 1939* (American Express, 1938): cover, American Express folder, OCPC, SC; *Aerogram* (Pan American Airways, ca. 1930s): cover, folder 21, box 287, accession 1, PAAC, SCRL; *Jesse Rogers' Song Collection and Souvenir from Old Mexico, XEPN-XELO Rio Grande B.C.S. and Victor Recording Artist* (n.p., n.d.): cover, DL; Gordon T. McClelland and Jay T. Last, *Fruit Box Labels: An Illustrated Price Guide to Citrus Labels* (Santa Ana, Calif.: Hillcrest Press, 1995): 121 (bottom), "Gasparilla" brand.

6. *1937 West Indies Cruises, Hamburg-American Line/North German Lloyd* (October 1936): 8, Hamburg American folder 8, KMEC, HL; *Raymond-Whitcomb Cruises West Indies 1926* (Raymond-Whitcomb, 1925): 27, Norddeutscher Lloyd folder 42, KMEC,

HL; on race and erotic imagery, see Vera M. Kutzinski, *Sugar's Secrets: Race and the Erotics of Cuban Nationalism* (Charlottesville: University Press of Virginia, 1993); Micol Seigel, *Uneven Encounters: Making Race and Nation in Brazil and the United States* (Durham, N.C.: Duke University Press, 2009): 67–94, 136–178; Jayna Brown, *Babylon Girls: Black Women Performers and the Shaping of the Modern* (Durham, N.C.: Duke University Press, 2008).

7. For a similar argument about portrayals of "native" women, see Mathur, "Wanted Native Views."

8. Charles B. Reynolds, *Standard Guide to Cuba: A New and Complete Guide to the Island of Cuba, with Maps, Illustrations, Routes of Travel, History, and an English-Spanish Phrase Book* (Havana: Foster & Reynolds, 1913): 21.

9. Reynolds, *Standard Guide to Cuba*, 24; William Seymour Edwards, *On the Mexican Highlands, with a Passing Glance of Cuba* (Cincinnati: Press of Jennings and Graham, 1906): 247 (sometimes, of course, a cigar is just a cigar); Philip Sanford Marden, *Sailing South* (Boston: Houghton Mifflin, 1921): 155–156.

10. Reynolds, *Standard Guide to Cuba*, 24–25; Cora Hayward Crawford, *The Land of the Montezumas* (Troy, N.Y.: Nims and Knight, 1890): 26.

11. Langston Hughes, *The Collected Works of Langston Hughes*, vol. 13, *Autobiography: The Big Sea*, ed. with an introduction by Joseph McLaren (Columbia: University of Missouri Press, 2002): 72; Crawford, *Land of the Montezumas*, 70.

12. Crawford, *Land of Montezumas*, 169; Hughes, *Collected Works*, vol. 13, 71, 72.

13. Crawford, *Land of Montezumas*, 69; Hughes, *Collected Works*, vol. 13, 73, 72; Harry L. Foster, *A Gringo in Mañana-Land* (New York: Dodd, Mead, 1924): 82; see also Reynolds, *Standard Guide to Cuba*, 24.

14. Javier Troncoso y Gama, "Feminine Types Below Rio Grande," *Lands of Romance* 1:6 (February 1936): 14.

15. J. T. Boumphrey, *Down Where There's No To-morrow* (Los Angeles: House of Ralston, 1928): 54, 82–83, 137 (quotations), and see also 79–86, 136, 139–141.

16. Clark, *Cuban Tapestry*, 205, 204.

17. Jonathan Peter Spiro, *Defending the Master Race: Conservation, Eugenics, and the Legacy of Madison Grant* (Hanover, N.H.: University of Vermont Press, pub. by the University Press of New England, 2009): 99; Bederman, *Manliness and Civilization*; Lake and Reynolds, *Drawing the Global Colour Line*, 95–113; Hoganson, *Fighting for American Manhood*; Kaplan, *The Anarchy of Empire*, 92–120; Anderson, *Colonial Pathologies*.

18. Ellsworth Huntington, *Civilization and Climate* (New Haven, Conn.: Yale University Press, 1915), 32; Ellen Churchill Semple, *Influences of Geographic Environment on the Basis of Ratzel's System of Anthropo-Geography* (New York: Henry Holt, 1911): 10; on this topic, see Stoler, *Carnal Knowledge*; Briggs, *Reproducing Empire*; Suárez Findlay, *Imposing Decency*; Christine M. Skwiot, "Genealogies and Histories in Collision," in Tony Ballantyne and Antoinette Burton, eds., *Moving Subjects: Gender, Mobility, and Intimacy in an Age of Global Empire* (Urbana: University of Illinois Press, 2009): 190–210;

see also Warwick Anderson, *Cultivation of Whiteness: Science, Health, and Racial Destiny in Australia* (Durham, N.C.: Duke University Press, 2006): 83–84.

19. Kaplan, *The Anarchy of Empire*, 92–120, makes a related point.

20. O. Henry, *Cabbages and Kings* (New York: Doubleday, Page, 1912): 35, 35–36, 38, 44, 45. On heterosexual romance as the solution to the problems of colonization, capitalism, and nationalism, see Mary Louise Pratt, *Imperial Eyes: Travel Writing and Transculturation* (New York: Routledge, 1992): 86–107; Doris Sommer, *Foundational Fictions: The National Romances of Latin America* (Berkeley: University of California Press, 1991); Kaplan, *The Anarchy of Empire*, 92–120.

21. Sommer, *Foundational Fictions*.

22. O. Henry, *Cabbages*, 7, 39–90, 241–252.

23. Isa Urquhart Glenn, "Tropical Heat and White Men," *Scribner's Magazine* 77:4 (April 1925): 361, 362.

24. Glenn, "Tropical Heat," 360–361, 364, 366, 367. I suspect the illustrator, like me, was rooting for Paquita.

25. Glenn, "Tropical Heat," 361.

26. Julian B. Carter, *The Heart of Whiteness: Normal Sexuality and Race in America, 1880–1940* (Durham, N.C.: Duke University Press, 2007): 98–107; Christina Simmons, *Making Marriage Modern: Women's Sexuality from the Progressive Era to World War II* (Oxford: Oxford University Press, 2009); Lary May, *Screening Out the Past: The Birth of Mass Culture and the Motion Picture Industry*, with a new preface (Chicago: University of Chicago Press, 1983), 200–236.

27. Emma Lindsay Squier, *Gringa: An American Woman in Mexico* (Boston: Houghton Mifflin, 1934), 9, 17.

28. Squier, *Gringa*, 17, 18, 35. For a more accurate account of the Yaqui people, see Evelyn Hu-DeHart, *Yaqui Resistance and Survival: The Struggle for Land and Autonomy, 1821–1910* (Madison: University of Wisconsin Press, 1984).

29. Foster, *Gringo*, 83–84 (quotation on 84); Clark, *Cuban Tapestry*, 28, 29, 30. Squier, *Gringa*, 58, also notes that the women condemned to arranged marriages and seclusion in the household "will become placidly fat" and allow their husbands to conduct affairs at will.

30. Simmons, *Making Marriage Modern*; Carter, *The Heart of Whiteness*.

31. Squier, *Gringa*, 79–80, 3–5, 198–282 (the dance is on 282). On the Tehuana, see Deborah Poole, "An Image of 'Our Indian': Type Photos and Racial Sentiments in Oaxaca, 1920–1940," *Hispanic American Historical Review* 84:1 (February 2004): 37–82; Analisa Taylor, "Malinche and Matriarchal Utopia: Gendered Visions of Indigeneity in Mexico," *Signs: Journal of Women in Culture and Society* 31:3 (2000): 815–840; see also Margaret D. Jacobs, *Engendered Encounters: Feminism and Pueblo Cultures, 1879–1934* (Lincoln: University of Nebraska Press, 1999).

32. Squier, *Gringa*, 58.

33. *Coast to Coast* (Panama Pacific Line, 1928): inside fold, Panama Pacific folder 1, KMEC, HL; *Raymond-Whitcomb Cruises*, 7.

34. *One Hundred Golden Hours at Sea* (New York: Southern Pacific Atlantic Steamship Lines, 1910): 7, 8, Southern Pacific folder 1, KMEC, HL. The 1907, 1910, 1915, 1926, 1930, and 1938 editions are also available in the KMEC. The 1907 brochure features a photograph of the "ladies' parlor and library" on 6 and mentions smoking rooms on 51; evening entertainment involving dinner and singing at the piano appears on 9 in 1907 and 15 in the 1910 version. In the 1910 brochure, the mother and children go for a walk on deck after breakfast while the father goes to the smoking room (15).

35. *One Hundred Golden Hours at Sea*, 3; *Six Superb Cruises to the West Indies* (Holland-America Line, 1933): inside fold, Holland America folder, OCPC, SC; *Year Round Vacation Trips*, inside fold.

36. "Be a Pleasure Pirate," advertisement for Hamburg American Caribbean cruises, *Chicago Daily Tribune* (November 17, 1929): H11; Marcella Seiden Scrapbook, HM.

37. Philip Dawson, *Cruise Ships: An Evolution in Design* (London: Conway Maritime Press, 2000); John Maxtone-Graham, *Liners to the Sun* (New York: Macmillan, 1985).

38. *Ships and Ports of the Great White Fleet* (United Fruit, ca. 1930s), 5, United Fruit folder 3, KMEC, HL; *We're Cruising to California on a Panama Pacific Liner!* (Panama Pacific Lines, 1934): 4, Panama Mail folder 2, KMEC, HL. For the change in social spaces, see *Coast to Coast* (Panama Pacific Line, 1924), Panama Pacific folder 1, KMEC, HL; *Coast to Coast: We Go Tourist on the Panama Pacific Line* (Panama Pacific Line, ca. 1930s): 6–7, Panama Mail folder 2, KMEC, HL.

39. *A Manual of Instructions for Pursers—Cruise Conductors: How to Conduct Cruise Programs Aboard Passenger Ships of the Great White Fleet* (United Fruit Co., ca. 1930s–1941), 9, 34 (quotations), United Fruit folder 36, KMEC, HL; on beauty contests, see *Coast to Coast* (1928), 3–4; "Bathing Suit Parade (Ladies)," 3:00 P.M., Wednesday, September 6, 1933, daily program of entertainment, Cunard Line folder 137, KMEC, HL.

40. *Manual of Instructions*, 11, 29; *Tropical Chatter* 0[sic]:12 (S.S. *Ecuador*, 1930): 11, Panama Mail folder 7, KMEC, HL. This is the same Mrs. Alvarez who won the prize for best costume at the masquerade ball (see Chapter 2).

41. *Tropical Chatter*, 19 (both quotations); Manuel Touissant to Luis Montes de Oca, June 11, 1937, doc. 28761, file 311, LMDO, CEHM; Clare Sheridan, *My American Diary* (New York: Boni & Liveright, 1922): 142.

42. Passenger List for West Indies Cruise on the S.S. *Veendam*, Holland America Line, February 15, 1928, in West Indies Cruise Photo Album, SC. Two of the women were maids accompanying their employers. The equal and even numbers of single men and women are no accident; they reflect the fact that passengers traveling alone typically shared rooms with persons of the same sex.

43. Passenger list for a voyage on the S.S. *Santa Elena* from New York to Los Angeles and San Francisco (Grace Line, 1936), Grace Line folder 42, KMEC, HL.

44. *Tropical Chatter*, 19; Jon Sterngass, *First Resorts: Pursuing Pleasure at Saratoga Springs, Newport and Coney Island* (Baltimore: Johns Hopkins University Press, 2001), 132–137; Cindy S. Aron, *Working at Play: A History of Vacations in the United States*

(Oxford: Oxford University Press, 1999): 85–86; "At the Resorts," *Chicago Daily Tribune* (August 16, 1891): 12.

45. *The Exclusive Grace Cruise Route* (Grace Line, 1935), 3, OCPC, SC; Dave Cain, "On the Good Ship 'Ecuador,'" *Tropical Chatter*, 5 (the Hotel Belmar was in Mazatlán, Mexico); Madeline Allen to her family, March 21, 1931, AFA; West Indies Cruise Photo Album, 16, photograph on the bottom right; *Sailing from New Orleans*, n.p. (inflation calculated using http://www.westegg.com/inflation/, accessed January 15, 2012); for very similar Havana tours, see Clark, *Cuban Tapestry*, 23–39; George W. Seaton, *Let's Go to the West Indies (How to Get the Most out of Your Trip)* (New York: Prentice-Hall, 1938): 66–73.

46. Clark, *Cuban Tapestry*, 38–39; Oakley, *Behold the West Indies*, 44; Seaton, *Let's Go to the West Indies*, 70.

47. "An Exciting Shore Leave," *Tropical Chatter*, 15. The incident is reminiscent of the more consequential "watermelon slice" incident in Panama nearly eighty years earlier; see Aims McGuinness, "Searching for 'Latin America': Race and Sovereignty in the Americas in the 1850s," in Nancy P. Appelbaum, Anne S. MacPherson, and Karin Alejandra Rosemblatt, eds., *Race and Nation in Modern Latin America* (Chapel Hill: University of North Carolina Press, 2003): 87–107.

Chapter 6. Spontaneous Capital Invisibly Exported

1. José Vasconcelos and Manuel Gamio, *Aspects of Mexican Civilization, Lectures on the Harris Foundation 1926* (Chicago: University of Chicago Press, 1926): 19, 20, 21. Clifford Gessler, *Pattern of Mexico* (New York: D. Appleton-Century, 1941): 1–2, similarly refers to "spiritual differences" as the motive for tourism. Susan Hegeman, *Patterns for America: Modernism and the Concept of Culture* (Princeton, N.J.: Princeton University Press, 1999): 5, notes that many U.S. thinkers identified the material with "civilization" and the spiritual with "culture."

2. Partha Chatterjee, *Nationalist Thought and the Colonial World: A Derivative Discourse?* (London: Zed for the United Nations University, 1986).

3. Dina Berger, *The Development of Mexico's Tourism Industry: Pyramids by Day, Martinis by Night* (New York: Palgrave Macmillan, 2006), and "Goodwill Ambassadors on Holiday: Tourism, Diplomacy, and Mexico-U.S. Relations," in Dina Berger and Andrew Grant Wood, eds., *Holiday in Mexico: Critical Reflections on Tourism and Tourist Encounters* (Durham, N.C.: Duke University Press, 2010); Dennis Merrill, *Negotiating Paradise: U.S. Tourism and Empire in Twentieth-Century Latin America* (Chapel Hill: University of North Carolina Press, 2009); Helen Delpar, *The Enormous Vogue of Things Mexican: Cultural Relations Between the United States and Mexico, 1920–1935* (Tuscaloosa: University of Alabama Press, 1992); James Oles, *South of the Border: Mexico in the American Imagination, 1914–1947* (Washington, D.C.: Smithsonian Institution Press, 1993); Christopher Endy, *Cold War Holidays: American Tourism in France* (Chapel Hill: University of North Carolina Press, 2004), and "Travel and World Power: Americans in Europe, 1890–1917," *Diplomatic History* 22:4 (Fall 1998): 565–594.

4. Banco de México, S. A., Oficina de Estudios Económicos, *El Turismo Norteamericano en México, 1934–1940* (Mexico City: Gráfica Panamericana, 1941): 25; *The First Inter-American Travel Congress, San Francisco, CA, April 14–21, 1939: Program and Regulations* (n.p., 1939): 1 (López de Mesa quotation), CL; on "invisible export" and "invisible import," see J. Rodolfo Lozada, *El Turismo: Lazo Espiritual y Fuente de Progreso* (Mexico City: Ediciones "Piramide," 1941): 69; August Maffrey, *Oversea* [sic] *Travel and Travel Expenditures in the Balance of International Payments of the United States, 1919–38*, U.S. Department of Commerce, Bureau of Foreign and Domestic Commerce, Economic Series No. 4 (Washington, D.C.: Government Printing Office, 1939): 56; Kenneth Street, "Invisible Import," *Jamaica and West Indian Review* (September 11, 1943): 3; F. H. Robertson of the Jamaica Tourist Trade Board, "Memorandum Relating to Tourist Trade Development in the West Indies" (September 1941): 1–2; both Street and Robertson in folder Vacation Travel Survey, 1943–July 1944, box 44, AACC, 1940–46, Caribbean Commission, 1946–1948, records of international commissions, RG 43, NARA II.

5. The literature on tourism in Mexico is now growing rapidly; see Berger, *Development of Mexico's Tourism Industry*; Berger and Wood, *Holiday in Mexico*; Merrill, *Negotiating Paradise*; Alex Saragoza, "The Selling of Mexico: Tourism and the State, 1929–1952," in Gilbert M. Joseph, Anne Rubenstein, and Eric Zolov, eds., *Fragments of a Golden Age: The Politics of Culture in Mexico Since 1940* (Durham, N.C.: Duke University Press, 2001): 91–115; Catherine Cocks, "The Welcoming Voice of the Southland: American Tourism Across the US-Mexico Border, 1880–1940," in Benjamin H. Johnson and Andrew Graybill, eds., *Bridging National Borders in North America: Transnational and Comparative Histories* (Durham, N.C.: Duke University Press, 2010): 225–248. Berger notes that studies published in Mexico to date have been anecdotal or hagiographic.

6. Benedict Anderson, *Imagined Communities: Reflections on the Origin and Spread of Nationalism*, rev. ed. (London: Verso, 1991); Eric Hobsbawm and Terence Ranger, eds., *The Invention of Tradition* (Cambridge: Cambridge University Press, 1983); Rudy Koshar, "'What Ought to Be Seen': Tourists' Guidebooks and National Identities in Modern Germany and Europe," *Journal of Contemporary History* 33:3 (July 1998): 323–340; John F. Sears, *Sacred Places: American Tourist Attractions in the Nineteenth Century* (New York: Oxford University Press, 1989); Marguerite S. Shaffer, *See America First: Tourism and National Identity, 1880–1940* (Washington, D.C.: Smithsonian Institution Press, 2001); John M. McKenzie, "Empires of Travel: British Guide Books and Cultural Imperialism in the 19th and 20th Centuries," in John K. Walton, ed., *Histories of Tourism: Representation, Identity and Conflict* (Clevedon: Channel View Publications, 2005): 19–38.

7. Glenda Sluga, *The Nation, Psychology, and International Politics, 1870–1919* (New York: Palgrave Macmillan, 2006); Walter Benn Michaels, *Our America: Nativism, Modernism, and Pluralism* (Durham, N.C.: Duke University Press, 1995); Mary Louise Pratt, *Imperial Eyes: Travel Writing and Transculturation* (New York: Routledge, 1992), 7; James Buzard, "Culture for Export: Tourism and Autoethnography in Postwar Britain," in Shelley Baranowski and Ellen Furlough, eds., *Being Elsewhere: Tourism, Consumer*

Culture, and Identity in Modern Europe and North America (Ann Arbor: University of Michigan Press, 2001): 299–319; Barbara Kirshenblatt-Gimblett, *Destination Culture: Tourism, Museums, and Heritage* (Berkeley: University of California Press, 1998); Rick A. López, *Crafting Mexico: Intellectuals, Artisans, and the State After the Revolution* (Durham, N.C.: Duke University Press, 2010); Christine Skwiot, *The Purposes of Paradise: U.S. Tourism and Empire in Cuba and Hawai`i* (Philadelphia: University of Pennsylvania Press, 2010); Mauricio Tenorio-Trillo, *Mexico at the World's Fairs: Crafting a Modern Nation* (Berkeley: University of California Press, 1996); Mark B. Sandberg, "Effigy and Narrative: Looking into the Nineteenth-Century Folk Museum," in Leo Charney and Vanessa P. Schwartz, eds., *Cinema and the Invention of Modern Life* (Berkeley: University of California Press, 1995): 320–361.

8. L. Lupián, "Turismo," 4, file 6, Asunto Actas y otros documentos relativos a la organización del Turismo, 1929, Consular Dept., IV-300-1: VI, SRE, AGE; John Torpey, *The Invention of the Passport: Surveillance, Citizenship, and the State* (New York: Cambridge University Press, 2000); Adam McKeown, *Melancholy Order: Asian Migration and the Globalization of Borders* (New York: Columbia University Press, 2008); Piers Brendon, *Thomas Cook: 150 Years of Popular Tourism* (London: Secker & Warburg, 1991); Lynne Withey, *Grand Tours and Cook's Tours: A History of Leisure Travel, 1750–1915* (New York: William Morrow, 1997).

9. Natalie Curtis, "An Old Town of the New World," *Travel* 8:5 (May 1905): 316; Leah Dilworth, *Imagining Indians in the Southwest: Persistent Visions of a Primitive Past* (Washington, D.C.: Smithsonian Institution Press, 1996); Erika Marie Bsumek, *Indian-Made: Navajo Culture in the Marketplace, 1868–1940* (Lawrence: University Press of Kansas, 2008); Sherry L. Smith, *Reimagining Indians: Native Americans Through Anglo Eyes, 1880–1940* (Oxford: Oxford University Press, 2000); Pratt, *Imperial Eyes*; Nicholas Thomas, *Possessions: Indigenous Art/Colonial Culture* (London: Thames and Hudson, 1999); Steve Clark, ed., *Travel Writing and Empire: Postcolonial Theory in Transit* (London: Zed Books, 1999). Partially protected by the legal concept of "domestic dependent nation," the Hopis maintain their own government and a distinct cultural identity; see the official site of the Hopi Nation at http://www.hopi-nsn.gov/.

10. Skwiot, *Purposes of Paradise*, notes the move away from colonization but offers no explanation for it; see also John Mason Hart, *Empire and Revolution: The Americans in Mexico Since the Civil War* (Berkeley: University of California Press, 2002): 106–130; Louis A. Pérez, Jr., *Cuba and the United States: Ties of Singular Intimacy*, 2d ed. (Athens: University of Georgia Press, 1997): 113–148.

11. "Editorial," *Real Mexico* 1:1 (April 1932): 5 (this magazine was published by the Consolidated Railroad and Pullman Company Tourist Service and Mexico's Departamento del Distrito Federal); Enrique Ortega, director, *Annual Report of the Institute of Tourism, Fiscal Year Ending June 30, 1938* (San Juan, P.R., 1938): 45, Folder Institute of Tourism 1938, box 986, 9-8-88, Puerto Rico, Reports, Annual, Institute of Tourism, OTCF, 1907–1951, RG 126, NARA II; Luis G. Mendoza, mission statement, *Comisión Nacional para el Fomento del Turismo, Memoria Anual, 1928–1929* (Havana: 1929): 1, CL.

12. Nancy Leys Stepan, *"The Hour of Eugenics": Race, Gender, and Nation in Latin America* (Ithaca, N.Y.: Cornell University Press, 1991).

13. Rebecca Earle, *The Return of the Native: Indians and Myth-making in Spanish America, 1810–1930* (Durham, N.C.: Duke University Press, 2007); Marilyn Grace Miller, *Rise and Fall of the Cosmic Race: The Cult of Mestizaje in Latin America* (Austin: University of Texas Press, 2004); Nancy Leys Stepan, *Picturing Tropical Nature* (London: Reaktion Books, 2001); George Reid Andrews, "Brazilian Racial Democracy, 1900–90: An American Counterpoint," *Journal of Contemporary History* 31:3 (July 1996): 483–507; Harvey R. Neptune, *Caliban and the Yankees: Trinidad and the United States Occupation* (Chapel Hill: University of North Carolina Press, 2007); José Vasconcelos, *La raza cósmica/The Cosmic Race*, trans. Didier T. Jaén (Baltimore: Johns Hopkins University Press, 1997). The Mexican thinker did have some followers in the United States; see Benjamin H. Johnson, "The Cosmic Race in Texas: Racial Fusion, White Supremacy, and Civil Rights Politics," *Journal of American History* 98:2 (September 2011): 404–419. A similar process of appropriation occurred in Australia and New Zealand; see Nicholas Thomas, *Colonialism's Culture: Anthropology, Travel and Government* (Princeton, N.J.: Princeton University Press, 1994), and *Possessions*.

14. Merrill, *Negotiating Paradise*, 29–102; Hart, *Empire and Revolution*; Ed Fletcher, "Our Trip to Baja California and to Gulf of California" (March 1919): 6, 79, folder 5, box 74, EFP, ca. 1870–1955, mss. 081, MSC, UCSD. Fletcher had bought the land with the approval of Presidents Díaz and Madero, which probably meant that he had received an exemption from the Mexican law barring foreigners from owning land along the country's borders and coasts; the early revolutionary governments rescinded such exemptions.

15. Manuel Tello, "Informe especial sobre el Turismo en Alemania," 1, file 4, Asunto Actas, file IV; Paul J. Vanderwood, *Satan's Playground: Mobsters and Movie Stars at America's Greatest Gaming Resort* (Durham, N.C.: Duke University Press, 2010); Merrill, *Negotiating Paradise*, 36–40; Eric Michael Schantz, "All Night at the Owl: The Social and Political Relations of Mexicali's Red-Light District, 1909–1925," in Andrew Grant Wood, ed., *On the Border: Society and Culture Between the United States and Mexico* (Lanham, Md.: SR Books, 2001), and "Behind the Noir Border: Tourism, the Vice Racket, and Power Relations in Baja California's Border Zone, 1938–1965," in Berger and Wood, *Holiday in Mexico*, 130–160; Rachel St. John, "Selling the Border: Trading Land, Attracting Tourists, and Marketing American Consumption on the Baja California Border, 1900–1934," in Alexis McCrossen, ed., *Land of Necessity: Consumer Culture in the United States-Mexico Borderlands* (Durham, N.C.: Duke University Press, 2009): 113–142; "Ley Cubana sobre el Fomento del Turismo," appendix A in Guillermo Andreve, *Cómo Atraer el turismo a Panamá* (Panama City, 1929): 35–44; Skwiot, *The Purposes of Paradise*.

16. Tello, "Turismo en Alemania," 4; Manuel Álvarez, "Asunto: Turismo. Exp. 861.7, La Habana, agosto 11 de 1928," 3, file 4, Asunto Actas, IV.

17. S. J. Treviño, "Turismo," 1, file 4, Asunto Actas, IV; Alejandro V. Martínez,

"Informe Especial sobre el turismo del consul de México en Phoenix Ariz," 1, file 4, Asunto Actas, IV; Lupián, "Turismo," 2–3, file 6, Asunto Actas, VI.

18. Lupián, "Turismo," 2; A. Casarín, "Turismo," 2, file 6, Asunto Actas, VI; Moisés González Navarro, *Los Extranjeros en Mexico y Los Mexicanos en el Extranjero, 1821–1970*, vol. 2 (Mexico City: el Colegio de México, 1994): 87–88; Edgardo L. Bruchell, "Informe sobre el turismo, consul en Providence, RI, 25 de julio 1928," 1, file 4, Asunto Actas, IV; Maffrey, *Oversea Travel*, vi, 34 (table 15). In this table, Maffrey is counting specifically those border crossers categorized as "visitors," a distinction that U.S. border officials made beginning in 1919. For earlier years, it was impossible to distinguish visitors from immigrants in U.S. government records.

19. Rafael Aveleyra, "Turismo," 10–11, file 6, Asunto Actas, VI, SRE, AGE; Tello, "Turismo en Alemania," 1–2; Edmundo González Roa, "Turismo," 1, 2, 3 (quotation), file 5, Actas y demas documentos, V.

20. Martínez, "Turismo del consul de México en Phoenix," 2; Ismael S. Vázquez, "Informe Junio de 1928. Turismo," 1–2, file 4, Asunto Actas, IV; Tello, "Turismo en Alemania," 4, 7, 9; González Roa, "Turismo," 4, 6.

21. T. Philip Terry, *Terry's Guide to Mexico: The New Standard Guidebook to the Mexican Republic, with Chapters on Cuba, the Bahama Islands, and the Ocean Routes to Mexico*, rev. ed. (Boston: Houghton Mifflin; Mexico City: Sonora News; London: Gay and Hancock, 1923): ccxxxiv; *Mexico: The Faraway Land Nearby* (n.p.: Asociación Mexicana de Turismo, ca. 1930s): 12; for a good overview of U.S. travel writing on Mexico, see Andrea Boardman, *Destination México: "A Foreign Land a Step Away": U.S. Tourism in Mexico, 1880s–1950s* (Dallas: DeGolyer Library, Southern Methodist University, 2001).

22. Sonia Lombardo de Ruiz, *El Pasado Prehispanico en la Cultura Nacional (Memoria Hemerografica 1877–1911)*, vol. 1 (Mexico City: Instituto Nacional de Antropología e Historia, 1994); Enrique Florescano, *Imágenes de la Patria* (Mexico City: Taurus, 2005): 189–252; Christina Bueno, "Teotihuacán: Showcase for the Centennial," in Berger and Wood, *Holiday in Mexico*, 54–76; Tenorio-Trillo, *Mexico at the World's Fairs*. I am one of the millions of tourists who have visited Teotihuacán, having spent a morning there during a research trip. It's stupendous. You really ought to go.

23. [Arturo César Castillo], *Archaeology in Mexico Today; Prepared and Distributed Free by Pemex Travel Club* (Mexico City: Petroleos Mexicanos, ca. 1940): 8, 27. *Mexico: Guia Ilustrada de Turismo* (np: nd), probably dates from the 1930s; a stamped notice on an interior page states "Asegurado Conforme a la Ley. 1934." The drawing on the front is unlabeled, but it features two large pyramids that might represent those of the sun and moon at Teotihuacán, although they seem to have swapped places. Alternatively, it could be a fantasy of Tenochtitlán, whose ruins lie under Mexico City.

24. J. de D. Bojórquez, "Sugestiones Pro-Turismo," *Revista Nacional de Turismo; Organo de la Comisión Nacional de Turismo* (June 1930): 63, I.300.IV:VI, file 6, Consular Dept., Asunto: Folletos relativos a la organización del Turismo, 1929, SRE, AGE; *Mexico: The Faraway Land Nearby*, 39; on folk art and nationalism, see Mary Kay Vaughan

and Stephen L. Lewis, eds., *The Eagle and the Virgin: Nation and Cultural Revolution in Mexico, 1920–1940* (Durham, N.C.: Duke University Press, 2006); López, *Crafting Mexico*; Mary K. Coffey, "Marketing Mexico's Great Masters: Folk Art Tourism and the Neoliberal Politics of Exhibition," in Berger and Wood, *Holiday in Mexico*, 265–294; Andrew Grant Wood, "On the Selling of Rey Momo: Early Tourism and the Marketing of Carnival in Veracruz," in Berger and Wood, *Holiday in Mexico*, 77–106; for examples of images, see *Guia Ilustrada*, photographs of "Churubusco: Typical scene in the old convent," featuring folk icons charro and china poblana, and indigenous dancers in ritual dress in an unpaginated section at the end of the volume; Xavier Sorondo, "The 'Three Falls' at Ixtapalapa: Drama of the Calvary Is Enacted Yearly in This Ancient Village near Mexico City," *Real Mexico* 1:1 (April 1932): 33.

25. González Roa, "Turismo," 6; *Guia Illustrada*, 51, and also the description of the national cathedral in Mexico City, 31; Lisa Pinley Covert, "Colonial Outpost to Artists' Mecca: Conflict and Collaboration in the Development of San Miguel de Allende's Tourist Industry," in Berger and Wood, *Holiday in Mexico*, 183–220; Marjorie Becker, *Setting the Virgin on Fire: Lázaro Cárdenas, Michoacán Peasants, and the Redemption of the Mexican Revolution* (Berkeley: University of California Press, 1995).

26. Charles Dudley Warner, *On Horseback: A Tour in Virginia, North Carolina, and Tennessee; with Notes of Travel in Mexico and California* (Boston: Houghton Mifflin; Cambridge: Riverside Press, 1889): 297; C. M. St. Hill, *Pocket Guide to Mexico* (n.p.: n.d.): 4–5, in Alice D. Perkins Scrapbook of trips to Colorado, California, and Mexico, 1882–1920, HL; Frances Toor, *Mexican Popular Arts* (Mexico City: Frances Toor Studios, 1939): 12 (the map in Fig. 12 appears on 23); Erna Fergusson, *Fiesta in Mexico* (New York: Alfred A. Knopf, 1934): v (quotation); on the promotion of crafts, see López, *Crafting Mexico*; Coffey, "Marketing Mexico's Grand Masters"; on souvenir shops, see, for example, ads for "The Popular Art of Old Mexico," "Lechuga's Curio Stores," and "Tlaquepaque," *Real Mexico* 1:1 (April 1932): 47; "La Abeja," "Cia. Orfebrera Mexicana," "Foto Mexicana," and "Casa Weston," *Real Mexico* 1:2 (June 1932): 45.

27. Adele Townley, "Six Glorious Weeks at America's Oldest School!" *Lands of Romance* 1:6 (February 1936): 14; Matt Garcia, *A World of Its Own: Race, Labor, and Citrus in the Making of Greater Los Angeles, 1900–1970* (Chapel Hill: University of North Carolina Press, 2001): 121–154; Diana Selig, *Americans All: The Cultural Gifts Movement* (Cambridge, Mass.: Harvard University Press, 2008); Catherine Cocks, *Doing the Town: The Rise of Urban Tourism in the United States, 1850–1915* (Berkeley: University of California Press, 2001): 174–203; Brad Evans, *Before Cultures: The Ethnographic Imagination in American Literature, 1865–1920* (Chicago: University of Chicago Press, 2005); Hegeman, *Patterns for America.*

28. Álvarez, "Asunto: Turismo," 3; this document is Álvarez's response to criticism of his original report by the head of the Bank of Mexico. On Cuba, see Merrill, *Negotiating Paradise*, 103–176; Skwiot, *Purposes of Paradise*; Rosalie Schwartz, *Pleasure Island: Tourism and Temptation in Cuba* (Lincoln: University of Nebraska Press, 1997). The growing number of U.S. residents with Mexican roots and the centrality of Mexicanness

to tourism in the U.S. states along the border also complicated efforts to maintain the nationality of Mexico's spontaneous capital.

29. Banco de México, S. A., Departamento de Turismo, "Turismo," June 27, 1928, file 4, Asunto Actas, IV; the financing of hotels and tourist camps was a frequent concern of Bank of Mexico president (and later secretary of the interior) Luis Montes de Oca and his many correspondents; see, for example, doc. 28684, folder 311/493, file 1/132, June 1937, documents 28683–28815, LMDO, CEHM. Berger, *Development of Mexico's Tourist Industry*, and Merrill, *Negotiating Paradise*, also address this issue.

30. Director of the Confederación de Cámaras Nacionales de Comercio e Industria to Luis Montes de Oca, March 12, 1937, doc. 28086, folders c. 304/496, file 1/99, documents 28005–28104, LMDO, CEHM, on this law; on Barbachano, see documents 28228 and 28279 in the same file; on Puerto Rico's predicament, see Ruth Hampton, acting director, DTIP, Department of the Interior, to Charles W. Schreiber of the Schreiber Travel Bureau, March 6, 1940, folder Tourist Development—General, box 1012, 9-8-92, Puerto Rico, Tourist Development, OTCF, 1907–1951, RG 126, NARA II.

31. E. Narváez, cable dated July 24, 1928; file 4, Actas y demas documentos, IV; González Roa, "Turismo," 4–5; Berger, *Development of Mexico's Tourism Industry*. The substitution of an automobile club card for a passport was quite common at the time, reflecting the limited number of well-to-do people who owned automobiles, their desirability as tourists, and the absence or inadequacy of systems of national identification.

32. Gaillard Hunt, *The American Passport, Its History and a Digest of Laws, Rulings, and Regulations Governing its Issuance by the Department of State* (Washington, D.C.: Government Printing Office, 1898), 3; Torpey, *The Invention of the Passport*.

33. Torpey, *Invention of the Passport*; Radhika Viyas Mongia, "Race, Nationality, Mobility: A History of the Passport," in Antoinette Burton, ed., *After the Imperial Turn: Thinking with and Through the Nation* (Durham, N.C.: Duke University Press, 2003): 196–214; McKeown, *Melancholy Order*. A quick glance at the passport requirements of the American republics reveals that another major aim of border controls was to prevent the spread of contagious disease.

34. González Navarro, *Los Extranjeros en México*, vol. 3, 34–35; A. J. Norval, *Tourist Industry: A National and International Survey* (London: Sir Isaac Pitman & Sons, 1936): 101, 165–167; *Insignia de la Federación Sudamericana de Turismo, Conocer y Hacer Conocer America es Contribuir a su Grandeza* (flyer published on the occasion of the 4th congress of the federation, meeting in Montevideo, Uruguay, in 1933), CL; *The First Inter-American Travel Congress*; for Mexico's participation in the Alliance Internationale de Tourisme, see the *Boletin Nacional de Información* of the Asociación Mexicana Automovilística, doc. 29176, folder 316/493, file 1/91, July 1937, documents 29175–29282, LMDO, CEHM.

35. "Cuarta Conferencia Comercial Panamericana: Memorandum sobre el Tema 6 del Programa 'Fomento del Turismo como Factor en el Desenvolvimiento del Comercio'" (Washington, D.C., Pan American Union, October 5–12, 1931): 2, CL; Norval, *Tourist Industry*, 101; "Discurso del Señor Elmer Jenkins Gerente de la Oficina de

Turismo Nacional de la Asociación Americana de Automovilistas (October 7, 1931, Washington, D.C., 4th Pan American Commercial Conference): 3, CL; Maffrey, *Oversea Travel*, vi. According to Norval, 101, the countries in my study earned much less than the top destinations, with Cuba taking in $28.4 million and the United States $163 million. U.S. tourists spent between $10 and $16 million in the British West Indies each year in 1929, 1932, and 1933. Most tourists in Canada were from the United States, and most tourists in the United States were from Canada. Yes, these figures did make me wonder why I wasn't studying tourism across the U.S.-Canada border.

36. Folder 52082/50, MLR A1-9, box 414, files 52082/031–52082/070, RG 85, Records of the Immigration and Naturalization Service, Subject and Policy Files, 1893–1957, NARA I; McKeown, *Melancholy Order*; Andrea Geiger, "Caught in the Gap: The Transit Privilege and North America's Ambiguous Borders," in Johnson and Graybill, eds., *Bridging National Borders in North America*, 199–222.

37. "[Public—No. 139—68th Congress.] [H.R. 7995.] An Act to Limit the Immigration of Aliens into the United States, and for Other Purposes," vol. 3, box 3, Instructions for Foreign Service Officers, RG 59, general records of the Department of State, NARA II; more accessible is "An Act to Limit the Immigration of Aliens into the United States, and for Other Purposes," *American Journal of International Law* 18:4, supplement: "Official Documents" (October 1924): 208–227.

38. González Navarro, *Los Extranjeros en México*, vol. 3, 33, 39; *Ley de Migración de los Estados Unidos Mexicanos*, August 30, 1930, articles 37 (quotation), 35, and 51 par. IV. I have not been able to get a copy of the 1926 law, but as González Navarro points out, it represented a significant innovation; for a long time the Mexican constitution specifically denied the government the power to require passports because doing so would violate the liberal principle of freedom of movement. The new law distinguished between immigrants and colonists because in Mexican usage the latter were specifically those going to establish or work in new farming communities.

39. For a copy of the forma 11, see "Ponencia de la Secretaría de Gobernación sobre el Tema #6 'Fomento del Turismo como Factor en el Desenvolvimiento del Comercio', en la forma aprobada como instrucciones a la Delegación Mexicana que representará al Gobierno de México en la IV Conferencia Comercial Panamericana," Asunto: Turismo. Proyecto de Bases Para una Convención Interamericana sobre Fomento del Turismo, de la Unión Panamericana, 1931, III-192-9, SRE, AGE; articles 77 and 78, *Ley de Migración y Reglamento: Decretos y Circulares Relativos Acuerdo de 16 Febrero de 1934* (Mexico City: Editorial Derecho Nuevo, 1934): 73–74; *Documents Required and Visa Fees for Tourists Entering Latin American Republics; Also, Requirements for Leaving These Countries* (Washington, D.C.: Pan American Union, 1931): 16–17. As late as October 1929, border officials were interpreting the ban on the immigration of people of African descent to Mexico to mean that none could enter the country for any reason; the Department of Foreign Affairs advised that black U.S. tourists should be allowed to visit Mexico for three days as long as they stayed within three miles of the border and paid a fee; see "Informe sobre turistas norteamericanos de raza negra," 1929, IV-169-34, SRE,

AGE. Neither the 1930 law nor the regulations implementing it specify undesirable racial groups (whether tourist or immigrant), leaving it up to the secretary of the interior to determine whether the applicants "belonged to races that, by their social conditions, may easily be assimilated to our environment, benefitting the race and the economic conditions of the country" (article 50 of the 1930 *Ley de Migración*, 17–18). The 1930 law thus may or may not have made it easier for nonwhite U.S. residents to visit Mexico.

40. *Requirements for the Entry of Aliens into the Latin American Republics* (Washington, D.C.: Pan American Travel Union, 1936): 10–11, 21; on allowing transportation companies to vouch for their passengers, see Gonzalo Vázquez Vela, Immigration Dept., June 1, 1928, to the president of the Ward Steamship Line; and A. de la Garza, memorandum from the Public Health Dept. to the Combined Commission on Tourism, January 22, 1929, both documents in file 5, Actas y demas documentos, V.

41. *Requirements* (1936), 30, 80; Pan American Airways district manager, traffic, Havana, to special representative for Caribbean, Havana, September 26, 1936, re "Cuba—Proposed New Immigration Law," folder 7, Cuba—Laws—Immigration Law (Proposed)—1939, box 727, PAAC, accession 2, SCRL; Torpey, *Invention of the Passport*, 9–10. Cuba required married women to apply for visas in person and show written permission from their husbands, a once common requirement that many nations had dropped by the 1930s. Restrictions on women traveling alone (long presumed to be prostitutes) were also being eliminated.

42. Letter from Silvestre Guerrero, subsecretary of the interior, to the secretary of foreign relations, January 6, 1932, IV-400-27, 1932, SRE, AGE; letter from the director of the Accounting Department to the consul in San Diego, December 14, 1920, 23-21-227, 1920, SRE, AGE. The consul in Del Rio, Texas, also mentioned an earlier tourist card, forma 5, which required a photograph and so was more expensive and time consuming to get for users, with the result that most locals chose to cross the border somewhere other than the official gateway; see L. Peña, "Informe por junio de 1928, Turismo," file 4, Asunto Actas, IV; St. John, "Selling the Border"; Berger, *Development of Mexico's Tourism Industry*.

43. Minutes, Combined Commission on Tourism meeting, July 30, 1929, 1, file 6, Asunto Actas, IV; S. Deborah Kang, "Crossing the Line: The INS and the Federal Regulation of the Mexican Border," in Johnson and Graybill, eds., *Bridging National Borders in North America*, 183–187; *Inter-American Travel Statistics: Movement of Travel in the Americas, January–December 1939 and 1940* (Washington, D.C.: Pan American Union, n.d.), table 3, footnote 4 (quotation), folder 4, box 12, PAAC, accession 1, SCRL.

44. "Touring in Mexico: Lower California as an Example," in *'Mexico' guía de turismo* (Interior Dept., July 1929): 25, file 6, Asunto: Folletos relativos, VI; Lozada, *El Turismo*, 10, 13; Andreve, *Cómo atraer el turismo a Panamá*, 5.

45. Alfredo L. Bofill, "Proyecto de Bases para una Convención Interamericana sobre 'Fomento del Turismo como Factor en el Desenvolvimiento del Comercio,'" and "Resolución sobre turismo aprobada por la Sección I y sometida a la Sesión plenaria," in "Cuarta Conferencia Comercial Panamericana" in Asunto: Turismo. Proyecto de Bases

Para una Convención Interamericana sobre Fomento del Turismo, de la Unión Panamericana, Año de 1931, III-192-9, SRE, AGE; *Special Handbook for the Use of Delegates, First Inter-American Travel Congress* (Washington, D.C.: Pan American Union, 1939), 6, 28, 29, CL; *The First Inter-American Travel Congress*, 8. It also seems likely that few American nations had adequate systems for identifying all their citizens, a prerequisite for this plan. The United States supported the resolution but abstained from voting for it because its government was prohibited from joining such multilateral treaties.

46. "United States Department of the Interior Memorandum for the Press," November 25, 1938, file no. 0-201-13, National Parks General, Travel Bureau, October 1940–December 1947, box 134, RG 79, NPSCCF, 1933–1949, General, NARA II.

47. "Why a Travel Bureau?" *Official Bulletin of the United States Travel Bureau, National Park Service* 1 (October 1938), 4, in file 0-201-13; *The United States Tourist Bureau* (Washington, D.C.: Government Printing Office, 1937): 3, file no. 0-201-13; "The United States Tourist Bureau, A Radio Address by James W. Gerard," aired on the Columbia Network, October 13, 1937, file no. 0-201-13. See also Ruth Bryan Rohde, "US Travel Bureau Filling a Long-Felt Need for Service," clipping from the *Christian Science Monitor*, June 8, 1939, and "Government Tourist Bureau Will Aid the Travel Industry; Thirty of Forty-Eight States Now Organizing to Share in Five-Billion-Dollar Industry," clipping from the *Boston Transcript*, June 19, 1938, both in file no. 0-201-13.

48. "United States Travel Bureau Functions and Objectives," file no. 0-201-13; *Official Bulletin of the United States Travel Bureau, National Park Service* 1 (October 1938), file no. 0-201-13; "International Networks," in file no. 0-201-13. Alaska and Hawai`i became states in 1959.

49. "Major Immediate Propaganda Objectives," June 5, 1941, draft #2," folder American Social Surveys Export Information Bureau #8, box 137, Reports and Surveys, Regional, Commercial and Financial, OFIAA, general records, central files, RG 229, NARA II; letter from Dr. Hedley Cantril, May 7, 1941, "Comments of Readers to Advertising Program from Chile," in "Excerpts from Various Letters Commenting on the Travel Advertisements of the Inter-American Travel Committee," folder American Social Surveys Export Information Bureau #8; letter from *United Press*, Caracas, Venezuela, May 1, 1941, in folder American Social Surveys Export Information Bureau #8. See also doc. 36174, minutes of a meeting of the Mexican Tourism Association, 3–4, folder 396/493, file 1/199, October–December 1940, documents 36149–36248, LMDO, CEHM.

50. "Major Immediate Propaganda Objectives," 6. This list was obviously composed by a Yanqui.

51. Robert M. Lovett to Guy J. Swope, director, DTIP, October 27, 1941, file DTIP—Virgin Islands—Tourist and Winter Residence Development—General, box 1313, Virgin Islands Tourist Development, 9-11-42, OTCF, 1907–1951, RG 126, NARA II; Coert DuBois, "Travel Facilities and Vacation Opportunities in the Caribbean Area," 5, folder Vacation Travel Survey, 1943–July 1944, box 44, AACC, 1940–1946, and Caribbean Commission 1946–1948, records of international commissions, RG 43, NARA II; see also Frank Fonda Taylor, *To Hell with Paradise: A History of the Jamaican Tourist*

Industry (Pittsburgh: University of Pittsburgh Press, 1993); Lawrence Culver, *The Frontier of Leisure: Southern California and the Shaping of Modern America* (Oxford: University of Oxford Press, 2010).

52. John L. Morris, "Report on the Investigation of a Proposed Inter-American Trade Mart," 3 (quotation), 4, 11 (quotation), 12, box 134, Commercial and Financial—Regional—Reports and Surveys, OFIAA, general records, central files, RG 229, NARA II; see also Mark Souther, *New Orleans on Parade: Tourism and the Transformation of the Crescent City* (Baton Rouge: Louisiana State University Press, 2006).

53. Charles W. Taussig, Lt. Col. A. F. Kibler, and Lt. Comm. W. S. Campbell, "Report of the United States Commission to Study Social and Economic Conditions in the British West Indies, Appointed by the President of the United States on November 13, 1940," 72, binder Historical—Taussig Report to President, box 1, AACC, 1940–1946, and Caribbean Commission, 1946–1948, records of international commissions, RG 43, NARA II; Neptune, *Caliban and the Yankees*; Taylor, *To Hell with Paradise*; Skwiot, *Purposes of Paradise*.

54. Krista Thompson, *An Eye for the Tropics: Tourism, Photography, and the Framing of the Caribbean Picturesque* (Durham, N.C.: Duke University Press, 2006); Polly Pattullo, *Last Resorts: The Costs of Tourism in the Caribbean* (London: Cassell, 1996); Mimi Sheller, *Consuming the Caribbean: From Arawaks to Zombies* (London: Routledge, 2003); Culver, *Frontier of Leisure*.

Chapter 7. The Most Ideal Winter Resorts

1. Jean Lane, "Panama Mail Cruise Between New York and California Ports," *San Francisco, Los Angeles, . . . 30 Delightful Days at Sea* (Panama Mail, ca. 1920s): 1, Panama Mail folder 1, KMEC, HL. Lane was billed as a "satisfied customer," but the style of the account suggests she was also a professional travel writer.

2. Lawrence W. Cramer to Harold L. Ickes, secretary of the interior, December 15, 1937, 3, file DTIP—Virgin Islands—Tourist and Winter Residence Development—General, box 1313, Virgin Islands Tourist Development, 9-11-42, OTCF, 1907–1951, RG 126, NARA II. About half of St. John was indeed turned into a national park; see http://www.nps.gov/viis/. I do not know if Cramer's concern that the residents retain the right to harvest wood for fuel was addressed.

3. Ward M. Canaday, chairman of the Board of Willy's Overland Motors, Inc., Willy's Americar, to Harold L. Ickes, secretary of the interior, February 25, 1941 (Canaday also contacted several members of Congress and other federal officials about developing the Virgin Islands, apparently to no avail); Louise Redding, vice president, Jordan and Parker Travel Bureau, Inc., to Ruth Hampton, acting director, DTIP, Dept. of the Interior, January 5, 1940, p. 2; Louis E. Tuffin to Secretary of the Interior Harold Ickes, undated, stamped received by Dept. of the Interior May 18, 1938, 2 (Tuffin's letter is notable for its anti-Semitism; he felt Florida had been ruined because Jews were allowed to patronize many luxury resorts there). All three letters are in file DTIP—Virgin Islands—Tourist and Winter Residence Development—General.

4. Paul M. Pearson to John H. Edwards, assistant secretary of the interior, October 23, 1931; Oscar Chapman, assistant secretary of the interior, to Ralph E. Church, House of Representatives, December 19, 1939, 1; Dept. of the Interior memorandum for the press, February 19, 1939, 3; Robert M. Lovett, acting governor of the Virgin Islands, to Guy J. Swope, director, DTIP, October 27, 1941; Chapman to Church. At the same time, the Civilian Conservation Corps, a federal jobs program, improved road and water infrastructure: Ernest Gruening, director, DTIP, to the secretary of the interior, December 14, 1938. All of these items are in file DTIP—Virgin Islands—Tourist and Winter Resident Development.

5. *Sailing Schedule, Cunard White Star Line/Donaldson Atlantic Line* (No. 1, January 2, 1936), Cunard folder, OCPC, SC; *Six Superb Cruises* (Holland America Line, 1933), OCPC, SC; *Grace Line 16 Day Cruises to the Caribbean* (April 1938): back of poster; Grace Line folder 8, KMEC, HL (see the August 1938 and November 1938 editions for other seasons); *Great White Fleet . . . Winter 1936–37*, United Fruit Company folder, OCPC, SC.

6. August Maffrey, *Oversea [sic] Travel and Travel Expenditures in the Balance of International Payments of the United States, 1919–38*, U.S. Department of Commerce, Bureau of Foreign and Domestic Commerce, Economic Series No. 4 (Washington, D.C.: Government Printing Office, 1939), 40, table 21 (numbers include both U.S. citizens and resident aliens. The total of all cruise passengers returns was only 92,781 in that year, demonstrating how much more popular, or at least affordable, short cruises to the Caribbean were than longer ocean cruises); *Inter-American Travel Statistics: Movement of Travel in the Americas, January–December 1939 and 1940* (Washington, D.C.: Travel Division, Pan American Union, n.d.), table 1, in folder 4, box 12, accession 1, PAAC, SCRL (travel to Mexico is not reflected in these numbers, and Bermuda was included in the figures for the West Indies. In each case, the number of people taking cruises is much lower than those traveling on regular liners, so the total volume of travel was considerably higher. Numbers include both U.S. citizens and resident aliens).

7. U.S. Department of Transportation Maritime Administration, *North American Cruise Statistical Snapshot, 2nd Quarter 2009* (September 2009): 4, table 3 (these numbers exclude Bermuda, the Bahamas, Mexico, and transcanal travel; they include all passengers, not just U.S. citizens), electronic document, http://www.marad.dot.gov/documents/North_American_Cruise_Statistics_Quarterly_Snapshot.pdf, accessed September 23, 2010; A. J. Norval, *The Tourist Industry: A National and International Survey* (London: Sir Isaac Pitman & Sons, 1936): 101; U.S. Dept. of the Interior memorandum for the press, February 19, 1939, 1–2 (for all dollar figures), file DTIP—Virgin Islands—Tourist and Winter Residence Development—General.

8. Corporación Nacional del Turismo, "Informe que presenta a los Miembros del Consejo Superior de la Corporación Nacional del Turismo, el Dr. Luis Machado, a nombre del Comité Ejecutivo" (Havana, July 29, 1938): 8, CL.

9. Frances Jones and Dorothy Smith, "Vacations with Pay," *Monthly Labor Review* 47:2 (August 1938): 269, 271 (only a small proportion of workers at these firms would

have had the seniority to be eligible for paid vacation time); *1937 West Indies Cruises, Hamburg-American Line/North German Lloyd* (October 1936): 3, 5, Hamburg American folder 8, KMEC, HL.

10. The magazine of the Automobile Club of Southern California, *Touring Topics* (today *Westways*), celebrated the construction and paving of roads and featured tales of early automobile adventurers from 1909; the best-known result of Florida's road building was a flood of "tin-canners" living out of cars or mobile home; see Nick Wynne, *Tin Can Tourists in Florida, 1900–1970* (Charleston, S.C.: Arcadia, 1999): 7–8; Warren Belasco, *Americans on the Road: From Autocamp to Motel, 1910–1945* (Baltimore: Johns Hopkins University Press, 1997); *A New 2 Weeks Vacation Trip to CALIFORNIA: How to Do It, What to See and Do, What It Will Cost* (All Year Club of Southern California, May 1933): 3 (quotations); Julius Weinberger, "Economic Aspects of Recreation," *Harvard Business Review* 15:3 (Spring 1937): 455, 456. Weinberger also calculated vacation spending by type of transport; travel by automobile grew far faster than travel by rail or airplane and constituted 57 percent of all vacation travel spending in 1935, suggesting that most U.S. vacationers remained in mainland North America. After domestic destinations, Canada remained the chief beneficiary, but Mexico gained considerable ground thanks to its extensive road building and publicity in the 1930s.

11. Ed Fletcher, March 1919, diary with photos, "Our Trip to Baja California and to Gulf of California," 6, 79, folder 5, box 74, EFP, ca. 1870–1955, mss. 081, MSC, USCD; H. W. Keller, "The International Pacific Highway," in *Transactions of the First International Pacific Highway Conference, Held Under the Auspices of the Automobile Club of Southern California, at Club Headquarters, Adams at Figueroa Street, Los Angeles, California, October 15–25, 1930*, folder 1, box 46, H. W. Keller Collection, HL. The quotation is from p. 5 of the address, which appears after p. 16 of the booklet. The Mexican officials attending the conference politely agreed with their hosts, but during the 1930s their priority remained building highways in the more heavily peopled northern and central regions.

12. Coert DuBois, "Travel Facilities and Vacation Opportunities in the Caribbean Area," 1, 3, 4, transmitted with Circular No. 58/44, AACC (British Section), dated July 29, 1944, folder Vacation Travel Survey, 1943–July 1944, box 44, AACC, 1940–1946, and Caribbean Commission 1946–1948, records of international commissions, RG 43, NARA II.

13. DuBois, "Travel Facilities," 5, 30, 31; see also Andrew Sackett, "Fun in Acapulco? The Politics of Development on the Mexican Riviera," in Dina Berger and Andrew Grant Wood, eds., *Holiday in Mexico: Critical Reflections on Tourism and Tourist Encounters* (Durham, N.C.: Duke University Press, 2010): 161–182; Lawrence Culver, *Frontier of Leisure: Southern California and the Shaping of Modern America* (Oxford: Oxford University Press, 2010).

14. George Yúdice, *The Expediency of Culture: Uses of Culture in the Global Era* (Durham, N.C.: Duke University Press, 2003), focuses on the post-1945 era and the role of international financial institutions in promoting tourism as an economic development strategy.

INDEX

abolition. *See* slavery

acclimatization, 18, 31, 40, 99, 135

Adam, 20, 96, 118, 145

African Americans, 8, 9, 71, 87, 104, 112, 113, 167, 170, 181n15

African descent, people of, 3, 10, 12, 20, 25, 69, 71, 90, 109, 124, 128–130, 148, 167, 175–177, 179, 208n66, 235n39

aging, 20, 84, 85, 89, 149. *See also* rejuvenation

agriculture. *See* horticulture

Aguas Calientes (Mexico), 3, 97, 109

air conditioning, 81, 82

air travel, 11, 64, 240n10

alcohol, 23, 61, 65, 147, 156

Allen, Madeline, 68, 69, 99, 106, 147

All Year Club, 46, 182

Alps, 49, 83

altitude, 3, 22, 39, 46, 77–78, 81

Álvarez, Manuel, 157, 164

Alvarez, Mr. and Mrs., 64, 145, 227n40

American Automobile Association. *See* automobile clubs

American Express, 87, 147–148, 179

American Riviera. *See* Riviera

American Social Surveys, 18, 193n5

Americas, ix, 12, 16, 19, 20, 49, 55, 71, 112, 154, 157, 160, 173, 177, 178, 211–212n23

Andreve, Guillermo, 95, 172

Anglo-American Caribbean Commission, 175, 176, 183

archaeology, 159, 160, 165, 232n23

architecture, 4, 74, 92–93; of cruise ships, 59, 60, 142; Latin American, 129–130, 159–160, 161, 178

Australia and Australians, 24, 40, 105, 112

Automobile Club of Southern California. *See* automobile clubs

automobile clubs, 167, 234n31; American Automobile Association, 88, 168; Automobile Club of Southern California, 91, 183, 240n10; Mexican Automobile Association, 166

automobiles, 11, 68, 69, 102, 166, 182, 214n43, 240n10

autumn, 20, 48, 78, 81, 122, 180

Awes, Addison, 24–25

Bahamas, 3, 44, 45, 58, 76, 78, 79, 87, 88, 212n25, 239n7. *See also* Nassau

bananas, 31, 32–33, 36, 37, 39, 51, 88, 90, 127, 130, 197–198n38

Bank of Mexico, 151, 153, 164, 233n28, 234n29

Barbachano, Fernando, 165

Barbados, 25, 68, 208n61

bathing, 53–55, 60, 69, 97, 100–104, 108, 177, 216n9. *See also* bathing suits; bathrooms; swimming; tanning

bathing beauty, 104, 107–111, 144, Plates 4 and 5

bathing suits, 12, 95, 96, 100, 102, 103, 104–111, 117–119, 122, 143–145, 216n10, 218n20, Plates 4 and 5

bathrooms, 53–55, 60, 63, 65, 66, 182

beaches: 5, 12, 13, 37, 97, 100, 103, 109, 112, 121, 158, 159, 216n8; bathing suits and, 12, 103, 105–108; Caribbean, 100, 104, 147, 218n17; Florida, 41, 75, 101–102, 104, 105, 121, 142; Jamaica, 100; men, 101, 107, 108, 109; Mexico, 102, 104, 165, 217n16; Panama, 103; Southern California, 39, 47, 101–105, 142, 217n14; tourism and, 95, 100–104; segregation, 104, 217n16; swimming, 103–105; tanning and, 112, 114–115, 118, 122, 123; whites and, 103–104; women and, 101–105, 110, 123, 216n10

ACKNOWLEDGMENTS

The publication of this book is highly improbable, and I am deeply grateful to everyone who made it possible. I owe Peggy Shaffer the greatest intellectual debt for telling me that my project was about the relationship between nature and culture. This insight freed me from other, less fruitful rubrics and galvanized my writing. She and Bob Lockhart then found a place for my work in the Nature and Culture series at the University of Pennsylvania Press and, along with the anonymous reviewer, copy editor Robert Milks, and project editor Noreen O'Connor-Abel, helped to make this book far better than I was able to do alone. Peggy was also one of a handful of people who believed me when I said I would remain a historian while making a career outside of academia. Alan Lessoff and James F. Brooks took me at my word as well and showed their support in practical and material ways. Their friendship constantly sustains me.

Many people offered me valuable sources, opportunities to present and publish my work as well as to comment on that of others, rigorous critique, moral support, breakfast, lunch, dinner, or a place to stay: Stephen Aron, Robin Bachin, Sharon Block, Peter Blodgett and Sue Hodson, Peter Boag, Matthew Bokovoy, Dominique Brégent-Heald, Jennifer Brier, Erika Bsumek, Jessica Cattelino and Noah Zatz, Andrea Cremer, Michael Dawson, Mark B. Feldman, Samantha Yates Francois, Andrea Geiger, Susan Gillman, Andrew R. Graybill, Philip Gruen, Carolyn Halladay, Karen Halttunen and Deborah Harkness, Kristin Hoganson, Michel Hogue, Hsuan L. Hsu, Benjamin H. Johnson, Deborah Kang, Kevin Leonard, Michele Mitchell, Jennifer Morgan, Molly O'Halloran, Carolyn Podruchny, Monica Rico, Bethel Saler, Andrew Sandoval-Strausz and Cathleen Cahill, Sarah Schrank, Peggy Shaffer, Monica Smith and James Snead, Sherry Smith, Jennifer Spear, John Torpey, and Phoebe Young. Heather Allen Pang gave me copies of letters her grandmother wrote on a 1931 cruise and also the greater gift of staying in touch despite our diverging lives. Marit Munson demonstrated great generosity of spirit when I most needed and least deserved it.

I owe many thanks to Elliott Young and Pamela Voekel for inviting me to attend and to serve on the board of the Tepoztlán Institute for the Transnational History of the Americas. They and especially Reiko Hillyer, Micol Siegel, and Jolie Olcott made me feel welcome and modeled transnational scholarship for me. Though the shortcomings of my work in that respect will disappoint them, it would have been even less adventurous without their example.

I am deeply grateful to the staff scholars at the School for Advanced Research, especially Rebecca Allahyari, James F. Brooks, Linda Cordell, John Kantner, and Nancy Owen Lewis, and many visiting and local scholars, especially Ted Edwards, Barbara Rose Johnston, Ivan Karp, and Corinne Kratz, who heard and read some early, unformed versions of my work and were kind about its failings. My coworkers at the School for Advanced Research buoyed my spirits and broadened my narrow horizons; many thanks to all of them, particularly Cynthia Dyer, Jonathan Lewis, Diane McCarthy, Jason Ordaz, Jean Schaumberg, Leslie Shipman, and all those mentioned above. In addition to keeping me practical and making me laugh, Lynn Thompson Baca and Carol Sandoval showed me that it's possible to live well and do good even when your dreams don't come true. I hope they know how much I admire them. Jane Kepp and Peg Goldstein proved good friends and invaluable allies in my brief freelance career. For hail and lightning at ten thousand feet, the opportunity to carry a large bag of dirt six miles up and down a canyon, and many a dinner in the best of company, I cannot thank Willow Roberts Powers and Bob Powers enough. Willow especially, but also all the usual suspects who attend their regular salons and hiking parties, nourished my mind and body.

At the University of Iowa Press, Maggie Brigl, Holly Carver, Karen Copp, Lydia Crowe, Jim McCoy, Allison Means, Joe Parsons, Faye Schillig, and Charlotte Wright made me feel at home and offered me welcome new challenges. On the shortest of notices Karen also scanned and cropped images for me, and Elisabeth Chretien arrived just in the nick of time.

Three institutions supported my research financially. The Huntington Library awarded me the Giles W. and Elise G. Mead Foundation Fellowship in 2005 and the Andrew W. Mellon Foundation Fellowship in 2009–2010. The Autry National Center granted me a visiting scholar fellowship in 2008, and the School for Advanced Research provided me with generous research funds during my employment there. Without these resources and the logistical support of Peter Blodgett, Fraser Cocks, Hanley Cocks, Linda Cordell, Mario

Einaudi, Marva Felchlin, Catherine Herlihy, Laura Holt, Len Leschander, Manola Madrid, Liza Posas, Kim Walters, and other librarians and archivists at institutions whose many names have given the endnotes an impressive bulk, I would not have been able to pursue this project. I owe Mario a particular debt for allowing me to use the Kemble Maritime Ephemera Collection before he finished processing it, thus enabling me to cover a major aspect of tourism in the period I study—the Caribbean cruise—which I otherwise could not have done nearly so well. A fine scholar himself, Peter Blodgett is the eminence grise behind many a successful career in U.S. history, and so I'm especially thankful to have his support.

Above all others, I am thankful for Catherine Herlihy, Fraser Cocks, and Hanley Cocks. Better even than their generous material support, they always give me a place to rest when I need one.

If you should have seen your name here and didn't, please forgive me. My spirit is grateful, but my memory is weak.

I thank Duke University Press for granting me permission to reprint those parts of the introduction and Chapters 5 and 6 that appeared, in a different form, in "The Welcoming Voice of the Southland: American Tourism Across the US-Mexico Border, 1880–1940," in Benjamin H. Johnson and Andrew R. Graybill, eds., *Bridging National Borders in North America: Transnational and Comparative Histories* (Durham, N.C.: Duke University Press, 2010): 225–248. I am equally grateful to Wayne State University Press for its permission to reprint those parts of Chapters 1 and 3 that appeared, in a different form, in "The Pleasures of Degeneration: Climate, Race, and the Origins of the Global Tourist South in the Americas," in *Discourse: Journal for Theoretical Studies in Media and Culture* 29:2–3. Copyright © 2009 Wayne State University Press. Used with permission by Wayne State University Press.